Elena

Strengthened *Through* Trials

ISBN: 978-1-885270-29-0

Cover design: Gloria Miller

Fifth printing: February 2013

Printed in the USA

Published by:
TGS International
P.O. Box 355
Berlin, Ohio 44610 USA
Phone: 330·893·4828
Fax: 330·893·2305
www.tgsinternational.com

TGS000630

Elena

Strengthened *Through* Trials

Harvey Yoder

Table of Contents

Dedication

First, I dedicate this book to God for His glory. Next, I want to honor the memory of my family members who are in heaven, especially my grandmother who planted seeds about Jesus and salvation in my heart.

I also thank:

My large, loving family, especially my mother who is a faithful example by her patient love, her prayers and fastings, and her undying trust in God through her difficult life.

All my friends in Romania and the USA who helped me grow strong in Jesus after I became a Christian.

Cornel, my husband, who supported and helped me very much with this book project.

—Elena (Boghian) Marza

Foreword

A special thanks to Elena and her husband, Cornel, for taking me to parts of Romania that figured so largely in her story. I not only treasure the experience of hearing Elena's story, but also actually seeing many places she told me about. During this process, Cornel, Elena, and her family became more than mere characters in a book; they became my special friends.

Bumping along rough roads in the western part of Romania, visiting prisons where Elena had been incarcerated, talking with people who had known her as a student, I kept studying the woman who tirelessly kept telling me the story of her life. The strength and courage of Elena amazed me, not only as she related her story, but also in the vivid accounts she gave of her life in communist Romania.

That strength was born through trials. It was not enough that Elena's grandparents and parents had received strength from their faith in the Lord Jesus Christ, but she too had to come to her own personal faith in Jesus. Then, as her faith unfolded and she searched for ways to serve Christ, a deep inner strength began to give meaning to her life. Again and again, I was impressed how she longed to "do something for Jesus," however insignificant it might have seemed. God saw the desire of her heart and began moving her to where she could find satisfaction in serving Him by serving others.

Elena needed God's strength that was deep inside her during years of persecution and imprisonment. When it seemed she could no longer endure the hardships, the Lord always provided some form of encouragement and allowed her to sense His presence. That was, and continues to be, the source of her strength.

Elena . . . a story of poverty and deprivation during childhood. Yet, even more, it is a story of faith and triumph by turning what seemed to be for evil, into good. May her story inspire us all to gather strength from our Lord and Savior, Jesus Christ.

For any inaccuracies that appear in this book, I take full responsibility. I tried to present the facts as they happened and as Elena remembered them, yet I am fully aware that others may remember things in a different manner. Where memory failed, I used writer's liberties to fill in the empty spaces.

Elena mentioned repeatedly that she does not want the spotlight to focus on her, but rather that God would receive all glory. I, as the author, echo that desire.

—Harvey Yoder

1

The Lord Has Taken Away

. . . THE LORD GAVE, AND THE LORD HATH TAKEN AWAY; BLESSED BE THE NAME OF THE LORD.

JOB 1:21B

Slowly dropping toward the western horizon, the Romanian sun sent comforting warmth on the back of the woman in the garden. *Viorica** pulled the sprouting weeds from the row of new spring onions.

The garden lay behind the low barn that housed their cows. A shed connected the barn to the house, and the three buildings formed an ell around two sides of the courtyard. From where she was working, Viorica could not see the house, but she had no qualms about leaving two-week-old baby *Rodica* in the house with *Elena.* At two years old, Elena already felt a responsibility for her baby sister.

From the neighboring yard came the shouts of children playing. Dogs barked, roosters crowed, and an occasional horse and wagon rattled past on the village street. But a sense of peace settled over Viorica as she worked in the garden. The three oldest children were spending the day at their uncle's house. Viorica's husband *Gheorghita* was working in the field, as were his parents, who lived with them in the two-room, mud-walled house. The day had been uneventful for Viorica, and she had welcomed the solitude of only seeing to the baby's needs and looking after little Elena. She had felt so rested that she decided to go to the garden to check for early spring onions. They would add a welcome taste of summer to their skimpy evening meal of soup.

Ahh! Here was a fat little onion. Viorica could almost taste the stinging flavorsome vegetable. She hunted for more as she pulled the ever-invading weeds.

She paused as the smell of wood smoke reached through her reverie. Straightening her back she looked toward the house but could see nothing.

* *See glossary on pages 235-238 for pronunciations of italicized words*

Perhaps one of the neighbors was burning their trash. Viorica bent to her task once more.

In the house, baby Rodica lay on her parents' bed. Elena sat cross-legged beside her, brushing away any stray fly that wanted to settle on the sleeping infant. The house was quiet. Through the window above the bed, Elena could see across the board fence and into the neighbor's yard. Several chickens pecked in the dirt and a rooster strutted importantly among them. A strong breeze fluffed the chickens' feathers into fans as they turned against the gusts.

Elena picked up the block of wood that her big sister Lidia used for a doll. A scrap of fabric pinned around the middle made do for a dress. Elena glanced at her sleeping sister, then gently cradled the wooden doll in her arms.

Across the room, Elena could see out a second window that overlooked their courtyard. She watched as swirls of smoke eddied around inside the enclosure then whipped over the fence to disappear into the air. But there was no cause for the two-year-old to be alarmed. She turned back to her doll.

The shed that connected the house to the barn was filled with wood. Quite dry wood, in fact. Gheorghita and his parents had slowly been collecting lumber for several years, storing it in the shed for the time when they could build a new house. A bigger house for Gheorghita and Viorica's growing family, with room enough for the grandparents too.

All the buildings were connected by the tinder-dry roof. There had been no recent rains, and the stiff breeze and warm sun had sapped all moisture from the overlapping wood shakes.

In the garden, Viorica continued her search for spring onions. Facing away from the buildings, she worked her way down the long row. Quite often, she moved away from the onion row to inspect other vegetables that were pushing their way up toward the light.

It was so good to be outside again. The sun warmed more than just her back, it seemed to warm her on the inside too. The long winter months of waiting for the baby were over. The baby was healthy, and though food was rather scarce, the potatoes from last year's harvest should see them through until a new crop was ready in late summer.

But then, she must not overdo herself. Gheorghita had warned her just that morning to continue to take it easy. "This is your fifth child in seven years," he had told her. "You must take care of yourself!"

"Oh, Gheorghita," she had protested. "What about you? You are working too hard!" Viorica had looked at his tall figure. His clothes hung loosely on his big frame.

"I am still young," he had said with a smile. "God has blessed me with strength and good health!"

Viorica paused in her work, remembering the conversation. Again, she smelled smoke, stronger this time. Whatever was burning was getting hotter. Viorica straightened quickly and looked toward the barn.

A cry of alarm rose in her throat! The entire roof of the barn was in flames!

Standing up so quickly from her bent-over position, combined with the shock of seeing the burning roof, was too much for Viorica's still-weak body. Her head whirled. Helpless, she felt herself falling. Falling into a black void. Viorica crumpled down among the onions. A slight moan escaped her lips as she lay on the soil, oblivious to what was happening.

The baby slept peacefully. Elena continued crooning to her doll, rocking back and forth on the bed. She patted the wooden body as carefully as she would have her baby sister, had she been awake.

Fanned by the breeze, the flames spread from the barn toward the shed. Fire licked at the stacked wood, finding easy prey for its voracious appetite. The heat increased ten-fold.

In a little restaurant around the corner, the mayor and several of his cronies were taking a break. They sat with their bottles on the table in front of them, discussing local happenings and conditions of life.

The door burst open. A villager's tousled head and frantic eyes appeared for a brief moment as he yelled, "Fire!"

Instantly, the men were on their feet. They stampeded out the door, the mayor in the lead.

They heard the screams of the neighboring women even as they saw the clouds of smoke billowing from the *Boghian* household. They raced around the corner.

"Is everybody out?" the mayor shouted above the noise of crackling flames and shrieks from the women. Getting no answer, he entered the smoke-filled yard and tried to get to the front door. But the intense heat made it impossible to go farther. He turned and went around the side of the house. Making a frame of his hands, he pressed his face against the window.

"The babies are inside!" he yelled in horror. He tried to open the window, but it was stuck. Grabbing a piece of wood, he cracked the glass and quickly removed the broken window. Smoke was already sifting into the room from the open door.

"Anybody in here?" he called. He looked for an adult figure but saw none. Only the two children on the bed under the window.

Grabbing the blanket that the children were on, the mayor drew it towards himself. Waiting hands reached for the baby as soon as he got her out the window. Then, he wrapped the blanket around Elena and drew her to himself. He handed her, blanket and all, to a man behind him.

"Anyone else in here?" he yelled through the thickening smoke. "Viorica! *Raveca!*"

There was no answer. The smoke engulfed him, making him cough. He withdrew his head.

The street was filled with people. Buckets of water were being thrown over the wooden fence, wetting the outside of the buildings. But the fire continued to grow hotter.

"Call the fire department!" the mayor yelled above the noise.

"We already did," someone shouted back. The call must have been made from the school around the corner.

The mayor knew it would take at least half an hour for the fire department to respond from the next town. Their entire village might be consumed by the inferno.

"Save the adjacent houses!" he yelled to the horrified throng. "Wet the roofs! Get blankets! Anything!" The villagers scattered to defend their dwellings from the raging flames.

With a moan, Viorica regained consciousness. She sprang to her feet, taking in the terrible scene before her. Again her head whirled, but she grimly held onto her consciousness.

"My babies! Oh, Lord, protect my babies!" Her scream of anguish was lost in the roar of the flames and the cries of the people on the street.

Viorica raced toward the house, darting through the neighbor's garden and into their yard. She ran out their front gate into the street.

"Viorica! There she is! Where are the other children?" The women crowded around her with cries and exclamations of alarm.

"Where is my baby? Where is Elena?" Viorica felt faint.

"Here!" The baby was thrust into her hungry arms. "And here is Elena!"

Viorica began to sob with relief. She pressed her crying infant to her breast.

"Where are the other children?" the women kept insisting.

"They are not here. They are at *Vica's* house!"

A babble of relieved voices surrounded the mother as she gathered her two youngest to her bosom. They were safe! Praise the Lord, her babies were safe!

"Someone is coming," Gheorghita told his parents. All three stopped hoeing and watched as a figure hurried toward them.

"It's *Ana!*" *Bunica* exclaimed as she recognized Viorica's sister-in-law. "Something must have happened!"

"Gheorghita!" Ana yelled as soon as she came within yelling distance. "Hurry home!"

Gheorghita dropped his hoe and ran toward the messenger. "Ana! What happened?"

Ana gasped in huge breaths of air. She shook her head. "Just hurry home, Gheorghita!"

He took hold of her arm. His parents came up behind him. "Ana, is it something terrible? Did something happen to Viorica? To the children? Are they dea . . . are they all right?"

Ana nodded her head. "They're all right. Just hurry home!"

Gheorghita insisted. "Tell me!" His voice was sharp with intensity.

"Fire!" Ana gasped with a look of terror in her dark eyes. "Your house is burning!"

With an exclamation of alarm, all three turned their eyes toward the village, almost two miles away. Across the flat landscape, they could clearly see smoke rising from the burning buildings.

"Viorica! My children! Is everyone safe?" Gheorghita's voice came out in a strangled gasp.

"Yes, everyone is safe. I told you!" Ana said. "Just quickly go home to them!"

Gheorghita sprang off across the field. His long legs sprinted across the newly planted field, his heart surging in his breast. His family was safe! But his house was burning! He must rush to be with Viorica!

Mosu and Bunica quickly hitched the wagon to the cows and hurried home. They tried to urge the cows to go faster, but it was in vain. They only ambled at cow speed.

By the time the grandparents arrived, the fire had died down only a little. Smoke still swirled above the village, and the street around their home was packed with people.

"God have mercy!" Bunica breathed, as the people made way for them. They tied the cows to a fence and hurried to their son and daughter-in-law.

All eyes focused on the Boghian family. The aged couple stood beside their son and his wife. The older children had arrived and were gathered around their parents.

Tragedy had struck. Everyone knew that. Everyone watched to see what reaction the family would have.

The Boghians were Christians. *Repentants*, the villagers called them. There were other Repentants in the village, but not many. The small band of Christians was not at all popular. The state government despised them—after all, they were ignorant people who served an invisible, unknown, non-existent God. The Orthodox church hated them—they had left the established church and that made them heretics. The common people simply did not like them—the Christians' joy and peace made the villagers aware of what they were missing in their own lives and made them feel threatened.

Now the whole village watched this family who had lost the few earthly possessions they had managed to own. The little two-room house had not been much for nine people, but it had been shelter. Their wheat, corn, and flour supplies had been small, but at least there had been enough to stand between hungry children and starvation until the next crops ripened. Two pigs and three lambs were not much livestock, but it had been that much. Thankfully, the two cows were outside and did not perish with the pigs and lambs in the barn.

Everyone knew the difficulties the Boghian family faced. And everyone wondered what reaction these Repentants would have. Would they cry and scream against the injustice of the devastating fire? Would they curse and swear as they themselves did when tragedy struck?

The Boghian family knew what to do. Oblivious to the watching people, they bowed their heads in front of the smoldering ruins and prayed.

"Lord Jesus, we come to You in our calamity. We bless You for Your faithfulness!" Bunica's strong voice rang out to the listening ears.

"Amen!" Gheorghita echoed.

Mosu picked up the prayer. "God, we know You are the Creator of all things. It is You who has given us everything we ever had, and You who has taken them away. Yet, we will trust in You. In all of our want, You have still blessed us. We thank You for your love!"

The people watched. They listened. Some shook their heads. How could such prayers come from a family who had lost everything?

As news of the calamity spread, the group of Repentants from the village worked their way through the crowd to the stricken family.

"Brother! Do not be dismayed by what has happened. Trust God!" The brethren and sisters comforted the Boghians.

"Come to our place!" Sister *Ligheria* urged them. "You can stay in the room where we used to gather for worship. It is not a big room, but you can sleep there. Bring everything you have saved and come!"

"Yes, go with them," Gheorghita instructed the women. "Mosu and I will stay here and watch over the smoldering flames. There might be some things we can still save."

Bunica's strong arm supported Viorica as they trudged down the slope to their neighbor's house. The children trailed along silently.

"What shall we eat for supper?" Viorica worried as she stumbled on the stony road. The sinking sun emphasized the lateness of the day. Her thoughts went briefly back to the garden where she had been gathering onions.

"Viorica, we will trust God to provide for us. He has never let us go hungry. Remember, He knows just what has happened." Bunica's voice was strong and confident. This was not the first trial she had gone through. Her faith was strong.

And God did provide. The Christians came with food. Some gave milk from their cows. Some brought bread. From their own meager stores, they shared.

When darkness clothed the village and Mosu and Gheorghita finally joined the family, food was waiting for them. Yes, the room was crowded with nine people in it, and supper displayed very little variety that night, yet it was with grateful hearts that the family prayed over the evening meal.

How they would fare in the coming days, none of them knew. It was beyond their comprehension how they would be able to replace the clothes and bedding that had been burned, or ruined by water from the fire truck that had finally come. They simply had no idea what to do next.

But they were sure of one thing. The God they trusted for their salvation had not changed. He would still be with them and assure them of His love regardless of what lay ahead.

2

Tata's Accident

For I reckon that the sufferings of this present time are not worthy to be compared with the glory which shall be revealed in us.

Romans 8:18

"Viorica, I must go. I see no other way out." Gheorghita spoke softly into his wife's ear.

"Somehow I have to make some money to buy materials to finish the house."

Viorica buried her head against her husband's shoulder. She did not speak but clung more tightly to him.

It was dark in the little room, and the children were sleeping.

"Viorica, I will be here to help you. Mosu and I will be right here with you." It was Bunica, speaking softly from her cot by the wall. "God will be with us through this separation."

"It is for the best," Mosu agreed. "Gheorghita must go to the mountains. We must prepare for the next winter."

"Yes," Viorica sighed. "I know it is the right thing to do. It is just . . ." Her voice trailed off into the darkness.

"I know, dear," Gheorghita said softly, stroking her hair with gentle hands. "I trust it will not be for too long. Maybe no longer than a year."

The darkness swallowed up his words. Everyone knew he would have to work long and hard to earn the money they needed.

It had taken them over a month to clean away the debris and ashes from the fire. The stacked lumber had smoldered and burned a long time before they could even begin to clear away. Trip after trip, the cows had pulled the wagon loaded with ashes down to the river where they would be dumped. Mosu and Bunica had worked alongside their son as they labored to clear the courtyard.

At first they had thought they could repair the burned-out house. The mud-brick walls were still standing after the fire. Christians from their village and neighboring ones had come to help them put a simple roof on the walls. Even that had been difficult. A soaking rain had drenched the mud walls, and they had needed to wait until those dried out before they could cover the house. Finally, the family had moved into the two rooms again. The roof would shelter them from the elements and the stove would keep them warm.

Then, they had decided to start all over and build a new house. The old house was just too small and the walls were deteriorating. It was a difficult decision, but a necessary one. They were still young and their growing family needed more room.

"Will you be able to find work?" Viorica asked. Her thoughts whirled. How could she endure the separation from her husband?

"Yes, *Ilie* promised me I could find work there. We will be working in the forest, bringing logs down to the railroad tracks. He said I could stay with him."

"It makes me feel a little better, knowing that you can stay with your uncle."

Gheorghita stretched himself out on the cot and pulled his wife down beside him. "It is time to rest. The morning will soon be here."

Quietness settled over the room. The children's soft, regular breathing intermingled with the longer breaths of Mosu and Bunica. But for the young couple, sleep did not come easily. Gheorghita finally dropped off to sleep, his tired body demanding rest. At last Viorica, too, felt sleep claim her consciousness.

Gheorghita shivered in the icy wind. Gusts of snow swept down the mountainside, blurring his vision. The stack of logs was ready to be pushed down the slippery slope on their journey to the railway.

"All ready!" Gheorghita heard the foreman yell. Gheorghita pushed his pole under the log nearest to him and heaved. The log moved forward. He moved his pole to get a better grip.

A noise behind him caused Gheorghita to jerk his head around to see what was happening. To his horror, he saw the stack of logs sliding down the slope toward him.

"No!" he yelled in fear. He scrambled desperately to get out of the way.

The mass of logs caught his leg just above his ankle. Gheorghita was thrown forward by the impact. He tried to catch himself by grabbing onto a log with his hands. Something snapped sickeningly in his lower leg.

The jumble of logs stopped. Gheorghita tried to pull his leg free, but he was imprisoned by two logs wedged against each other.

"Help!" he yelled.

"We'll be right there!"

The foreman and two other workers rushed up to him. They took in the situation immediately.

"Put your poles on either side of his leg," the foreman instructed. "Now push gently uphill."

They pushed. But the weight of the logs pushing downward was too great. The log pile did not move.

"Be careful!" the foreman warned. "The stack of logs might bear down on him and crush him!"

"Dear God, please help me!" Gheorghita prayed out loud. Sweat beaded his forehead as pain shot up his leg. "Lord, protect me. Please, let me see my family again!"

"We must move the lower log," the foreman decided. "Place the poles on each end and push gently."

It worked. Gheorghita pulled his leg free in spite of the increasing pain that surged through him.

"Here, lie down on my coat." The foreman spread the garment. "We will take you down to Ilie's house."

Gheorghita, carried by the two workers, bore the agony of the trip down the mountain. When he finally collapsed on his cot, relief washed over him. Ilie hurried off to find someone to take Gheorghita to the hospital. Everyone knew the leg was broken.

"Lord," Gheorghita groaned aloud, "why did this happen? How is it possible that more calamities can visit us? Viorica and my parents are already doing all they can to provide for our family. How can they possibly take more suffering? This will be another cross for us to bear." Gheorghita dashed away a threatening tear. He was glad he was alone. The pain in his leg intensified his emotional state. "Why, Lord?"

"I must go home," Gheorghita said to the old man. "There is nothing I can do here."

Ilie looked at him steadily. "How can you? And what can you do at home?"

Gheorghita looked at the white cast on his leg. It was now two weeks since the accident. Ilie had brought him his meals and faithfully taken care of him.

"I will go by train."

"Does the train stop in your village?"

Gheorghita did not answer. Instead, he said, "At least at home I can be with Viorica and the children and my parents. I miss them much more now that I can't work."

"If you leave, I shall miss you," Ilie said quietly. "I will miss your songs and the talks we have. Perhaps you will come back when you are well."

"I don't know." Gheorghita shook his dark head. "Three years I have worked here in the mountains, Ilie. Three years is a long time to be away from my family. Even though I have been going back as often as I can, the weekends are never long enough.

"Since we have another baby, Viorica needs me at home more than ever. Not that I can do much," he looked woefully at his leg.

Then Gheorghita straightened himself up on the cot. "Tomorrow, I will go home. If you help me to the train, I will get off at the station nearest *Patrauti* and send word to Viorica to come and fetch me. We will make it somehow."

Ilie's face wrinkled into a grin. "I can see you are determined. I'll help you. Now, since this is your last night here, why don't you sing? Perhaps I can remember your songs after you are gone."

Softly at first, and then with greater fervor, Gheorghita began to sing.

Going forth with weeping, sowing for the Master,
Tho' the loss sustained our spirit often grieves;
When our weeping's over, He will bid us welcome,
We shall come, rejoicing, bringing in the sheaves.

Ilie listened to the words and, beyond them, the sincerity in the singer's voice. He knew he would miss Gheorghita. Somehow, when Gheorghita was there, it made his small house seem like a holy place.

"Where did Mama and Lidia go?" five-year-old Elena wondered. She remembered hearing a lot of talk after someone from the village had come to their house, and suddenly Mama and Lidia were no longer there. However, the house was far from empty. The older children had come home from school and the two little ones, Rodica and *Lucia,* were bouncing on the bed. Bunica was busy at the stove stirring *mamaliga,* their usual supper.

"They went to the train station," *Vasile,* her oldest brother, told her. "Bunica said they went to bring *Tata* home. He has . . ."

The rest of the words did not register. Tata was coming home! For almost as long as she could remember, Tata came home only once or twice a month. It always brought joy to little Elena. She loved her father.

Elena did not notice how often Bunica looked out the small window of their new two-room house. She did not even pay much attention to what Bunica was saying as she worked by the stove. She was used to hearing Bunica pray as she went about her work.

". . . cold to be coming home so late," Vasile was saying to Bunica. "I wonder if they are all right."

"We must ask God to protect them," Bunica said softly, giving the mamaliga another stir. "All we can do is trust God to meet our needs."

Then the door to their room opened. Bitter winter air swept into the room.

"Hurry! Help us get Tata to the stove! I'm afraid he's almost frozen!" Mama's voice burst into the room.

A flurry of activity followed. The sled Mama and Lidia had used to pull Tata the five miles from the train station was too big to drag into the house, so the adults helped Tata hobble into the warm room. The snow that came along in was ignored.

"Tata!" The children crowded around their father.

"Let me see my family!" Tata laughed as he unwrapped the blankets around him. "I can hardly breathe! Oh! The stove feels so wonderful!"

"Tata, why is your leg so big?" Elena stared at her father's right leg, swathed in blankets.

Helped by his wife onto the cot closest to the mud stove that warmed their room, Gheorghita lay back against the pillows. His face, though flushed from the cold, was drawn with fatigue and pain.

"My leg was broken in an accident," Tata told his children, crowded around him. "I can't walk on it and I can't work."

For Elena, it was hard to understand. If something was broken, it was usually no longer good for anything. Would Tata have to throw his leg away?

"It'll take several months for it to heal. The doctor said it was a clean break and it should heal all right." Tata answered the unasked questions he saw in the solemn eyes looking at him.

Bunica bustled into action. "Vasile, sweep the snow together. We don't need melted snow making puddles on the floor. Lidia, come over here by the stove. Viorica! You must sit down and rest. You have worn yourself out!"

Indeed, the toll of pulling her husband across the snow on a sled showed on Viorica's face. Her face was lined with weariness. Lidia, too, felt exhausted. She leaned her head against the warm side of the stove.

"I will get you hot tea," Bunica told the homecomers. "That will warm your insides and give you some energy."

Elena helped carry the steaming tea to her parents. She set Tata's cup on a chair close to his cot. She was so glad Tata was home again.

From his prone position, Gheorghita looked around the familiar room. His eyes took in the crowded conditions. With concern, he noticed the worry lines on Viorica's forehead. He gave an involuntary sigh.

Bunica, who was giving Mosu his cup of tea, heard the sigh and looked over at Gheorghita. "Son, how did this happen?" Her voice was soft and kind.

As Gheorghita told them about the accident, Elena and the older children listened intently. The story made a vivid impression on their young minds. They could picture the heavy, cruel logs, pinning their father's leg between them.

"I was almost in despair for several hours after the accident," Gheorghita related. "I thought it couldn't be that this had to happen. I kept asking God why He allowed such a calamity to happen to our family after we had suffered from the fire. I'm afraid my faith was rather weak at first.

"Then, as I prayed, I felt the presence of God come over me. His Spirit began to comfort me and I could rest in Him. I still don't know why the accident happened, but I can now rest in the care of my heavenly Father." He ceased speaking and everyone sat in silence.

Their situation looked grim. It was the middle of winter and food was scarce. The pile of lumber that Gheorghita had been able to accumulate was still not enough to build the new house. Now, the accident had put him out of work for months. There would be no income.

Bunica was undaunted. "This is no time to be discouraged. We will continue to trust God and allow Him to provide for us as He always has."

A smile crossed her face as she recalled an earlier moment. "I remember so well when *George Oltean* told us that we could trust God in everything. That made a tremendous impression on me then. I think that was one reason I was willing to accept what he was saying. That we can trust God even when things are happening beyond our control is a sense of joy and peace that has never left me." Bunica wiped her eyes with a corner of her apron.

Mosu took a sip of tea from his cup. "We still thank God for the Good News that Brother Oltean brought back to us from America. We were hungry for the truth."

"Was Brother Oltean the one who gave you your first Bible?" Viorica wondered.

The elderly couple nodded their heads. "We learned so many things from that Book," Mosu continued. "It was like a well of fresh water to us. Our boys were young and we wanted to find a better way of life for our family. We spent hours and hours reading from the Word."

"That is why you went to prison," Lidia said quietly from the corner of her cot. She had heard the story before.

"Well, not exactly," Mosu said soberly. "Reading the Bible showed us how we must live and why we had to stop doing some of the things we were doing. It was when we followed the teachings from the Bible that others made life difficult for us and sent us to prison."

Bunica broke in. "We spent many nights reading and praying. After we had become true believers, the Spirit showed us so many truths! We could scarcely wait to see what else we would find in the Scriptures. It was, and still is, a glorious life! I have never regretted for a single moment the choices we made almost 40 years ago. I would do it all over again! I continually pray that we'll remain faithful to our Savior until our dying day!"

Gheorghita looked fondly at his parents. His eyes lingered on his children and came to rest on his wife. "The faith of my parents has shone like a beacon in my life. Even as a young boy, I saw that my parents had a faith they were willing to suffer for. I remember when Tata refused to kiss the hand of the priest. In the events that followed, I knew that my parents would stay true to their faith. Even though it meant prison."

Elena looked wide-eyed at the adults. She knew what prison meant. Being locked up, away from family. Suffering. Hunger. Beatings. The very idea of being shut up in prison terrified her.

"You have never talked much about your time in prison," Mama said turning to her mother-in-law.

"Prison life is nothing to talk about," Bunica said softly. "The Lord allowed me to go through experiences that have drawn me closer to Him, though I would never wish those experiences on anyone. But there were many others who suffered worse than I ever did."

"Come, all of you," Mosu spoke up, "let's pray. It is time we turn our thoughts to God and rest in His love. Even Gheorghita breaking his leg, and the troubles we are afraid may come with that, are not too much for God. Nothing is impossible with Him. Let's carry our problems to Him, then rest in His love." Mosu moved slowly and stiffly as he knelt by the stove.

One by one, the children knelt on the floor. Bunica sank to her knees in gratitude. Viorica knelt beside her husband's cot.

They did not wait on each other, or take turns. Each heart, as it turned in supplication to God, began praying. Their voices, including those of the older children, rose in a symphony of cadences as they prayed to their Lord and Savior. And the trust they put in Jesus was not in vain, for as they prayed, they felt their hearts warmed as God wrapped His warm blanket of peace around their souls.

3

The Prodigal Son

For this my son was dead, and is alive again;
he was lost, and is found.

Luke 15:24a

"Tata, here is your *borsch,"* Vasile offered a bowl of the steaming soup to his father.

"And here is your tea," Elena piped up. She placed the cup carefully on the little table beside the cot.

"Thank-you, children," Gheorghita said. "It makes me feel better just to be at home with my family. I don't deserve so many blessings."

Bunica bent over to place her hand on her son's forehead. "Yes, isn't God wonderful to us? He gives us much more than we deserve."

Gheorghita reached up and caught his mother's hand. He looked deep into her eyes. "You believed in me even when I was rebellious and wayward. You trusted that I would come to know the Lord. Thank-you again for your prayers."

Bunica wiped her eyes. "My dear son! To know that you now serve Jesus with all your heart brings such great joy to me." She smiled tremulously. "God truly is good to us."

Elena listened intently as she observed the tender moment between her father and her Bunica.

Bunica sighed as her thoughts turned further back in time. "One of the hardest moments of my life," she recalled, "was when I returned from prison and there was no one at home. I found only an empty house. The neighbors had thought our entire family was never coming back, so they had taken some things and sold them." She paused in her musing, remembering the bleak moment. "I had no way of knowing that Mosu would soon be released from prison too. I only knew I was all alone. My heart nearly broke. If I had not had Jesus to turn to, I don't know what I would have done." Bunica shook her head. "It was harder to come home to an empty house than it had been to be in prison."

"But Tata," wondered Dan, "where were you?"

Gheorghita looked at his family. He shifted his leg with his hands. Outside, the wind swirled snow around the little house.

Leaning back against a pillow, Gheorghita addressed the children. "I want to tell you about a difficult time in my life. A time when I brought much grief and pain to your grandparents." Sensing a story, the children crowded around their Tata.

"I was about nine years old when my parents became Christians." He smiled at Vasile. "Just about the age of Vasile. I saw that something had happened to their hearts. Whenever they read the Bible and prayed, I watched them. Young as I was, I knew they had found what they were looking for. They had found Jesus.

"Well, soon some other people in the village repented, and my parents and these people began meeting for Bible study and church. At first I attended too. I was young then, but as the years went by, I began to develop other interests.

"I stopped going to church regularly. I knew this hurt Mama and Tata very deeply, but life was too exciting to waste time in church. I thought I was having the best time of my life."

Elena moved closer to her father. The tone of his voice held her spellbound. She crossed her restless legs and gazed up into his face, fascinated with this story of a Tata she never knew.

Tata went on. "I joined the army. I was the right height and build, so I was made a guard at the king's palace. I had a real nice position—a nice place to sleep and fairly decent food."

Vasile and Dan looked at each other, eyes wide. Their father had been a guard in the king's palace! They smiled.

Gheorghita saw the exchange of glances between his sons. He said soberly, "That good position did not last. When World War II broke out, I was sent to fight in the Romanian army. At the time, we were fighting with the Germans against Russia." He paused for a moment and closed his eyes. Everyone in the room was quiet, listening. Viorica was holding little Lucia; Mosu was fashioning willow whips into a basket. Bunica was tending the fire. Even the little ones were listening to their father's story. Tata opened his eyes and continued.

"During the war, I was taken prisoner by the Russians. There, I endured the worst conditions in my life. I won't tell you everything, but I will tell you this—I really learned what hunger is. We prisoners got so hungry that we ate anything we could get. Sometimes we would carefully sort through the garbage to find something to put into our empty stomachs."

Gheorghita took a deep breath. He sipped his tea. Then he continued, almost as though he had forgotten his family was listening.

"Fish bones. One time we found some bones left over from an officers' dinner of fish. The bones were soft, and to us they tasted delicious. If we could find potato peelings or egg shells, we were thankful. All around us, prisoners were dying. Almost every day, we had to bury the dead.

"Life was merely a hopeless existence. I had reached the bottom." His voice trailed off as he relived those terrible days. But as his children sat spellbound, eyes glued to their father, his face brightened with a remembered hope.

"It was then that I remembered the things I had heard in my parents' Bible Study. I remembered the prayers, the songs, the joy and tears I had seen as the Christians gathered for church services. And there in that prison, I cried out to God. With the little strength I had left, I prayed.

"I told the Lord, 'I know I don't deserve any mercy, but I will serve You the best I know how. If You deliver me from this prison and allow me to see my family and my country again, I will surrender my life completely into Your hands.'

"One day we were put into a cattle car. Our captors locked the door, and for days we were on the train. No one told us anything. I thought we were probably being sent to Siberia to starve. There was no food, only a little water, and terrible, unsanitary conditions. Our water ran out. Once when the train stopped, the door to our car opened and we were given some water and a little food. While the door was open, I heard our Romanian language! Hope surged within me! Perhaps we were back in our country!

"God was good," Gheorghita's voice shook with emotion. "We were released at a train station and told we could return to our homes. I couldn't believe what I was hearing. I thanked God for His mercies.

"But when the door opened and we were told to get out of the car, I was blind! I could tell the others were all moving toward the door, but I couldn't see anything! My heart sank like a stone. Had I been released from one prison only to be delivered to a prison of blindness? I wished I had died in prison. Right then I reminded God: 'O Lord, I promised to follow You if I would be able to see my country and my family again!'

"We were given some food and, after I ate, my vision started coming back. New hope surged in my heart! I knelt and thanked God for healing me. Now I wanted to go home to my parents and tell them what God had done for me!"

"Gheorghita," Bunica interrupted gently. "Eat your borsch. It is already cold." He picked up the bowl and spoon.

"Did you get home then?" Lidia asked eagerly. "Was anyone at home?"

Bunica cleared her throat and answered for her son, now eating his food. "Yes, I and your Mosu, who had been released from prison by that time, were at home, when we heard a knock on the door. When I went to the door, I saw an emaciated boy standing there. His clothes just hung on him, and he looked so pale and ill. His eyes were sunken deep into his head." Her eyes filled with tears.

"It was only after he said 'Mama' that I knew who it was. I recognized his voice.

" 'Gheorghita!' I cried out. Quickly, I helped him into the house, calling for Mosu. '*Costache*, Costache! Gheorghita is home!' Together we put our son to bed, then we knelt beside his cot and thanked God for sending one of our sons home to us. Gheorghita was so nearly starved. At first, he was so weak that he could only take milk. Like a baby."

By now, Tata had finished his borsch. "I have memories of mostly sleeping and eating those first weeks. I was so thin and weak that Mama and Tata kept me hidden. People would have been shocked to see me and, besides, I was too weak for visitors.

"It was during this time of recovery that I told Mama and Tata that I wanted to live for God. I told them about my experience in prison. I told them I wanted to repent and ask the Lord Jesus to save me. We prayed together. I wanted to be true to my promise to God.

"Gradually, I became stronger. One Sunday, my parents had gone to church and I was at home alone. I felt strong enough to go outside. It was summer time and I wanted to feel the sun on my face again.

"I had scarcely sat down on the bench outside the door when some of my old friends came by. They stopped, shocked, when they saw me. 'Gheorghita, is that you?' they exclaimed. 'We didn't know you were back!' They came into the yard and we visited for awhile. I told them about my time in prison. Before long, they got up to leave.

" 'Come with us,' they invited me. 'We're going to a party.' At first I told them I was finished with things like that. I told them I had stopped drinking. 'Oh, that's all right,' they said. 'You don't have to drink. Just sit at our table and eat with us.'

"It had been such a long time since I had been able to do anything, and now I felt so good that I decided to go with them. I sat with them and they started drinking plum brandy."

Gheorghita paused in his story telling. He looked at all his children, listening wide-eyed in rapt attention. His voice faltered once more. Then he continued.

"I failed. They kept encouraging me to drink, and finally I gave in. That brandy almost killed me. I became terribly sick—so sick I thought I was going to die. My whole body seemed to be on fire.

"My friends saw that my weak body had reacted to the alcohol, and they got scared. They quickly carried me home and left. When my parents came home from church and saw me, they knew immediately that I was very sick. I could not even talk."

"We took him to the hospital with the horse and wagon," Mosu remembered. "We didn't know if he was going to make it or not. At the hospital they gave him a shot and took him into a private room. We couldn't stay with him."

"In the hospital I had a vision," Gheorghita told his children. "I thought I was burning in hell. When the doctor was giving me a shot, I thought it was the devil with a pitchfork. I yelled out, 'Devil! Don't prick me with your fork!'

"In my vision I saw a group of Christians with our pastor. I yelled, 'Brother Vasile, save me!' They were standing in a cloud, singing. I yelled again, 'Help me! Save me!' In the dream, I saw Bunica pleading with them to pray for my salvation.

"Then, in my vision, I remembered what I had heard about the blood of Jesus cleansing our hearts from sin. So I began crying out to Jesus to save me by His blood. Just before the vision ended I heard the people in the cloud rejoice, 'One more soul is saved from hell.' Then I lost consciousness.

"When the doctor saw my body relax, I guess he must have thought I died. They had restrained me with bands when I was thrashing around, but now they untied the bands and covered me with a sheet.

"When I became conscious again, I was shocked to find myself lying in the morgue, completely covered with a sheet. Even in my horror I was too weak to do much, but when I heard someone mopping the floor, I asked,

'Why did they put me in here?'

"There was a yell from the cleaning lady, and she rushed out of the morgue. Soon someone came, dressed me, and put me back into a bed. I stayed in the hospital for several days before my parents took me back home."

Mosu nodded his head. "When we came to pick up your father to take him home, the doctor asked us, 'Who is Vasile? Your son yelled for him to save him from the devil.' I think this experience had shaken the doctor."

Elena moved her leg. Sharp needles of pain prickled her skin. Her heart was beating fast. Her Tata had almost died! She shivered.

"But children," said Tata, very much alive now, "that experience taught me so much. I learned it was extremely dangerous to not be obedient to the will of God. When I drank that whiskey, I was going against what God wanted for me. Yet, in His mercy He saved me. When I cried out for the blood of Jesus to save me, God heard my prayer.

"After that, I gave my life completely into God's hands. I held nothing back. I loved going to church and singing and praying with my parents and the other Christians. We had a group of about eighteen families that met regularly. We became like a family. Many times, the Orthodox priest tried to stir up trouble against us, but that didn't keep us from getting together. Our love for each other and for God was too great."

"The priest still tries to make trouble," Lidia murmured. "He still doesn't like us."

The children all knew that. They had suffered many times from the taunts of other children in the village and felt the scorn heaped on the whole family whenever they met the priest in the streets.

"Jesus told us we would go through these things," Bunica said simply. "The Bible says that all who live godly lives will suffer persecution. We count it an honor to suffer for the name of Christ."

"Did they beat you in prison?" Elena asked softly. "Did they beat you with a stick?"

Tata stroked her hair. He saw the fear in his daughter's eyes. Nearly six years old, she was old enough to understand what suffering meant.

"Elena, my child, do not worry. God always gives us strength when we need it. He has promised never to leave us nor forsake us."

"I—I don't think I could stand being beaten," Elena's voice was low and hesitant. "It would hurt too much."

"We pray that you will never need to suffer that," Tata assured her. "I pray all the time that my family would be protected from harm and evil." He smiled reassuringly at his children.

A sense of peace flooded over the little room. The crowded house, the meager food supply, the day-to-day struggle for survival—these things receded into the background. The Boghian family had few earthly riches, but their blessings from heaven were very real as Gheorghita shared his testimony with his family. God had blessed them with the greatest gift given to man—a living faith and a close relationship with Jesus Christ. Indeed, they were rich.

4

We Need Our Land!

Humble yourselves therefore under the mighty hand of God, that he may exalt you in due time: Casting all your care upon him; for he careth for you.

I Peter 5:6-7

"Mosu! Bunica! What is wrong?" Elena heard alarm in her father's voice as he came into their little house. She turned to see what was happening.

A sheet of paper was spread on their little table, and her grandparents were staring at it with unseeing eyes. Gheorghita strode across the room. Looking over their shoulders, he began to read. His shoulders slumped.

"It has happened." His voice sounded flat and defeated. He picked up the paper. "First, they took the land away from the rich. Now, they are taking the land away from the poor."

Mosu said reflectively, "When they took away *Solonar's* farm right here in Patrauti, we understood that they would leave everyone at least 4 *hectares* of land. Solonar had 18 hectares, so they took 14 hectares and left the rest to him. Next, they are confiscating all the land anyone owns over two hectares. I never imagined they would demand this much!"

Elena's eyes were glued to her Bunica's face. What was happening? What was all this about "they" taking away land? Their land?

"Call the children," Bunica told her son. "Call Viorica and all the children. We will take this letter to the Lord as Hezekiah took his letter before the Lord."

"Elena, call the children and tell them to come inside," Gheorghita instructed immediately. He turned his back toward his parents and stared out the window.

Elena dashed outside toward the garden where Lidia, Vasile, and Dan were working. Panting, she ran between the rows of potatoes her siblings were hoeing.

Vasile grinned at her when she arrived. "Are you coming to help?" he teased.

Elena did not smile back. "Come! We must go inside! Someone is taking our land!" Elena blurted out her message.

"What?" Lidia exclaimed, her brows drawn together in consternation. "What do you mean? Are they here now?"

Elena shook her head. "There is a piece of paper that says it. A letter."

The children shouldered their hoes and headed toward the house. Silence settled over them. What new storm cloud was gathering over their home? Apprehensively, they entered the house.

"Come, children." Gheorghita drew his older children to himself as he knelt on the simple wooden floor. "We do not know what trouble is coming into our lives. We will take our need to God."

Mosu and Bunica were already on their knees, praying. Mama and the little children had joined the circle on the floor.

Elena squeezed her eyes shut. She listened to the prayers of her grandparents and her parents. She heard Lidia and her older brothers praying. She, too, began to pray.

Her voice was almost drowned out by the prayers and weeping of the others, but she prayed anyway. "Dear God, please help us. Don't let anyone take away our land. Don't let them take away our garden."

She imagined someone coming with big trucks and shoveling up all the dirt around the house and hauling it off. What would happen to the house? Where would they live? Questions swirled through her mind, but there were no answers. Then she heard Tata's prayer:

". . . we put our trust in You." His strong voice carried easily to Elena's listening ears. "We don't know what all is going to happen, but we will not stop trusting You for our needs. We love You because of Your great gift of Jesus Christ as our Savior. We want to say, Your will be done."

She felt reassured. If Tata could pray with such confidence, surely God would hear them and not let anyone take away their land.

"It's getting worse," Mosu said, coming in the door after work. His shoulders drooped with a weariness from more than just the days' work. "They have taken *Viorel's* land, and I heard that a man was beaten because he refused to sign his land over to the state." His face was haggard with worry.

Bunica lifted her hands from the table. "Oh Lord, look down on Your children! What will happen to all of us?"

When Gheorghita returned, he brought more distressing news. "People are getting notices to come to the village headquarters and sign forms to give up their land. The forms state that the owners voluntarily give their land to the state. In turn, they are promised secure jobs and free medical care."

"Our people have yet to see any benefits from what is happening," Mosu said slowly. He sat on a wooden chair and rested his head in his hands.

"We were hoping for a good harvest so we could afford to finish the house," Viorica said thoughtfully. "It's nice to be in these two rooms but we need more room. How can we give up our land?"

Elena paused from setting bowls on the table. She frowned. There it was again. This talk of someone taking their land. How could they take it? What would be left for them around the house?

"What would be left for us?" Bunica asked the men. "Anything?"

Gheorghita shook his head. "I don't think anything will be left. They're taking all the land along the road to *Suceava*. Already I have seen heavy tractors at work not far from our fields."

"What of the crops that are already planted? There is still a month before the potatoes are ready for harvest!" Viorica voiced all of their thoughts.

"Virginia said at school today that her family was digging what they could get," Lidia said in a small voice. "She said the potatoes were still quite little."

Bunica drew in her breath sharply. Then she bowed her head. Her lips moved and she closed her eyes. A heavy silence settled over the room.

"I will not sign," Mosu said firmly. He faced the young government official in the mayor's office. "I will not voluntarily give my land away to anyone. This land has belonged to my family for years and years. We need the land to provide for my family and for my son's family."

"Hah!" the official sneered. "You're an old man! You aren't able to work the land anymore. All the land in this area is going to be taken by the State. If you do not sign this paper, we have ways to make you glad to sign." The threat hung in the air.

"I will not sign," Mosu reiterated. "It is our land."

"We will see about that!" He made a note on the files in front of him. "Now get out of here!" The official rudely motioned him away.

Mosu turned and left the room. He reached for the iron railing to steady himself as he went down the steps and out onto the street.

"Good day," he said politely to the men on the street.

Not many answered. A cloud of oppression hung over the group. Mosu slowly made his way home.

"What did the teacher say?" Vasile asked, his nose wrinkling up in bewilderment. "Why are we being sent home?"

Lidia shook her head. "He just said we can't come to school until our grandparents and parents cooperate with the authorities. He told us not to come back without an official document from the government office."

"But—school?" Dan was puzzled. "What does signing over our land have to do with us going to school?"

"I don't know," Lidia said. "But I need to finish my exams to get ready for high school. They have to let me come back!" She shook her dark hair emphatically.

Elena and Rodica followed the older three children down the sidewalk to their front gate. The Boghian house was just around the corner from the village school where all the children attended until they graduated from eighth grade. Lidia was in her last year of grade school. Next year, she hoped to attend high school in Suceava.

"What?" Viorica stared at the five children as they walked slowly into their home. "Why are you coming home? What has happened?" Her eyes searched the faces of her school children.

"They told us we can't come to school anymore," Lidia told her mother. "They said we can't come back until we have government papers saying we cooperate with them."

"Until we give our land away!" Viorica's hand flew to her throat. "They are trying to force us through our children! Oh! What will become of us?"

The Boghian children were subdued that day. The unexpected holiday was not one of freedom. Uncertainty hung over their heads and clouded anything they normally would have enjoyed.

When their grandparents returned from their work in the fields, they, too, were subdued and quiet. Only after Gheorghita returned from his job in Suceava did they begin to talk.

It was after supper and they were all still sitting around the table. Mosu cleared his throat. "I am to report to work at the new collective farm tomorrow."

"Surely not!" Gheorghita stared at his father. "They are not forcing you to work at your age!"

Mosu nodded his head slowly. "I must. People are being beaten if they do not obey the new rules."

"*Dorel* has committed suicide," Bunica said with tears. "His widow says he told her he would rather die than give up his land and go work on the collective farm. They took his land, his cow, and his pigs. They only left a few hens."

"They won't let us attend school anymore," Lidia said, close to tears. "They sent us home today."

The adults' eyes turned to the children. "They are trying to force us to sign over the land," Mosu said softly. "They will not give up."

"But how can we give the land away?" Viorica was close to tears. "We need our land to provide food for the family! What will become of us?"

"Shh!" Bunica said lovingly. "Has not God promised that He will look after us? I will put my trust in Him. Gheorghita, why don't you read to us from Revelation 21? We need to turn our minds away from earthly trouble and think of our future in Heaven where none of these troubles will exist. No one can take away our heavenly mansions!"

"Come on, old lady. Sign here. Your husband signed and now you must sign too." The government official stood threateningly over Bunica. He had rudely entered their house and shoved a paper in front of Bunica.

Viorica and the children were crowded into the opposite corner. Elena felt her heart beat rapidly. What would he do to their Bunica?

"I will not sign," Bunica said softly. "The land is our land and we need it. This says we voluntarily give our land to the government. That is not true. I cannot sign to a lie."

How could Bunica be so calm? How could she speak in such a measured, even serene voice? Elena trembled inside. She crowded closely against Lidia.

"You must sign. Your husband and your son have already signed. Can't you see their signatures?"

Bunica squinted at the paper. She saw her husband's name "Costache

Boghian." Had he really signed this? It looked like his signature.

The official jiggled the paper impatiently. "Come, come. Your husband is the head of this home, is he not? If he has consented to our request, surely you must comply."

Bunica sighed. "I wish Costache were at home. I don't know what to do!"

The official waited. He cleared his throat importantly. "This will be to the benefit of everyone. We will all share everything with everyone."

"But this is not right to force people to give away their land!" Bunica tried to reason. "You are making us do what is not right for our family!"

"Lady, everyone has to comply. We cannot make any exceptions. I explained this to your husband and son and they finally understood. Just sign the paper they already signed."

With a sigh, Bunica picked up the proffered pen. She shakily signed her name, "Raveca Boghian" beneath her husband's name.

"Now you, ma'am," the officer addressed Mama.

Viorica looked at Bunica and then at the paper.

"Sign right here under your husband's name." The official pointed to a space beneath his signature.

There was something about the signature that did not look quite right. It looked smaller than Gheorghita's usual signature.

Reluctantly, Viorica signed her name.

The official snatched the paper almost gleefully. He hurried out the door without another word.

"I don't know if we should have signed," Bunica turned to her daughter-in-law. "Something just doesn't seem quite right. I can't imagine what would have persuaded the men to change their minds and sign away our land!"

"I did not sign," Mosu said wearily that evening. "They must have forged my signature. And now our land is gone. They have taken it by force."

"We must hurry and harvest the potatoes," Tata told the family as soon as he came home from work and found out what had happened. "We must salvage what we can. Some families lost their entire harvest because they hadn't dug the potatoes before the government plowed the land."

"How could they ruin people's fields?" Dan burst out. "Who would be mean enough to drive the tractors and ruin people's potatoes and corn?"

"There are those who gladly do it," Tata replied. "People who had very little or nothing before this now run the machinery. They are suddenly in a position of power. They gladly obey their superior's orders to plow under the crops.

"But we must hurry. Vasile, hitch the cows to the wagon. We will all go and work until dark. All except Bunica and Mama and the little ones."

"Gheorghita, I must come too." Viorica pled with her husband. "The little children will be all right with Bunica. We must hurry! We need the potatoes for next winter!" Desperation put a pleading note into her voice.

Gheorghita hesitated.

"I will be all right," Bunica said firmly. "Take her, Gheorghita! She is right. You must harvest all you can. The potatoes will be small enough as it is."

Elena hurried down the row with her basket. With nimble fingers she picked up the potatoes that Tata and the boys had dug with their hoes. She carried the full pail to the wagon and dumped the potatoes on the bed. Then she hurried back.

All over the surrounding fields, families were working in a frenzy, harvesting whatever they could. Toward Suceava, the huge tractors had already turned over scores of family plots. The soil lay raw and exposed in the evening light.

For years, each family had tilled their own plot and harvested their crops from the rich Romanian soil. Now, one by one, the land was being confiscated by the government. With tears and laments, the villagers mourned. They felt forlorn and beaten. A dark shadow had fallen over the land.

Three men in uniform entered the Boghian yard. They marched up to the door and knocked. The warm midday sun beat down on the roof.

Bunica opened the door. She looked calmly at the three. "Yes!" she said pleasantly.

"We are here under orders to collect agricultural implements for the State farm." He glanced at his paper. "You have a total of 12 people living here, is that correct?"

"Yes," Bunica replied calmly. Viorica came to the door and looked out over Bunica's shoulder.

"We will take your agricultural equipment. In addition, you will be responsible to provide a quota of goods to the State farm. Here is the list."

Bunica looked at the paper. Eggs. Milk. Meat. Wool. They were to give a quota of the production of what little they had. How could they meet this and still feed everyone in their large family?

"You are to bring these goods to the village office. You will be checked for compliance with the government." Then he and his companions turned and walked toward the little barn the Boghians had built after the fire.

Bunica and Viorica watched them as they walked away. "I guess you won't need our spoons and forks, too, will you?" Bunica asked dryly.

The spokesman turned sharply. "You had better watch out! Your tongue can cause you a lot of trouble!" Then he turned to his task.

The children watched silently through the window as the men hunted through the barn for any "agricultural" tools the State farm could use. What could they take? Their hoes? Their spade? Would there be no mercy in their poverty?

The family watched in disbelief as the men pulled the old wagon into the courtyard. They heaved the plow and the cultivator into the wagon. Then they pulled the wagon out the gate and into the street. The gate clanged shut behind them.

"They take even from the poorest," Viorica said in a trembling voice. "How can they be so heartless? How can we feed our family?"

Elena heard the despair in her mother's voice. A cold hand of fear clutched at her insides.

"Surely, these are the end times," Bunica said soberly. "When even the few things we have are taken away."

Then she straightened her shoulders. "But we will not complain! The Bible tells us these things will happen. One thing they can't take from us is our faith in Jesus Christ!" A smile broke out over the wrinkled face of the elderly woman.

"And thank God, they didn't take any of the livestock! They must have taken into consideration that there are twelve of us. Some of our neighbors have not been so blessed. The government has confiscated horses, cows, sheep, pigs, and even chickens from people they thought had too many. At least we have our animals! Thank-you, Jesus!"

The sun broke out from behind the clouds and beamed through the windows in the little cottage. A warming ray rested lightly on Elena's cheek. She looked at her grandmother with trusting eyes, her fears of the moment forgotten.

"Of course your children can go back to school! Here is the document they need! Since you have cooperated with us, there is no reason why they can't attend again." The officer sounded almost chatty as he handed Gheorghita a document stamped with an official seal.

Gheorghita silently accepted the folded form and left. He joined his waiting children and accompanied them across the road to the school.

"Oh, Mr. Boghian! How are you?" The principal's cheerfulness sounded forced. He could not bring himself to meet Gheorghita's eyes.

"Here is the document from the mayor's office, allowing my children to attend school again," Gheorghita said flatly, handing the paper to the principal.

"Yes, yes!" The principal took the proffered document and unfolded it rapidly. He glanced over it and then addressed the children.

"You may go to your usual classes. Thank-you, Mr. Boghian."

Gheorghita watched his children hurry down the hall, then he turned and left the school. He would have to explain to his boss why he was late. Not that it would do much good. He headed toward the bus stop.

5

Two Widows

A FATHER TO THE FATHERLESS, AND A JUDGE OF THE WIDOWS, IS GOD IN HIS HOLY HABITATION.

PSALM 68:5

"Lidia, what is the formula for finding the area of a triangle?" Dan asked, frowning at his geometry book.

"Area equals one half the base times height," Lidia answered automatically, not lifting her eyes from her history book.

Vasile yawned and stretched his arms above his head. He winked at Elena who had lifted her head from her homework when Dan had spoken.

Elena glanced around the single room that served as their family's kitchen and living room by day and their bedroom by night. Then, she busied herself with her third-grade homework at the table in the middle of the room.

The five oldest children were doing their homework while their mother fixed supper. The three youngest children played by the brick stove that warmed the room.

Elena heard the door of the small, front entry open. She listened intently for Tata's footsteps. When the door into their room did not open, she dropped her eyes to her book again. It must be Mosu coming home from work and going into the only other finished room in their new house. At least Bunica and Mosu now had their own private room. It was smaller than the room the rest of them lived in, but it was warmed by the stove and comfortable for the old couple.

"Children, clear the table. Tata should soon be here," Mama said as the April twilight slowly died away outside. "Boys, make sure there is wood stacked up on the porch for the stove. Lidia, could you finish stirring the mamaliga? I need to feed the baby. Elena, please set the table."

Viorica picked up her youngest child, *Maricica.* Just over a year old, Maricica cuddled up against her mother's breast. Viorica sat on a cot with a sigh. It felt good to be off her feet.

Elena set eleven bowls and spoons around the table. Little Maricica did not eat at the table yet. Even though two-year-old *Nicu* still sat on Tata's lap to eat, he recently had insisted on his own bowl and spoon too.

"Viorica." Bunica came in the door of their room. "I will just take a bowl of mamaliga in to Mosu. He has been hauling manure with a wheelbarrow all day and is tired out. I'll eat with him in our room."

Just then Tata entered with dragging feet. He sat down at the table and rested his hands on his head.

"Son, is your job wearing you out?" Bunica paused in ladling out the hot mamaliga and looked at Gheorghita.

"We almost had an accident today," Tata said slowly.

"What happened?" Lidia asked quickly. All the children's eyes turned toward their father. Mama and Bunica gave gasps of dismay.

"We were digging the foundation for a basement in a part of the factory building. We had finished digging a ditch that was deeper than I am tall and had just started putting the wooden forms in when we heard dirt begin to fall." Tata paused and slowly shook his head. "It was a terrible sound."

"Did anyone—was anyone hurt?" Bunica interrupted.

Tata shook his head. "No. I was at the ladder and the men came screaming toward me. I held the ladder while they all scrambled out of there before the dirt caved in."

"Tata! Why didn't you climb out as soon as you heard the dirt cave in?" Vasile asked, a small line furrowing his forehead.

At first, Tata did not answer. Then he looked lovingly at his wife and each one of his children. He smiled at them.

"That was my first thought, children. When the dirt started falling, I was ready to spring for the ladder and get out of there fast. But something stopped me.

"I knew that the other men were not ready to die. Many times I have witnessed to them about being prepared for death, and they all just laugh at me. I know they are not prepared to meet Jesus. I couldn't make myself get out until I knew they were all safe."

For a long moment, no one spoke. Then Bunica said, "You did the right thing, son. Maybe this experience will cause them to think about their souls. They need to repent from their sins and believe on the Lord Jesus."

She spooned some more mamaliga into a second bowl. "How wonderful it is to have Jesus in our hearts and be ready to meet Him at any time. There have been so many accidents recently!"

It was true. Many times Tata came home with stories of fatal accidents on the job. A huge paper mill was being built in Suceava, and he and hundreds of other workers labored day after day at the construction.

"Come, sit down," Viorica called to the little children. "Your Tata is tired and I am sure he is hungry."

They bowed their heads. "Dear Lord," Tata prayed. "We are thankful to You for this food. Thank-you for loving us so much that we can have something to eat. We are thankful for our house and for the clothes we have. Much more, we are thankful for each other as a family. But most of all we thank You for our Savior, Jesus Christ. I thank You that You spared the lives of the men today. God, speak to them and help them see that they need to repent and turn to Jesus. Thank-you for sparing my life today. I know all our lives are a gift from You. Thank-you for letting us be together tonight. In Jesus' name, amen."

Elena studied her father's face. The care and tiredness that had earlier been so visible were gone. Instead, a deep peace seemed to glow from his eyes as he looked around the table at his family. Elena gave a little sigh. Something inside of her settled back to normal. She pushed her bowl forward for a helping of mamaliga.

"Something is wrong with Mosu!" It was Bunica hurrying into their room. "He had just eaten his supper and laid back on the cot when all of a sudden he began groaning and moaning in pain! Viorica, is there still some of the herbal tea in the container?"

Mama hastily stood up and headed for the cupboard. Tata rose and hurried to his father.

"Oh, Lord Jesus!" Elena heard her grandmother pray. "Please be merciful to my husband!"

"Here! Take this! No, wait! Let me make the tea and then we will bring it over!" Mama shoved the teakettle to the hottest part of the stove top.

Bunica hurried back to her room.

Through the closed door, the family could hear the moans of their grandfather. The little children looked at each other with wide eyes. Elena felt something hard rise up in her throat. She could not eat her mamaliga.

Tata called Vasile and spoke to him in the entry, then sent him out the front door. The rest of the children waited to see where Vasile was sent.

But they did not ask any questions. They quietly went about their tasks of clearing away the dishes.

Viorica went briefly into the other room and soon returned, her eyes wet with tears.

"Someone is coming!" Dan whispered as they heard the front gate open. The children peered out into the dark.

"It's Pastor Vasile! And some more brothers from the church!"

"Yes, children," Mama answered behind them. "Mosu asked for anointing from the brethren. Our Vasile went to ask them to come."

Dear Mosu! Elena felt numb. He must be very sick! She felt her knees trembling.

"Children, I will go to pray with them. You must be very quiet. Lidia, see if you can get Maricica to sleep." Mama slipped out and closed the door behind her.

"I'm scared," Rodica said with a trembling voice. "What will happen to Mosu?"

Lidia took Maricica and sat on the cot. The other children crowded around their oldest sister. They heard Vasile come in. He took off his jacket and sat down, breathing heavily.

"We will pray for Mosu," Lidia said simply. "We will ask God to heal our Mosu!"

The children knelt on the floor. They began to pray, asking God to bring healing to their grandfather. Little Lucia, only five years old, knew how to pray. Even Nicu, not quite three, knew how to pray. They had all been taught to pray as soon as they could talk.

They ended their prayers as they had heard their parents and their grandparents do countless times. "May Your will, Lord, be done. Help us to accept whatever answer You give us."

"Come in!" Elena heard dear Bunica's voice in answer to her knock. She slowly pushed the door open.

"Oh, Elena! Come in and close the door." With tender tones, Bunica addressed her granddaughter. She turned from the little table where her open Bible was spread before her.

Elena began to cry. Sobs wracked her thin frame as she pressed her face against her grandmother's shoulder.

"There, there," Bunica's voice soothed her. Her own eyes were wet with tears. "Yes, we must cry, for we do miss dear Mosu so much! But we don't cry as those who have no hope for their loved ones. Elena dear, we must have joy for Mosu! He has gone before us! Even though we miss him, think where he is!

"Elena, I can see Jesus opening His arms and welcoming Mosu home! After all the pain and suffering Mosu had in his last five days, now he is in heaven with Jesus! We are happy for him!"

Elena nodded. But something still bothered her. "I can still see him in the casket, Bunica. I try to think of him in heaven, but my mind wants to tell me he is just buried in the ground."

"Yes, dear child." Strong but loving hands smoothed back Elena's dark hair. "I know it looks like Mosu is buried in the ground, but that is just his body. His worn-out body. His soul has gone to meet Jesus and he will be given a new body, just like it says here in the Bible." Bunica pointed to the open Book in front of her.

"Even in our sadness, there is joy! Joy to know that dear Mosu has gone to live with Jesus forever! Forever, Elena! Never will he have pain and suffering again. All his troubles are over! Now he can be with Jesus through all eternity!" The old lady's voice choked with emotion, her eyes sparkling through tears. "Thank-you, Jesus! Thank-you for our hope! For our salvation!"

Elena was caught up in the emotions of her grandmother. She knew that dear Bunica's faith was giving her strength through the ordeal of losing her husband. She was not grieving like many of the widows in their village when their husbands had passed away. No! Her grandmother had living faith!

All through the days of her husband's illness, Raveca had been steadfast in her faith. Her confidence in God had not wavered even after the doctor told her there was no hope of saving her husband's life.

To the very end, she had received her strength from God. When Costache had died, saying, "My Lord Jesus! My Savior!" Raveca had willingly surrendered her husband into the hands of their Lord and Redeemer. Her tears of sorrow had been washed away by the tears of joy that all griefs and sorrows were now over for her husband.

Now she comforted her granddaughter. Knowing the terror of death for a young girl, she opened the window of her heart and tenderly, through her own example, led the trembling girl to a greater understanding of life after death. The sting of death and the dread of the grave was softened for Elena.

"Son, you are not well." Bunica laid her hand on Gheorghita's head. She looked in concern at his sunken eyes and hollow cheeks.

Wearily, Gheorghita lifted his eyes and looked at his mother. "I must not get sick," he murmured in a low voice. "I have to keep working!"

Viorica hurried over to the table. "Gheorghita! You are ill! What is wrong?"

"I'm not sure." Limply, Gheorghita pushed the bowl away. Supper was over, and for some reason he could hardly move. "I just feel so weak."

"Come, you must rest." Viorica tugged on the arm of her husband. She helped him to the cot near the stove.

The children watched their father slump onto the cot. Elena dashed to lift his feet and put them up so Tata could rest comfortably. Suddenly, he looked old. Old and worn out. There was something about his face, lying still on the pillow, that reminded her of Mosu. Sudden tears sprang to her eyes.

Shaking her head against the unwelcome tears, she pulled a blanket up to her father's chin and smoothed away the wrinkles.

The next day, Sunday, Tata insisted he felt well enough to go to church. In the afternoon, he lay down to rest.

Bunica made some herbal tea for him to drink. Viorica asked the older children to take the little ones outside so their father could rest better.

Elena tried to brush away the cloud that hovered over her. She played with her siblings for awhile and then softly went inside. She could hear her Tata's deep breathing as he slept. Settling down on another cot, Elena read her books and tried to shut her mind to the dismal thoughts that wanted to crowd in.

The next morning, Gheorghita forced himself to eat breakfast. Viorica hovered over him. "Do you think you should go to work? Perhaps you should just stay at home for a day to rest."

"I can't," Gheorghita shook his head. "If I don't report for work, I could lose my job. We need the little wages this job pays. With another baby on the way, I can't get sick! I have to go!"

"How can you walk even to the bus stop?" Bunica, too, was worried.

"I will go on the truck that picks up the workers," Gheorghita tried to reassure them. "I won't have to walk very far at all."

"It will be cold on the open truck!" Viorica said in despair. "You must take the heaviest coat you have!"

Gheorghita prepared to leave. Bundled up against the cold October morning, he took his lunch box and turned toward the door. Viorica stood on tiptoe and kissed him good-bye. For a brief moment, the two stood in an embrace. Then Gheorghita left. He closed the door softly behind him.

"Ma'am, I came to tell you that your husband is in the hospital in *Burdujeni*. He became very ill at work, and the ambulance came to transport him."

Elena stared at the messenger. His left eye twitched as he delivered the news. He smoothed his hair.

"What's wrong with Gheorghita?" Viorica asked in dismay.

"Ma'am, I don't know. I just wanted to let you know why your husband is not coming home tonight. I would think he is well taken care of."

"There was no accident?" Bunica asked. "He just became ill?"

"That's right. He was sick in the morning and became worse during the day. They took him in the afternoon."

"Mama!" Elena grabbed her mother's arm. "You must go see him!"

The man was turning to leave. He heard Elena's plea.

"You cannot see him now," he said simply. "Visiting hours are Thursday and Sunday afternoons only."

The words fell heavily on the family's ears. This was only Monday. They stared in disbelief at Gheorghita's co-worker.

"I'm sorry, but I'm sure he will be well taken care of." In spite of his attempt to be cheerful, his voice lacked conviction. He turned and left.

"Come, we will pray for your tata." Bunica gathered everyone in a circle and prayed for her son. Viorica prayed for her husband. The children prayed for their father.

They prayed for healing. They prayed for strength. They prayed for grace to accept whatever might happen to them.

Elena knelt to pray along with the others. But the cloud of foreboding that was hovering over her became darker, heavier, threatening to smother her. She cried out to God to heal her sick father.

Viorica shifted her bag from one arm to the other. She cleared her throat. Gathering courage, she spoke to the guard on the other side of the gate.

"Sir, I came to see my husband. He is sick and I brought him food."

The guard looked at the village woman and saw the anxiety written on her face. He opened the gate to let her pass through. "Knock on the front door," he instructed. "Someone will meet you there."

Viorica passed through the gate and walked up the drive beneath the silent, outstretched arms of the trees lining the driveway. Her lips moved in silent supplication.

She was anxious to see her husband. She had asked *Sora Niculina* to check on him yesterday. Niculina lived near the hospital and had been glad to make the visit, paying the right people for the privilege of visiting outside of the established hours. Through Niculina, Viorica had known what food and personal items Gheorghita needed. The bag on her arm had been lovingly packed for today's visiting hours.

"Yes?" The white uniformed nurse who answered her knock stood blocking entry into the hospital.

A chill swept through the door along with the antiseptic smell of all hospitals. "I came—I came to see my husband."

"What is your name?"

"Viorica Boghian. I am Gheorghita Boghian's wife."

The nurse looked at her mutely for several moments. "You—you will need to speak to the doctor," she stammered and turned quickly. "Wait here."

It seemed like a long time to Viorica before the door opened and a man dressed in white opened the door. He looked down on the small woman waiting outside the door.

"You are Gheorghita Boghian's wife?"

Viorica nodded.

"Come into my office."

With a motion of his hand, the doctor indicated a chair. Then he began asking questions. "How many children do you have?"

"We have eight children."

The doctor raised both eyebrows. "How old are you?"

Viorica hesitated a moment. Why was the doctor asking all these questions? They did not seem pertinent to her. "I am thirty-eight."

"How is it with your family? How do you manage with so many children?"

"My husband's mother lives with us. We—we manage." What was happening? Was this questioning connected in any way with the inquiry of the police early this morning?

Viorica had been summoned to the door of their home by a knock. The village policeman, who lived across the street from them, had been there with a query. "Is Gheorghita at home?" he had asked.

After Viorica had told him, "No, my husband is at the hospital," the policeman had looked at her keenly and replied, "Oh! I thought he was at home."

There had been no more explanations. The policeman had gone home, leaving the family deeply puzzled over the incident. Now this questioning by the doctor. What was happening?

The doctor studied Viorica. Then he said simply, "Your husband is not here. He was transferred to Suceava."

Immediately Viorica stood up to leave. She clutched the bag of food to her breast. "Then I will go to the hospital there to see him."

"Lady, not to the hospital. To the morgue."

Viorica stared at the doctor. "What? Why did they send him there?" She was bewildered. "That is no place for a sick man! You mean . . ." Her words trailed off into a small gasp of disbelief. She turned and fled the hospital.

In shock, she sought help from her step-brother, *Nicolae*, and his wife, who lived in the city. "The doctor says they have put Gheorghita in a morgue!" Viorica cried to her relatives. "Why have they put him in a morgue?" Her mind refused to think logically.

Sister-in-law *Vighenia* immediately put on her coat. "We will go and see. Come, Viorica."

Nobody answered the door to their knock. The solid metal door guarding the entrance to the morgue stayed shut. The two knocked again and again.

"It's too late in the day," Viorica decided. "No one will come." She held herself rigid. Her breathing was rapid.

"The window!" Vighenia motioned to her. "Around the corner there is a window! We will look inside and see if he . . . what we can see."

They silently moved around the corner of the building. The morgue was at the rear of the hospital, and bare trees were the only spectators to what was happening.

"Viorica, lift me up so I can get a grip on the ledge."

Vighenia grabbed the edges of the window and pulled herself up as Viorica wrapped her arms around her and lifted her.

A small gasp escaped from Vighenia. "There he is! I see him!" She peered between the bars and shaded the window with her hands. "He looks like he is sleeping."

"Is he—dead?" Viorica could hardly make herself say the word.

"Viorica! Let me down! Viorica! I will help you look inside!"

Viorica bowed her head. "No, I—I can't!"

"Dear sister, you should! You can see how peaceful his face is!"

Viorica's racing heart thumped painfully inside her chest, just above her unborn baby. She opened her mouth and tried to breathe deeply.

"Here, Viorica! I will help you," Vighenia insisted.

With numb hands, Viorica held onto the ledge as Vighenia hoisted her up. She tried to peer through the window. She couldn't see. She cupped her one hand in front of her eyes.

There was Gheorghita. Her husband. His eyes were closed and his body was covered with a white sheet. He lay on his back, completely still. Viorica began to sob.

Lovingly, Vighenia helped her down. Viorica leaned heavily on the arms of her sister-in-law as the two moved around to the front of the brick building. Viorica's feet dragged with every step as they left the hospital compound. Low moans of pain escaped from deep inside of her.

Elena scarcely heard the conversation swirling around her. She stood with her siblings in a tight knot behind her mother and grandmother. Other relatives pressed around them.

"Please let his wife see his body!" Bunica spoke pleadingly to the caretaker.

"No! I am under orders that no one is to see him! His casket is to be sealed so the infectious disease he has can't be spread!" The caretaker was clearly under duress.

"What disease?" Bunica argued. "Yesterday they told Nicolae that the body would be released to us today. How is it possible that today we are denied access to his body?"

The caretaker hesitated. "I am under orders." His words came out by force of habit.

"Oh, Lord! Please soften this man's heart and let Viorica see her husband once more," Bunica prayed sincerely. "Create some miracle and open the door for my daughter-in-law!"

Elena heard her grandmother's prayer. She waited to see what would happen.

“Just the wife, then,” the caretaker said suddenly, looking over his shoulder. “And only for a few minutes. No crying, no wailing.” He opened the door.

Elena watched her mama enter as Bunica stood aside. And then, as if drawn by an irresistible force, the children surged toward the door. The caretaker was overwhelmed by the number of children and watched mutely as they followed their mother. Bunica brought up the rear with little Lucia in her arms.

A long, muffled sob tore at Elena’s throat as she looked on the face of her Tata. It looked as though he were merely sleeping. She wanted to cry out and wake the silent figure before her. Memories of her father surged through her. She could still feel the gentle touch of his hand upon her head, and see his brown eyes, now behind closed lids, that could make every corner of her heart warm and comfortable. Tears spilled out over her cheeks as she gazed longingly and lovingly at Tata’s body.

Through her grief, Elena became aware of the commotion around her. “Out! You must get out!” The caretaker was frantically trying to regain control of the situation. Elena saw some of her relatives inside the morgue. Someone took a picture of the family clustered around the coffin.

“No! You are not to take pictures! You must leave immediately!” The caretaker’s voice cracked under the strain of his predicament. His eyes wide, panic stricken, he darted around the group, pulling at their clothes, pushing them toward the door. “This is terrible! You must leave!”

Silently, they left. The panting caretaker swung the door shut and locked it.

There was nothing left to do except leave. Nothing to face but another funeral. Another grave. Another time of grief.

“I must tell you that when I saw Gheorghita, I was shocked by how he looked.” Sora Niculina told Bunica and Viorica. She sat forward on the cot in their house. “I knew something was wrong.”

“How—how did he look?” Elena heard the anguish in her mother’s voice. She tried to swallow the lump that refused to go away. She had worked on that lump all during her Tata’s funeral and the two days since.

“Well, his skin was so gray. And he told me that the doctor would inject him with ten vials of medicine all at once. He said he could not think clearly afterwards. This was on Wednesday that I saw him.” Gheorghita had been admitted on Monday.

"Do you think—" Mama's voice broke off, as if she was horrified at her thoughts. "Do you think they wanted him to die? Perhaps even killed him? But why would they do such a thing? He never harmed anyone!" The questions tumbled from Mama's mouth as she rocked in pain.

Bunica shook her head slightly. "He had his enemies. The bosses at the construction site did not like that he was telling the others about his faith. We may never know what really happened. But one thing we know—God does not make mistakes. Even allowing Gheorghita to die is for some purpose. Though right now it is very difficult to accept." Her head was bowed.

"I'm praying for you," Sora Niculina said with tears. "Surely God will look on you with mercy. Two widows and eight children." Then she looked at the sorrowing figure of Viorica. "And another one on the way. May God have mercy."

"We will not despair." Bunica lifted her head and quoted in a trembling voice, "'I will never leave you nor forsake you,' He said. I claim that promise for me, for Viorica, and for the children!"

A feeling of comfort stole over Elena's heart as she saw her grandmother's faith shine through the darkness. How God would care for them, she did not know. But she knew that the faith of her grandmother was comforting her once more.

6

Life Afterwards

For our light affliction, which is but for a moment, worketh for us a far more exceeding and eternal weight of glory.

II Corinthians 4:17

"There is no way you can afford to bring up another child, Viorica! You can't even afford to feed the ones you have! Your mother-in-law is an old woman. You live in an unfinished house. I tell you, you must consider what I am recommending." The strident voice of their neighbor reached to the kitchen where Lidia and Elena were washing the supper dishes.

"No," Viorica's voice was firm. "That would be a sin. I don't know how God will provide for us, but I have faith that He will not leave us without food and clothes."

"God! Where is God? Where was He when they took away our land, our animals, and our plows? You say you trust in God? You, who have no husband and no one left to provide for you! How will God provide for your eight living children, without you adding yet another one? If you went to the hospital and explained your predicament, you could have a free abortion."

Elena looked wide-eyed at her older sister. Whatever was *Tanti Aurora* saying? How could she be so cruel? Her mother would never consent to having an abortion, would she?

"That woman!" Lidia whispered vehemently. "I wish she would go home!"

There was no answer from Mama. The two girls listened intently.

The outside door opened into the little entry. Bunica's familiar footsteps came inside. She carried a pail of milk into the kitchen where the girls were working.

"Bunica!" Lidia burst out in a passion. "Tanti Aurora is in there with

Mama. She's trying to persuade Mama to get an abortion! She thinks we already have too many children!"

Without a word, Bunica turned to join her daughter-in-law. With sure steps she entered the other room.

"Good evening, Aurora! Ahh! Viorica! You are crying!"

"Oh, ah, good evening, Raveca," stammered the visitor. "I was just—just visiting with the new widow. I see things here are not going well at all. So many children, and now another one on the way." Tanti Aurora's words tumbled out in her haste to explain her position.

"Thank-you for your concern. But as you can see, God is providing for us. Just now I brought in a pail of milk that Vasile got from our cows. I tell you, I don't know that the cows have ever produced as much milk as they have this spring. In fact, ever since Gheorghita died, we have not gone hungry. And soon we will have more vegetables from the garden." Bunica spoke with a thankful heart.

"Oh, yes, I know your garden has always done well. No one else can raise produce like you do. Ever since you came back from prison, you've used different methods than the rest of us."

"God is good to us. I learned things from working in the prison garden that have been a great benefit to our family. My time in prison was not in vain."

"Really! Well, I should go, I guess. I was just telling Viorica I can't see how she will provide for another baby now that her husband is dead. It's just too bad."

"I'm sure Viorica looks at her unborn baby as a gift from God, friend. We are not asked to know just how God will provide for us. We are asked to have faith that God will take care of us. We are all looking forward to the birth of the child. Perhaps it will be a boy! A gift of life to bring cheer and comfort to us now that our husbands are gone." Bunica's voice was hopeful.

Elena and Lidia looked at each other with teary eyes. Oh, how they loved their grandmother! With her gentle and kind words, she had once more brought hope and peace to their hearts.

"I know I don't have the kind of faith you have. I still wonder if Viorica shouldn't consider an abortion."

"Aurora!" Bunica's voice held a tone of authority the girls recognized. "We all know that abortion is murder! The Bible clearly forbids murder, even of unborn children! Abortion is not an option for us Repentants. Every birth is a gift from God! Only He has the right to take a life away."

Each word was spoken with firmness and rebuke.

"Not everyone feels like that," the woman said defensively. "Many women abort their babies when there are already too many children in the family." She got to her feet and moved toward the front door. "I meant no harm," she muttered as she left the house.

The girls flew into the room. Lidia knelt by her mother's side and gently wiped away her tears. Elena shed her own tears as she watched the emotional struggle on her mother's face.

They could hear the shouts of the boys and the little ones outside at play. Time seemed to stand still.

"Come, girls," Bunica said gently. "We will pray. We will pray for Tanti Aurora first of all. She does not have Jesus to give her love and understanding. We must pray too, that we will not hold bitterness and hatred in our hearts toward her. God will help us love those who don't understand."

The two widows and the two girls bowed their heads. Elena slipped a hand into her grandmother's hand. She gathered strength and peace from the prayer as Bunica poured out her heart to God.

Yes, God would provide. Elena did not know how, but in her ten-year-old mind, she had perfect confidence in Bunica. And she trusted God because Bunica trusted Him.

"Oh, Bunica! You are tired! We must stop to rest!" Elena laughed as she watched her grandmother pull herself up the hill from tree to tree.

"Yes," Bunica puffed. "That is a good idea! My old legs can't run about as yours do." She stopped and sat on a fallen log, panting.

"Bunica, I love going with you! It's so beautiful outside in our beautiful country!" Elena darted up the slope to pick some wild flowers for her grandmother. She made a little bouquet and brought them back to where her grandmother was resting.

"Yes, God has made Romania beautiful! I often wonder if the Garden of Eden was not very much like our country in the summertime. So fertile and pleasant!"

Elena tripped away to the spring that bubbled out of the hillside. She drank deeply from her cupped hands. Brushing away the droplets that formed on her chin, she sprinted on her long, thin legs back to Bunica.

"Tell me again where we're going," she said as she plopped down on the grass at Bunica's feet.

"We're going to see an old friend of mine," Bunica explained. "Maria is very old and lives with her granddaughter. I met her in prison."

Elena felt a tightening in her chest whenever prison was mentioned. "Why—why were you in prison?"

"Oh, child. Has time gone so fast that I haven't told you about our past?" Her voice trailed away and she looked far into the distance.

"I still thank the Lord for sending Brother George Oltean to us from America. Through that good brother, the Gospel was sown in our village, and because of that, we found salvation for our souls. Oh, how good the Lord is! He has sent light into our lives!

"I still remember the joy and peace I experienced when I repented of my sins and asked Jesus to come in and be my Savior! The light! The joy!" Bunica's voice vibrated with passion.

"But Bunica, you were always a good person. You were always a Repentant!" Elena was puzzled. How could someone like her Bunica repent from her sins?

Bunica shook her head slightly and smiled at her granddaughter. "No, no, dear one. No one has always been good. Everyone needs to repent from their sins. And I, oh, how I needed to repent! I had many, many sins I needed to repent from. And, Elena, I still need to repent from sins whenever the Spirit convicts me of something I have done wrong."

This was more than Elena could comprehend. She could not imagine that her dear grandmother, so kind and patient, so Godly and loving, would ever have to repent of anything. Now Elena knew that she, too, had sins she needed to repent of.

"But you asked why I was in prison," Bunica continued. "Well, that is a story I must tell.

"After your grandfather and I became Repentants, we began living a different life from what we had lived before. We read the Bible that Brother Oltean had given us. Yes," she nodded her head to answer the question she saw in Elena's eyes, "the same Bible that I still have and love.

"Anyway, one Sunday we went to the Orthodox church with the rest of the people from the village. When we went forward to take communion, Mosu did not kiss the hand of the priest or the crucifix as is the custom of that religion. We were just learning many things from the Bible and had read in Isaiah that idols are dead. We realized that the crucifix is an idol and that it is wrong to kiss it. So, Mosu told the priest how we now believed.

"The priest got so angry at Mosu that he took the crucifix and hit Mosu on the head. The other people got angry, too, and they beat your grandfather. They threw him out of church.

"The priest was so angry that he filed a suit against us in court. Mosu was tried first, and sentenced to three-and-a-half years in prison." Elena shivered. Suddenly the forest around them seemed to take on a gloomy atmosphere. Yet she wanted to hear more.

"My trial was separate from Mosu's," Bunica remembered. "I was accused of setting myself up as a holy person, better than others." She shook her head. "I never wanted anyone to believe that. I only tried to live as I knew Jesus wanted me to live.

"Anyway, during the trial, the judge told me that he understands that those who are holy can take hot coals in their hands and not be burned. He asked if I was willing to do that.

"I didn't feel as though I was on trial. I felt that Jesus was on trial, and I knew that He could do a miracle to show these people that He really does live in my heart. I remembered how God delivered Daniel's three friends from burning in the fiery furnace. So I told the judge I would be willing to hold the hot coals.

"At first, the judge looked stunned. Then he turned to someone and told them something. The person left and I thought he would come back with hot coals.

"Elena, God gave me peace to wait without fear. I was willing to be put on trial for my faith in Jesus. I was willing to suffer even if God did not make a miracle for me.

"No one ever came back with hot coals. God delivered me from that. But I was sentenced to prison for a year and a half.

"It was there that I met Maria, the one we are going to visit. She listened to the Gospel, and before I was released she repented and believed in Jesus. Now, she is a dear sister whom I love."

No longer was the forest dark and menacing. Birdsong filtered down to the resting pair. Once more, Elena felt surrounded by love. God had been good to her dear Bunica.

"Come, I have rested. Let's continue on." Bunica pulled herself up. "We are two missionaries, going where God is sending us!"

Elena slipped her hand into her grandmother's hand and matched her steps to walk by Bunica's side. Together, they walked on up the hill.

"Come, *Margareta!*" Elena urged. "Come see the baby! He was born just yesterday!" Hand in hand, the two girls went into the Boghian house.

"Is he sleeping?" Margareta asked in a whisper. They tiptoed to the cot where Bunica was holding a little bundle.

"Yes, the dear child is sleeping," Bunica replied softly. "And Mama is sleeping too . . . dear daughter, she is worn out."

Little *George*, swaddled in a soft, white blanket, lay in his grandmother's arms. The girls peered at the little boy's red, wrinkled face. Margareta touched his cheek softly.

Bunica's head bent low over the baby. "Dear little boy," she crooned softly. "You are heaven's gift to us. God has given us back a George to take the place of the Gheorghita He took home to Himself in heaven. Thank-you, Lord Jesus!"

"Supper is ready!" Lidia called from the other room. At fifteen, Lidia was a tremendous help in the household. A capable cook, she took charge of the meals whenever Mama or Bunica were occupied elsewhere.

The girls left the room. The big table was already crowded with the Boghian family. "Sit down, Margareta!" Lidia invited. "Nicu, scoot over toward Lucia. Margareta, you can squeeze between Rodica and Elena."

The children paused while Vasile led in thanks for the food. Then they began to eat the boiled potatoes.

They had scarcely begun the meal when the door opened and Margareta's mother came in. "Oh, there you are, Margareta! I called you to come for supper, but when you didn't come, I thought you must be over here."

Margareta's mother looked at the children crowded around the table. She saw the pot of boiled potatoes sitting in the middle of the table and the slices of bread on each child's plate.

"Really, you shouldn't stay and eat here. There are already so many children to eat the potatoes." Then she looked sharply at Margareta's plate. "Margareta! So many potatoes! You don't even like boiled potatoes! Why are you eating them?"

"Mama! These potatoes are delicious!" Margareta's voice bubbled over with laughter. "They taste so much better here!" She looked at Elena and giggled.

"Oh, hello!" Bunica smiled a greeting at their neighbor as she entered the room. "I didn't know you were here! Did you come to see little George?"

"No, not really," Margareta's mother laughed. "I came to get my daughter. She shouldn't be eating your food. You have so many of your own to provide for."

"Ahh, yes," Bunica answered, smiling at the little girl. "Busy eating with the rest."

"I don't understand," Margareta's mother said with a rueful smile. "At home I can never get her to eat boiled potatoes, and now she says she loves them. She says your potatoes taste better. Look at her. Eating them without butter, she is."

Everyone knew that Margareta's family could afford much better food than the Boghian family. Margareta's father was the village policeman and could afford to buy good food.

"You know, it's the company your daughter enjoys. She is always welcome in our house and at our table," Bunica said graciously. "Come, why don't you take a peek at George? He's sleeping in his mother's arms."

The two women left to look at the new baby, leaving the chattering children busily eating boiled potatoes.

7

Away From Home

FOR THOU ART MY HOPE, O LORD GOD: THOU ART
MY TRUST FROM MY YOUTH.

PSALM 71:5

The double iron gates looked high and forbidding. *Like prison gates,* Elena thought. A cold feeling clutched the pit of her stomach.

"I need to see the director," Mama said hesitantly to the gatekeeper in the little gatehouse.

"Step inside," he answered. One gate opened enough to allow Mama, Elena, and Rodica to slip through. "Wait here."

Elena looked around the paved courtyard. A concrete wall blocked the courtyard from the street. Buildings formed the other three sides. There were no trees or flowers anywhere.

"Yes?" A lady strode briskly toward them, accompanied by the gatekeeper.

"I—I am here to enroll my two daughters. I have a letter from the Child Welfare Office from Suceava."

The director took the letter and read it. "Very well. Follow me."

The trio trailed in the wake of the director.

"Sign here," the director pointed to a document on her desk.

Mama signed her name, "Mrs. Viorica Boghian."

"Your girls will be well taken care of, Mrs. Boghian. Of course, you already know that since your sons were with us last year." She reached out and shook Mama's hand.

Elena clutched her small bag of possessions to her chest. Rodica, too, had one small bag.

"Good-bye, girls. I will see you at vacation time. Be good and remember what we have taught you." Mama gave each of the girls a brief hug and turned to leave.

"Come right this way," the director said. "Rodica, you will be sleeping in the dorm over there." Then she turned to eleven-year-old Elena. "Let's see, you are ready for the fifth form. That will put you in the dorm on this side."

"Miriam!" she called out to an older girl. "Take little Rodica and show her where she is to sleep. Elena, follow me."

Elena trailed along behind the director. She trudged up the winding stairs to the second floor. As she stepped into a huge room, they were greeted by long rows of beds that stretched to the far wall.

"Your bed will be the first one, right here," the director pointed to a narrow cot on the right side. "Here is a drawer for you to put your personal items in. Supper will be in ten minutes. You will hear the bell and you must come immediately." The director turned and left the room.

Elena's legs felt weak. She sat on the edge of her cot and looked around with frightened eyes. Her bag of personal items looked small and insignificant beside her. She looked at her skirt and blouse. This would be the last day she wore them. The boarding school provided uniforms for the students.

How had she ever ended up here? When Mama had asked her if she wanted to go to the boarding school like Vasile and Dan did, Elena had thought it would be an adventure.

During the previous school year, the boys had entered boarding school, come home for brief stays at holidays, and then spent the summer at home. They had talked about life in the boarding school: the classes, the food, and the sports they were involved in.

It had all sounded strange and exciting. Elena knew only village life and life in the surrounding forest and fields. Gathering berries on the slopes of the hills, collecting kindling for the stove, and hunting for mushrooms in the spring had been a part of her life ever since she was little. She knew nothing of city life. She could barely remember traveling into the city of Suceava. If perchance she did leave their village, life outside Patrauti always looked somewhat frightening.

But when Mama had asked her if she wanted to attend the boarding school, Elena had said yes.

"The school will provide textbooks, clothes, paper and pencils, and whatever you will need. You will have a place to sleep and food to eat," Mama had told her daughter. "The mayor encouraged me to enroll the boys, and now he thinks I should send you and Rodica there too. He knows how difficult it is for me to provide for all you children. I need Lidia after school to help with the little ones. Bunica is getting older and it's hard for her to help with the work while I'm gone."

After her husband had passed away, Mama applied for work at the factory where he had become ill. The work was hard, and Elena remembered the horrible time when Mama became ill and spent time in the hospital. The work had simply been too taxing for the mother of nine.

After she was well again, Viorica had asked for a cleaning job at the factory. This, too, was hard, strenuous work, yet it suited the small woman better.

Each morning at four o'clock, the group of workers left Patrauti for the factory. The men walked the eight kilometers briskly, and Viorica tried to keep up. She did not want to fall behind in the dark, especially in the winter. Stories of ravenous wolves had been handed down from generation to generation, and nobody wanted to be out alone. Elena had gotten used to having her mother at work when the children got up in the morning.

Reluctantly, Bunica had consented to the mayor's plan. The two women were having an extremely difficult time feeding and clothing the large family. More and more, Viorica had to take on the role of provider in the home, earning the meager wages they needed. Bunica tried to be a mother to her grandchildren. They all loved and learned to respect their grandmother, but it was not an easy task for the old woman. Suffering from ill health, Bunica was wearing out. Yet she worked as hard as she could to help her daughter-in-law and grandchildren.

A jarring noise woke Elena out of her reverie. The supper bell! She leaped to her feet, hastily shoved her bag into the dresser, and shut the drawer. Then she ran down the stairs toward the warning sound of the bell.

It was not hard to find the dining room. Rows and rows of girls, two by two, were filing toward a building. Elena trailed along behind.

There was no chattering and giggling. Educators accompanied each troop of girls, watchful for any sign of unusual behavior.

Supper consisted basically of macaroni. There might have been some cheese mixed in but barely enough to make a difference.

Elena could hardly eat. There was a bewildering, dizzying schedule for everything. Spoons clattered as the group ate quickly. It seemed as though they had scarcely begun eating when a warning bell buzzed and everyone finished their food rapidly.

Just once Elena caught a glimpse of her little sister and something inside her lurched as she yearned to run over to Rodica. Fresh tears began streaming down her cheeks. Then, another bell sounded and they all rose in one sweeping motion.

Before she quite knew what was happening, Elena was whisked outside along with the girls from her group. In the courtyard, there was a milling of children, boys and girls. Some immediately began games, others sat in groups. A group of girls disappeared through a doorway and soon reappeared with uniforms slung over their arms. They busily set to sewing on missing buttons or mending tears. A group of children were called in for kitchen duty.

Elena looked around for a glimpse of Rodica, or Vasile or Dan. She saw no one familiar. In the midst of all the activity, she felt alone, like a tiny island in the middle of a vast ocean.

"Hey! Who are you?" A group of boys her age sauntered up to where Elena was leaning against a building.

Elena felt threatened. She did not say anything and lowered her eyes. She could hardly breathe.

"I said, 'Who are you?' " One boy thrust his face close to hers. His breath made her draw back even farther.

"Leave her alone!" another voice called out. It was Vasile! "Clear out of here! She's my sister!"

"Aww, don't get upset, Vasile. We didn't know who the new kid was." The boys turned and left.

"Oh, Vasile," Elena whimpered. "This place is terrible! I want to—I want to go home to Mama!"

"Shh!" Vasile said in a low tone. "If you act scared, the children will give you a rough time. All the new ones go through it. You'll get used to it!"

Elena shook her head. Not her. She was too shy. Even in the village school she ran around the corner to her house during breaks rather than mill around the schoolhouse with the other children.

Before she could say anything more, a loud bell sounded. All the children began forming lines, two by two.

"Get in line!" an instructor yelled at her.

Elena sprinted across the courtyard and stepped in place beside another girl. The children waited until everyone was lined up, and then, under orders, they marched inside. They tramped up the stairs Elena had taken before and entered the dorm.

Elena was glad to see her bed. Just to be in a place where she had been before gave her a small feeling of comfort. But now she was surrounded by a host of girls. She was sure they were all looking at her!

The constant chatter was kept to a low hum as the girls got ready for bed.

Elena pulled her nightgown out of her bag. Already there was a uniform hanging on a hook, ready for her the next day.

How vastly different this was from anything Elena had ever imagined! Her mind had never even tried to imagine such a scene. At home, she always got ready for bed with her siblings and settled down for the night. Now, she was suddenly thrust into this huge room filled with complete strangers! Tears squeezed out of her eyes and ran down her cheeks. Her legs trembled and she felt cold all over. She pulled back the covers and lay down, feeling a cold wave of loneliness wash over her.

Her prayers! She had not said her prayers! Elena went rigid. For a moment, her tears dried up.

Bunica always made sure the children knelt by their beds and prayed before they went to sleep. From Lidia, all the way down to the youngest one who could talk, the Boghian children prayed every night. In fact, the first words of the children were often repeated words of prayers.

Elena quickly glanced at the girls close to her bed. Were any of them praying? Were there no girls who had been taught to pray?

What would the other girls say if they saw her kneeling? Would they laugh at her? Would they mock her as the village children did whenever someone spoke about the Boghian children attending the Repentant church?

Elena felt herself shrivel inside. Here, she was all alone. None of her siblings were there to protect her. No Vasile could come and make the girls leave her alone. She would have to face the scorn and ridicule alone. Elena trembled.

Elena, have you prayed tonight? Even at boarding school, far from home, Elena could hear her grandmother's loving voice speak to her.

Quickly, Elena slipped out of bed on the side toward the wall. She bent over the bed, burying her head in the covers.

She waited for the taunts, the laughter, but none came.

She drew a deep breath and began her prayers. It was difficult to think of the usual things to say. She had been suddenly thrust into such a different world that nothing seemed familiar.

But she asked God to be with her. To help her do the right things. When she began praying for her family, tears flooded her eyes. Hastily she brushed them away and finished praying. Then she slid into bed again.

The girl in the next bed was watching her. Elena tensed, waiting for the questions, the taunts.

"All in bed!" A loud voice from the doorway startled Elena. She jumped in fright as the lady's voice filled the room and hastened any laggards under the covers.

"Remember! Punishments for any talking or walking around! I want no one, I mean *no one*, to make the least disturbance!"

Elena lay quaking, too scared to cry. She was terrified at the mere mention of punishment! That was something she thought she could never endure. Even at home, whenever her mother or Bunica would ask her to do something, she would immediately do it. Just hearing the cries of the boys whenever they were disciplined was enough to bring respect and obedience into her life. She would even do her siblings' work if she suspected they were skipping chores and a punishment was imminent.

With a final shout of warning, the lady left.

The room was almost immediately very still. Only an occasional whisper was heard in the gathering gloom.

"There must be something more than just threats in her warning," Elena thought to herself as she huddled under the covers. "They must really punish for any misbehavior."

She couldn't help but compare her mother and grandmother's kind voices to the harsh warning that still hung in the air. Tears began flowing down her cheeks and onto her pillow. She felt so alone in the bed. Even though the cot was a single, narrow bed, it felt as big as a field to Elena. At home, she often slept between her sisters, all piled together in one bed.

She wondered where Rodica was. She had caught a glimpse of her younger sister only once that evening. Just the memory of her little sister's tear-stained face in the dining room brought a fresh flow of her own tears.

She stirred restlessly. Her pillow felt sodden under her cheek. She turned the damp pillow to the other side.

When you feel all alone, remember your heavenly Father is with you. Bunica's words came to Elena's mind. Again and again, Bunica told her grandchildren of the comfort that God gives to those who ask. *He will never leave you nor forsake you, regardless of your circumstances.*

"Please, God, be with me!" Elena prayed in desperation. Her mind repeated the cries of her heart over and over. Her trembling limbs gave but a glimpse into the agony of her soul.

The Lord gave His comfort and assurance of love to the lonely, panic-stricken, homesick girl. The tears continued to flow, but they were less heart-wrenching. Finally, exhausted both by the bus trip to the boarding school and the extreme emotional upheaval, Elena fell asleep in the middle of her lonely bed.

8

Childhood Prison

CASTING ALL YOUR CARE UPON HIM; FOR HE CARETH FOR YOU.

I PETER 5:7

"Get up!" The strident voice filled the still-dark room in a blast of sound.

Elena sat up in bed, startled and shaking. Where was she? A frightened look at her surroundings was no comfort.

Girls were rising from their beds in the dormitory. The windows, up high on the walls and covered with iron bars, let in a smattering of early fall light.

"Get up!" the girl next to Elena hissed. "Right away! You have to be ready to go wash in five minutes."

Then she saw the other girls make their beds. She quickly imitated them, her heart thumping in fear. This was all a nightmare. She could not believe she was in this place, so far away from home! The tears started again.

"Line up!" Elena jumped. A woman stood in the doorway, peering into their dorm.

The girls all stood at attention at the foot of their beds. They held their arms stiffly at their sides.

The instructor walked briskly down the room, inspecting beds. "*Livia*! Look at the wrinkles on your bed. Bathroom duty for you tonight!"

Cold prickles of horror crept up Elena's spine. She took a quick look behind her. Would her bed pass inspection?

"Eyes forward!" The dreaded voice boomed at her. Elena stared straight in front of her, rigid with terror.

"Wash!" The command came in a harsh tone. The girls obediently filed in twos toward the bathroom.

There was absolutely no time for dawdling. Everything had to be done with precision and speed. Each girl had only a few seconds to wash at the cold water spigot before they were shoved aside for the next one.

Then back to their dorm to get dressed. A few strokes of the brush through the hair was all the time given for grooming.

Elena had tried to keep back her tears through the entire morning schedule. But suddenly, standing at attention, waiting to leave the dorm, her tears spilled over.

"Quit your blubbering!" The instructor told her tersely.

"I want to go home! I want my mother!" Elena's words burst out in a torrent of tears.

"Be quiet! Now march!"

Through her tears, Elena stumbled along with the others. Not a glance of pity came her way. The other girls had nothing to offer the newcomer. In fact, there were other new girls going through the same experience. But not a word of comfort came their way. This was school. This was training ground for future citizens of Socialist Romania.

The stern visages of Marx, Engels, and Lenin looked down at the rows of girls as they filed down the halls. Their feet made scuffling noises on the hard floors as they shuffled outside.

The girls waited for a few minutes while a group of older girls finished their morning exercises. Then, at the sound of a commanding whistle, they took their positions.

Fifteen minutes of vigorous bending, marching in place, swinging their arms, and other maneuvers left Elena breathless.

Her stomach rumbled as the column of girls headed for the dining room. But one piece of bread with margarine and a cup of tea was all she got for breakfast.

The night before, Elena had been too distraught to eat. Now she wolfed her bread down ravenously and gulped the tepid tea.

Another line-up. Another march. Elena did not know where they were going, and she did not care. Her entire being cried out in protest at being in this strange place. Everything was new and unfamiliar. She was always being hurried from place to place.

Suddenly, she spied a woman entering a room across the courtyard. It was the lady who had admitted her the day before.

Elena darted out of line. She did not even hear the instructor screaming at her. With tears, she flung herself at the director. "Please let me go home! I want to leave here! I will walk home! Just let me leave!"

Rough hands grabbed her shoulders and jerked her away from the lady.

"Be quiet and stop that!" The educator forced her outside to rejoin the column of girls. The line advanced again. The instructor kept a firm grip on Elena's shoulder and marched her along with the rest.

Elena sobbed broken-heartedly. She barely noticed a line of younger girls until all at once she spied Rodica. With a feeble cry, she moved toward her sister.

The instructor was on guard. With a sharp slap to Elena's cheek, she forced her forward. There was no time for more than a hasty, pained glance at her little sister's tear-streaked face before they were past each other.

"Salute!" The sound of a man's voice filled the room. Everyone was packed into a classroom, standing at attention. The man began to sing. Accompanied by martial music from a speaker, the group of students joined in the patriotic song. Everyone stood rigidly, holding the salute until the song ended.

Most of the monologue that followed went over Elena's head. She heard all kinds of platitudes about the great leaders of communism and the strides their country was making for complete independence from the Soviet Union.

Following the speech, the girls were ordered to do their lessons.

The following hours dragged on in study, a march to the dining room for a slightly more substantial lunch, more study, and finally, after supper, the brief period of free time in the courtyard.

The first several days, Elena wept copiously and frequently. Her tears scorched more than her face; they burned deep furrows into her heart. She felt forsaken, lonely, and forgotten.

Why did Mama bring me to this horrible, horrible place? Elena's thoughts chased each other round and round. *Why didn't Vasile and Dan tell us how awful this place is? When can I go home? Will I ever see Mama and dear Bunica again?* Fresh outbursts of tears flooded her cheeks.

Elena pressed her face against the board fence that separated the playground from the street. She peered through the cracks.

A girl about her age and the girl's mother came walking down the sidewalk across the street. They were chatting and laughing.

Elena studied them. Something inside her tightened.

"Get away from the fence!" The yell from the instructor jerked Elena to attention. She whirled. But not fast enough.

"You know you are not allowed to get close to the fence!" The stick in the instructor's hand landed on Elena's back. Pain shot through her shoulders. She whimpered and ran to the middle of the yard.

A commotion at the other end of the courtyard caught Elena's attention. A fracas of some kind was going on in the middle of a cluster of girls. But before the instructor could break up the fight, everyone scattered.

Conflicts among the group were usually bitter, but brief. Elena made sure she was never caught in the battles. She was too scared of a beating. She had a dreadful fear of the sticks the educators and teachers carried.

The enforced rests on Sundays were perhaps the worst ordeals Elena could think of. After lunch, they all had to lie down on their beds and lie perfectly still for as long as the instructors thought good. This was usually a long time, for it was easier to keep control over the lively children when they were in bed than when they were enjoying free time in the courtyard.

"We're not babies!" *Nuti* whispered fiercely to Elena. "There is no way I can sleep!" She tossed angrily in her cot next to Elena's.

"Maybe we should try to act like babies," Elena suggested. "If we're treated like babies, let's act like babies!"

Nuti giggled. "Wah! Wah!" she cried softly.

Catrina heard her. "What are you doing?" she hissed.

"We're being babies!" Nuti whispered back. "We are supposed to sleep in the daytime like babies, so we will cry like babies!"

Elena and Catrina laughed softly as Nuti continued to "cry."

Elena gave a soft "Wah" experimentally. She laughed. Then she tried it again.

The three girls "cried" in the beds. And giggled.

In the middle of a cry, Catrina stopped abruptly. Her strangled cry made Elena look up.

The instructor was standing right next to Elena's bed. Her face was red with fury. "You girls are being impudent! Take that!"

Her stick fell in rapid blows on Elena's head and arms.

Elena tried not to cry out in fear. She huddled in a small heap on her bed. Her heart thumped uncontrollably and every nerve in her body screamed. Yet hardly a sound escaped her mouth.

Next, it was Catrina's turn, then Nuti's. "You girls! You beasts! You make my job miserable with all your disobedience! Take that! And that!"

Three cowed girls spent the rest of quiet time immobile on their beds. They dared not move.

Unbidden memories of home crowded into Elena's mind. She wondered if little George was crawling. Did Lidia miss her? Did Mama still leave for work early in the morning and arrive home at night, too exhausted to do more than eat and collapse into bed? She imagined herself running up the hills to gather sticks for kindling. A chore to many, to her it was always a delight, for then she could roam the hillsides and release her abundant energy.

Tears continued to spill out and run down over her cheeks and soak her flat pillow. She had been here for months now, and still she was not used to the grim conditions.

Day after day went by with no smiles, no laughter. If the girls got silly, they were severely reprimanded or even beaten. Their pent-up energy had hardly any outlets. They must march. They must sit. They must stay in line. So many rules! There was hardly ever time to be what they should have been—carefree, young children.

In the midst of her dreary existence, Elena found a bright spot in her days—running. Running track provided an outlet for Elena's emotions. Day after day, the girls were herded around the track, competing for first place.

At first, running was no different from any of the other exercises they did every day. But gradually Elena learned to love to run. Her wiry body toughened and her lungs expanded. Her long legs pumped up and down as she ran.

The wind in her face felt good. Her coach taught her how to pace herself and to save a burst of energy for the last lap. A feeling of exhilaration swept through her as she ran.

The daily exercise paid off. Soon Elena was consistently part of the group who finished the required laps before the rest of the girls. Within months she was usually crossing the finish line ahead of the rest—the winner.

But this was not good enough. Elena determined to win every time. She put her entire will into running, into winning.

Gradually, home became distant. Even though she eagerly looked forward to each vacation, the dismal existence was now brightened by her sport. She pressed on in her training.

"Tweedly-tweedly-tweet!" The little bird sang sweetly from the summer-green linden tree.

Elena paused from her dreary march to the dining room for lunch. She listened to the bird calling to her. For once, Rodica was beside her. The two sisters had spent as much time together as they could that sunny summer morning. Two weeks ago they had returned to the boarding school after spending half of summer vacation at home. They had not wanted to come back to school early, especially because Dan and Vasile were still at home. The girls rarely saw their brothers since the boys had been transferred to a different boarding school last year. But the director had only sent the girls home for the first half of vacation, and so they were back. Back in the monotonous routine.

"Tweedly-tweedly-tweet!" The bird sang again, inviting Elena to come closer. It sweetly put into song something that longed for expression in the lonely girl's heart.

"Come! Let's go look at the bird!" Like a swallow, Elena darted out of the long line of girls, clutching Rodica by the hand. Reaching the tree, both girls craned their necks and searched the leafy branches for a glimpse of the warbling songster.

"Elena! Rodica! Get back in line!"

Oh no! The instructor in charge had seen them dart out of line. Elena looked behind her in a panic.

The stick raised menacingly, *Doamna Turliuc* bore down on them, screaming in rage.

Reason left Elena. So terrified was she of the stick that without thinking she ran straight for the dormitory building. She flew up the stairs two at a time and arrived breathless at the top.

Below, she heard the wailing cries of her sister as she was struck again and again with the stick. With a whimpering cry of terror, Elena dove under a bed next to a wardrobe. She pulled herself up against the wall and forced her breathing into slow, even, quiet breaths.

She heard Doamna Turliuc come up the steps with purposeful treads. She heard her enter the room. "Elena!" The angry voice almost caused Elena to jerk. "Elena, come here!"

Elena scarcely breathed. She closed her eyes.

"Elena?" This time there was a slight question in the woman's voice. Perhaps she was not sure that Elena had come into the room. The building was large and there were many places a fleeing girl could hide.

As the instructor's footsteps died away, Elena opened her eyes. She was lying on the bare floor, dust tickling her nose. Down the long row of beds, a pattern of light and shadow made the familiar room a strange prison. She could hear the girls march into the dining room. Still, she did not move. She couldn't.

It was Sunday. Perhaps today they would be taken to the river for an "outing." It wasn't much of an outing, for they had to march in columns of twos all down the street, sit beside the river, do exercises, and then march back to the boarding school again. Elena enjoyed the brief look at the river, but she hated the stares of the passersby as the "orphans" were marched up and down the streets.

How could she get out of her dilemma? Elena did not know. One thing she knew, Doamna Turliuc would beat her when she found her.

Perhaps she could run away—run home to Bunica and Mama and Lidia and the little ones. She could try to climb over the high board fence and escape out of town. She could walk through the greening fields of spring and walk and walk until she got home.

Then she would never, never leave home again. She would go work in the fields to provide food for herself. She would work hard and eat very little. She would even be willing to beg in order to get something to eat. Anything would be better than staying here.

Elena heard more movement outside. She heard the students marching in line. They were going to the river. Perhaps now would be a good time to try to sneak out.

Why hadn't she thought of that before? During the walk to the river, she could have darted out of line and run up some dark alley. Now she would have to sneak out of the dorm, slip through the courtyard, and try to scale the fence without being caught.

Elena knew it would not work. The fence was too high. And there was always a guard by the gate. She sobbed quietly.

All afternoon, she hid. She heard the clatter of pots and pans as supper was prepared in the kitchen. She became acutely aware that she had missed her lunch. She was hungry.

The early spring light began to fade. The dark shadows under the bed became blacker. Fear gripped her. She couldn't stay here alone.

Just then, she heard the students coming back from the river. The scuffle of feet headed across the courtyard toward the dining room. Elena crept out from under the bed and softly stole down the steps. She would slip in at the end of the line. She rounded the door and walked outside.

But Doamna Turliuc had been watching for her. With a shout, she uprooted a puny sapling struggling for survival by the fence and triumphantly headed for Elena. Elena waited. She knew she couldn't run away again.

"Where were you?" The words were flung at her.

Something made Elena answer truthfully. "In the dorm."

"I looked there for you! Where were you hiding?"

"Under a bed."

Menacingly, the sapling was raised up against the evening sky. Some dirt still clung to the roots. "Why did you leave the line at lunchtime?"

"I heard a bird singing."

"You heard a bird! Such ridiculous nonsense! There was no bird. You ran away from me like a—like a goat! And then you hid from me all afternoon! You—disobedient—wretch!"

With sharp blows, the sapling whipped against Elena's legs. The educator seemed to lose control of herself as, in a near-frenzy, she beat Elena's bare legs. Elena tried to stand still in spite of the searing pain.

"Never do that to me again!" Doamna Turliuc panted as she flung the sapling into the yard. She wheeled and went into the dining room, leaving Elena behind in the deserted courtyard. Blood trickled down her legs.

With sudden resolve, Elena went to the director's office. A new director, a man this time, was at the desk.

"Sir," Elena said through her tears, "I want to go home. I have to go home!"

She stood, disheveled and teary-eyed, in front of his desk. She did not complain about the treatment she had just received. She did not beg. She just said, quietly and brokenly, "I want to go home!"

9

Growing Up

AND WE KNOW THAT ALL THINGS WORK TOGETHER FOR GOOD TO THEM THAT LOVE GOD, TO THEM WHO ARE THE CALLED ACCORDING TO HIS PURPOSE.

ROMANS 8:28

"Rodica!" Elena called out joyfully. "Oh look, Rodica! I can see our house!"

The two girls had traveled by bus from the boarding school in *Siret* to Patrauti. The two-mile hike in the summer sunshine through the village to their home was pure joy.

"I still can't believe the director let us come home!" Rodica gave a skip and a hop. "They let us come back four weeks before the new school term begins! And now we're almost home again!"

"God softened his heart," Elena said with conviction. "I didn't really believe he would let us come home, even if it's still vacation time. But I was so sad after my legs were switched that I didn't know what else to do. I didn't even care if he would punish me. But all at once he said, 'You may go home tomorrow.' "

"And this is tomorrow!" Rodica sang out.

Elena laughed at the thought. "Tomorrow never comes, but this time it did! Come on, let's run!"

The two girls began to run. Past the school, around the corner, and . . . they were home! Elena was first to push open the gate. With flying feet, she raced to the front door.

"Mama! Bunica! We are home!"

"Elena! And Rodica! Why—what? What has happened?" Stunned, Bunica lifted her wet hands from the bowl of potatoes she was peeling and tried to dry them on her apron.

But Elena and Rodica flung their arms around their grandmother, oblivious of her dripping hands. Elena lay her head against the familiar breast and gave a huge sigh. They were home!

"Where is Mama?" Rodica asked. "And the children?"

"Your mama is at work, of course," Bunica answered the questions. "The other children are playing in the garden. Didn't you see them before you came in?"

"No. We had to come in and see you," Elena answered in a contented voice. "It's so good to be home, Bunica! We missed you so much!"

"Come, Elena, let's go see the boys! And the little ones!" Rodica dashed out the door.

But when Elena turned to follow her younger sister, Bunica gasped. "Whatever happened to your legs, child?"

Elena turned to face her grandmother. She gave a quavering sigh. "I was switched," she said. At the memory, tears came to her eyes.

"Whatever happened?" Bunica asked sharply. "Whatever did you do? Were you sent home because—surely you were not misbehaving!"

"I just wanted to see the bird singing!" Elena said in a low voice. Perhaps she had truly been bad.

The door opened and Mama walked in. "Why, Elena!" she exclaimed.

"Oh, Mama!" Elena wrapped her arms around her mother. Tears streaked down her cheeks.

"Look, Viorica! Look at her legs!"

Elena tried to tell the story the best she could. Her voice shook with emotion as she described the singing bird, the angry educator, her panicked dash to a hiding place, and her foiled attempt to slip in line undetected. Then she told them how Doamna Turliuc had whipped her legs until the blood ran.

"Oh Lord, have mercy!" Mama moaned. "You poor child!"

Bunica had gotten some water and was gently washing Elena's legs. The dried blood came off on the washcloth and turned the water red. Gently, she spread ointment on the welts.

"I sent my children to the boarding school to get an education, not beatings," Mama said sadly. "The mayor convinced us this was the best thing to do. And now, look! This is not what I thought would happen there." She sat up straight. "Where is Rodica? Is she at home too?"

"Yes, Mama. She's outside with the little ones. But Mama! I asked the director to let us come home, and he did! Isn't that a miracle? Oh, it is so good to be at home again! I want to go see the little ones! Where is little George?"

After the door closed behind Elena, Viorica turned to her mother-in-law and said tiredly, "We must write a letter to the director. Elena and Rodica shouldn't have run out of line, but surely there was no need to switch Elena's legs until they bled. They shouldn't allow such actions in the school!"

"Daughter," Bunica said slowly. "Perhaps we shouldn't have allowed the children to leave home to go to the boarding school. Not only because of the kind of life they are experiencing there, but perhaps even more because of the teaching they are missing from a Godly home. Sometimes I worry that what they are taught in school will make a big impact in their lives. We know the teachers tell the students there is no God. That can do a lot of damage to a young soul."

Mama's shoulders slumped. "I don't know what else we can do. The money I bring home from cleaning at the factory doesn't even supply what we need. Your health is not good, and I feel like you have to be a mother all over again. You should not have to spend your days looking after little ones. It wears you out."

"I don't complain," Bunica said, picking up a potato and peeling it. "God has given me a strength that I do not have of my own. I told you of the dream I had one night soon after Gheorghita died. God gave me the assurance that I would live at least five more years. Five years to help out with the family. By that time, your little boy will be five years old."

"Mama!" Viorica turned a stricken face toward the old woman. "I trust the Lord will let you live more than five years! What would I ever do without your help?"

"We will trust in the Lord," Bunica said firmly. "My five years are not up yet." She placed the potatoes in a kettle of water and set it on the stove. "But I am looking forward to going to my heavenly home! I want to see my Jesus! And dear Costache, and Gheorghita, and all the other Repentants who are already in heaven! 'Even so, come, Lord Jesus!' "

The two widows prepared the simple evening meal. Outside, the children's voices rang with laughter, Rodica's and Elena's rising above the rest, ringing with a special joy. They were home for the whole summer!

Elena's heart thumped rapidly under her uniform. This was their first day back at the boarding school after summer vacation. The summer had been too brief, spent busily working in the garden, gathering sticks from the forest, and helping her brothers pick strawberries.

"Get out your textbooks. We will begin our classes with a review of the things we learned last year." Doamna Turliuc's voice was loud, but for some reason, she did not sound as harsh as Elena remembered from last spring.

She stole a quick glance at the educator, then dropped her eyes to her book in haste. Doamna Turliuc was looking directly at her!

"I know it is sometimes hard to remember everything from one year to the next," Doamna Turliuc continued. "So, the first several days will be spent in review."

"I wonder if she read the letter my mother wrote to the director," Elena thought. "Is she going to make my life miserable because we complained about the switching?"

Nothing unusual happened that day. Even though Elena had dreaded coming back to the boarding school, she found the familiar routine easier to bear since she was a second-year student. But she still expected some form of reprisal from Doamna Turliuc. Perhaps she would take her time and get back at Elena in a more subtle way.

"You are doing good work!"

Surprised, Elena lifted her head from her literature book. Doamna Turliuc was standing next to Elena's desk, so close that Elena could see her blouse rise and fall with her breath.

Elena cringed in spite of the kind words. She was relieved when the educator moved on up the aisle and rang the bell for dismissal. The girls all filed out of the classroom; Elena followed in a daze.

Doamna Turliuc could be kind! Elena was amazed at the very thought! She had praised her work! Nothing like that had ever happened to her in school. True, the director of sports bragged about Elena's capability in track and in gymnastics, but never had any of her teachers praised her school work.

Elena sighed. Was this just Doamna Turliuc's way of softening her so that her retaliation would be all the more harsh? What was her motive for this kindness?

The bewildering events continued. One day, Doamna Turliuc pressed five peanuts into Elena's hand as she left the classroom. Then one Sunday, she left Elena almost speechless with surprise.

"Elena, do you want to see where I live?" Doamna Turliuc actually smiled at Elena. "You are to come home with me for a visit."

It was right after a meager breakfast. Elena was dreading the enforced Sunday morning "study" time in the classrooms. Those hours seemed to stretch out for ages.

"You can stay with me until this evening. Then I will bring you back."

Elena could not speak. She just smiled a tight little smile and followed the lady out the door.

"Here, let me take your jacket," Doamna Turliuc said kindly as they stepped inside her apartment. "We'll hang it right here in the hall. Through that door is the bathroom where you can wash up. I'm going to make us some tea and serve some cookies my mother baked for me. I often stop at her house on the way from school, and just yesterday she sent these cookies along. They are still fresh!"

Elena softly closed the bathroom door behind her. The room was glazed in glistening white tile. The sink and tub were sparkling clean. A bottle of pink soap stood on a shelf next to a lovely vase of flowers. The large mirror reflected the bright light from the ceiling.

Elena turned on the spigot and washed her hands with the soap and warm water. She straightened her uniform collar and tried to smooth down her hair. Her large, brown eyes stared back at her from the mirror.

She smiled slightly at the girl in the mirror and felt herself relax. Opening the door, she stepped into the tiny kitchen. A cheery red tablecloth covered the small table in front of the window.

"Sit right here while I make the tea." Doamna Turliuc bustled about, chatting as she placed cups and saucers on the table. "I live here all by myself, so everything is just the way I like it, and nothing changes while I'm gone. Except, of course, what Tiger decides to destroy."

Elena glanced quickly behind her! What did she mean?

The educator laughed. "Oh, don't be scared. I don't actually keep a tiger in my house. Tiger is my cat. He will come out once he's used to having you here. He's a little shy at first."

The orange-striped cat that padded into the kitchen a little later stole Elena's heart when he ate a piece of cookie from her hand. Almost immediately he allowed her to pick him up and stroke him. His loud, rumbling purr gave a delightful note to the tranquil scene in the little apartment.

"Yes, Tiger is a great comfort to me," Doamna Turliuc said cheerfully. "After working all day at the boarding school under strict orders from my superiors, I find it so relaxing to come home and spend time with my cat."

The educator rambled on, talking about herself comfortably without seeming to notice that Elena found herself too tongue-tied to talk.

"Do you care for more tea? No? Then while I clear up the dishes, why don't you take Tiger into the other room. Perhaps you can find a book to read. We're going to take a walk down to the river this afternoon. It's such a beautiful day!"

The entire day opened up a completely new world for Elena. The leisurely walk to the river, the soft grass under her bare feet, the warm sun shining on her back as they rested on the bank, and the delicious late lunch the educator had prepared—all were part of an experience Elena never could have imagined. She felt as though she was another person completely. And Doamna Turliuc! Elena hardly recognized her anymore!

Was this the same person who had screamed so harshly at her just last spring? Who had cruelly switched her legs until they had been covered with bleeding welts? How was this change possible?

To find human kindness, and yes, even love, coming from the woman she had feared made a tremendous impact on Elena's young life.

After lunch, Doamna Turliuc handed Elena a gift. "Before we go back, I have a little present for you. I embroidered this handkerchief when I was thirteen years old, just like you. I want you to have it."

Elena stared at the delicate pink flowers stitched onto snowy white linen. The crocheted lace edge was neatly attached with tiny, even stitches. It was absolutely beautiful!

"Thank-you!" Elena managed to whisper. They were very nearly the only words she had been able to say all day. "Thank-you," she said again.

She looked up at Doamna Turliuc's smiling face. She was not only thanking her for the handkerchief, but also for the delightful day and, most of all, for treating her like a human being.

But she could not find the words to say what was on her heart. She just clasped the white handkerchief to her breast.

Doamna Turliuc smiled back at her. Then she turned abruptly toward the hall. "Get your jacket. It's time to take you back."

That night, Elena thanked God for the beautiful day He had given her. She prayed for her family as she always did. Then at the end, she prayed for Doamna Turliuc.

That night, in the first bed in the bleak dormitory, a happy girl fell asleep, carefully clutching a white embroidered handkerchief. Even at the boarding school, God had provided a bright spot in Elena's life.

10

Running to Live

Know ye not that they which run in a race run all, but one receiveth the prize? So run, that ye may obtain.

I Corinthians 9:24

The huge arena was bordered by the wide, 400–meter running track. The sun shone warmly on the grassy field and empty bleachers. A group of twenty girls jogged around the track, their arms and legs flashing in the sunlight.

Elena ran easily beside Ana. They led the group around the track. Pacing themselves, they passed the starting line for the second time.

"Breathe easily!" called *Sergiu*, their physical education teacher. "Conserve your strength!"

Elena loved to run. Every year, she trained religiously to gain strength, speed, and stamina. The pounding of her feet on the cinders sent exhilaration surging up her spine.

Another lap. Then another. She spaced her breathing to keep her limbs in an even stride. On and on she ran.

She could hear the beginning of labored breathing behind her. Some of the girls must be tiring. But not Elena! She had just gotten her second wind. She felt like she could run forever.

Ana, too, kept running easily. The two girls were evenly matched with a long, tireless stride that ate up distance with ease.

A shrill whistle from Sergiu indicated the end of their first training period of the year. The runners slowed and sprawled on the grass in the infield.

"The distance between the first and the last runners was too great!" Sergiu scolded them. "You last girls must keep up! Our school must be better than ever before! In less than two months, we will compete in the national sports competition, and I want each of you in top form!" Sergiu himself had been a star athlete and his energy overflowed into his coaching. He bounced on the balls of his feet as he lectured his charges.

"Elena and Ana, prepare for the sprint."

The two girls bounded to their feet. The brief rest had revitalized them, and they were ready to go.

They toed up to the starting line. Elena positioned herself with both hands on the ground, one leg stretched out behind her and the other leg bent in starting position. Ana settled herself in the same position, then grinned in friendly competition at Elena.

The whistle shrilled.

Instantly the girls were up and running. Side by side, they raced around the track, their feet pounding in unison. They rounded the first curve. Ana, on the inside, gained a slight lead.

As they rounded the last corner and began the homestretch, Elena threw back her head and drew from the energy she had reserved for this stretch.

Arms pumping rhythmically, long legs reaching forward with ever-lengthening strides, she gave herself up to the joy of running.

She was dimly aware that Ana was falling behind. Still, she ran. She ran with the wild abandonment of a colt on a green, grassy meadow. Her hair streamed out behind her and the wind felt cool on her face.

Even after she had crossed the finish line, a good length ahead of Ana, Elena felt as though she could run another lap around the track. She circled back to Sergiu who was waiting for them.

"Like a filly, you run," Sergiu said, allowing a rare, brief smile to rest on his stern features. To him, sports was serious business, not a pleasure. "But you must discipline yourself to concentrate on winning, not just running for the pleasure of it. In a few weeks you'll be competing with faster runners."

Elena glanced almost apologetically at her friend. Ana smiled back good-naturedly. She didn't mind that Elena was faster. To Ana, running was simply good exercise and something she naturally enjoyed.

Boarding school had not varied much from year to year. Elena had endured the relentless grind of demanding lessons, rigid schedules, and drab surroundings.

Summers had been short, glorious vacations at home with her family. Even before she was fourteen, the legal age for employment, she had begged to go with her brothers to pick strawberries to sell. She enjoyed the challenge of rapidly filling her containers and relished the satisfaction of taking a few coins home for their household. At times these earnings allowed their meager lunches of hard-boiled eggs or cold mamaliga to be supplemented by a piece of bread and a small slice of salami bought at the store. And what wonder of wonders when they unwrapped their lunches to find a small portion of cooked chicken that Mama or Lidia had saved for them! Even the bones were gnawed and savored!

High school was less rigid than boarding school had been. It also gave Elena new challenges to face. Already a good student, she had early showed considerable promise in sports, especially running. Training rigorously under Sergiu, she gave everything she had to become better and better. She worked diligently to maintain her status as the first-place runner in her school and, later, in her district. Running became her life.

"A letter! Oh, good, it's from Bunica!" Yet as she took the envelope a slight feeling of uneasiness swept over her.

Of course she was glad to hear from her dear grandmother! Bunica was the dearest on earth to her!

Elena walked across the courtyard in search of a private place to read the letter. Girls mingled while doing their evening jobs. Patching uniforms, studying for failed tests, or doing mundane tasks like sweeping the courtyard still occupied their evenings at boarding school. Elena finally sat down in a quiet corner.

A letter! It had been a long time since a letter had arrived from home. The first year Elena and Rodica had been in boarding school, letters from Bunica had arrived regularly. Like fresh water from the hillside spring, the words had always brought a sense of peace and comfort in the unreal world of boarding school.

Elena's mind went back to the last letter she had received from Bunica.

Why does your grandmother write such fairy tales? Years later, Elena could still feel the withering scorn in the director's voice.

Elena had been called from the supper table to the director's office. He was seated at his desk, holding Bunica's letter to Elena and Rodica. He read from the open page: " 'We pray every day for you girls and your brothers. We know that God is watching over you even while you are away from home. Never forget to pray every night before you go to bed and thank

Him for His care of you.' " He looked up, scorn written on his face. "Such nonsense! Your grandmother is a foolish old woman who still needs a God to give her comfort. We know there is no God. He is just a product of weak people's imaginations. Our government is showing the entire world what can be done when people turn away from such ignorance and support their leaders!" He glared at Elena. "I will destroy this letter. It is better not to fill your mind with such drivel!"

But Elena had begun to cry. Her dear grandmother's letter—destroyed? With her whole lonely heart, she had yearned to read the message Bunica had sent—yearned to gain comfort from the scripture verses Bunica included in every letter.

"Bah!" the director had burst out in disgust. "If it means so much to you, take the letter! Get back to your supper!"

Miraculously, the letter was thrown at her, and she had clutched it to herself as she hastened from the room. After that, no more letters had reached them during the boarding school days.

But now, years later, here was another letter from Bunica. Elena opened it carefully.

Dear girls,

"In all thy ways acknowledge Him and He shall direct thy paths." This verse from Proverbs will be the light to direct you every day. Remember, God will show you each path to take, each decision to make, if you give Him first place in your lives. Acknowledge means not only to recognize, but to give Him the center of your heart every day. There should not be a single day that you do not pray to Him and ask Him for direction. Girls, nothing is more important in all of life than giving God first place in our hearts.

You are in school, learning so many things. All of your subjects should teach you that God has created the world and that there is a purpose for your lives. Do not let the false teachings of atheism make any inroads in your lives. Your faith in Him will keep you from these pitfalls if you allow it to.

We are doing as well as can be expected. Your mother is still working at the factory and suffers from ill health. Lidia is very capable and runs the household much better than I can. The little ones grow up fast. Little George is now seven years old and, of course, he is doing well in first grade.

The lack of rain is serious. Daily, we pray to our God for rain. We know not why we are suffering from this drought but I think it is a sign from heaven against the sins of the people in forgetting God. I pray a famine will not overtake us.

I pray for you every day. Learn to trust Jesus as your Savior.
Much love, Bunica

Tears misted Elena's eyes. She was oblivious to the damp chill of the evening air. The concrete step she was sitting on was hard and uncomfortable, yet she did not move.

Her grandmother's world seemed so far away! Bunica wrote so easily about trusting God and praying to Him for their needs! Elena remembered the warm, comfortable feeling of nestling in Bunica's lap as they spent their evenings together so long ago. Now those times were gone. Time and years had managed to cut a chasm between home and her world at school.

What kind of faith did she have? Elena did not know. She still prayed every night, but her prayers had fallen into a regular pattern of familiar words. She still believed in God, but He seemed far away.

God was in heaven. Heaven was far away. From heaven, He ruled the world, caused the planets to orbit in their circuits, and made the stars to shine.

She was only one little speck on this earth. A little, insignificant speck. How could God care about her world? Did He concern Himself about her feelings, her life? Did He care about how well she did in sports, in running track, or in the pentathlon? She wondered.

The comfortable world of her childhood had vanished. Even going through the trauma of losing Mosu and Tata in her girlhood had not shaken the comfort she had always received from her belief in Bunica's God. In spite of their extreme poverty when they were young, they still had the security of knowing they were safe in their home. Bunica and Mama had provided a stability for them that kept the darkness from overtaking them.

Elena stared at the letter. She recognized that something had changed dramatically over time. Slowly her faith had eroded.

Resting her head on her knees, Elena wept. Wept for her childhood. Wept for her Tata. Wept for her home. But most of all, she wept for the emptiness she felt inside. Her tears fell on the letter in her lap.

One more lap to go. Elena paced herself among the other runners in the national competition in *Bucuresti*. She felt the familiar surge of adrenaline tingling through every part of her disciplined body.

Now! She moved slightly to the right of the runner she was trailing and began her sprint down the final stretch.

Faster, faster she pumped her legs. Past the bleachers crowded with spectators, past the white posts marking the course she sprinted.

Slowly she passed the runner to her left. She asked her body for more speed and drove every muscle in her body to peak performance.

The crowds in the stands cheered the contestants on, growing noisier as the race neared the end. Elena knew Sergiu was among the watching crowd, tense with anticipation as he watched his star pupil fly around the track.

Elena ran. As fast as she had ever run. She still loved to run, but she had also learned to run for the heady sense of accomplishment. And today, she *must* win!

Toward the finish line the young women flew. Elena drew on every ounce of energy and training she had, but she could not draw away from the knot of three other runners that crowded her field.

The finish line was just ahead! The white flag was still raised.

Her lungs screamed for air. Her legs drove on like pistons. Exerting every ounce of will, Elena ran.

At the last moment, two of her competitors raced ahead. The white flag dropped, signaling the end of the race.

Before the announcer declared the winners, Elena knew she had not come in first. Gasping in big drafts of air, she listened for the names.

". . . third place, Elena Boghian."

Third. She had only placed third.

Even though she knew it was a great honor to place at all, she felt a sharp stab of disappointment that she had not taken first prize. She had wanted to be the fastest eleventh grade runner in all Romania.

"Here, drink this!" Sergiu handed her a jug of water. He handed her a towel to wipe her streaming face.

"Good running, but of course, not quite good enough." His words came out in a staccato burst. "We must train more diligently. By next year, you will be taking the first prize."

Elena could not say anything. She wondered if Sergiu was not sure that she would ever be the fastest among her class of women, yet he was not going to give in to doubts. "Give your best and you will be the best" was his motto. He admitted no doubts about his pupil or his own training methods.

The rest of the track meet was a blur to Elena. A growing emptiness inside her kept her from thoroughly enjoying the rest of the sports competition.

"Elena, is this what you want to do with your life?" Mama asked in concern.

Dropping her eyes to the floor, Elena did not answer. She instinctively looked toward the corner where Bunica usually sat. But the corner was empty.

Her grandmother had died while Elena was in high school. Her long fight against the sicknesses was finally over. For over five years she lived with an ever-growing hernia. She had not wanted to go to the hospital, but the family insisted. When she finally allowed them to take her in, her illness was so advanced that she died in the hospital before the doctor could even see her.

So now there was no Bunica to encourage her. Elena thought the empty spot in her heart would never be filled. All of her securities were being swept away.

Subconsciously she knew that was why she had given herself so vigilantly to running in competitions. She needed some goal to live for. Some reason for life.

She had chosen running. Something about driving herself on in fierce competition seemed to push back the emptiness that struggled to overtake her.

"Mama, I don't know," she finally answered. "The agricultural courses I'm taking in school don't interest me. I only take the classes because I have to. Running has become—my life. Sergiu wants me to continue training this summer so I can compete again this fall. Universities all over Romania have asked me to come to their college and join their track team."

Mama looked with tired eyes at her daughter. "I'm concerned for you. You are giving your sport first place in your life. You no longer have time to go to church. You spend hours and hours training for something that will bring you no lasting results. Elena, put your life in God's hands. Give Him your heart!" Her voice was soft and pleading.

Tears dimmed Elena's vision. Her hands felt cold. As cold as her heart.

She stumbled out of the house. Down the dirt road that led to the river she walked, paying no attention to anything or anyone. With sure feet she crossed the log spanning the creek and quickly climbed the slope through the forest.

Her mind jumped back to her childhood when she and Bunica walked this very trail, on their way to visit someone ill or discouraged. Always, Bunica had carried some little gift, but now Elena realized that she had carried much more than a tangible gift. Bunica took her faith along and liberally shared it with everyone she could, everywhere she went.

"Oh, Bunica! If only I could speak to you now! If only you could help me!" Elena's silent cry seemed to fade among the trees. She scrambled up the steep sides of the "egg," as the local people called the jutting promontory that overlooked their village.

Exhausted, she dropped to the ground when she reached the top. The houses and streets of Patrauti stretched out before her. Yet it seemed as though she was hundreds of kilometers away from the village life of her childhood.

Who was she? What was she doing with her life? Where was she going?

Ever since grade school, she had made running a major part of her life. She had competed among the local schools, then in larger cities. Now, finally, she had competed in a national competition and had come in third.

But rather than feeling satisfied with her accomplishments, Elena felt empty. She thought she should feel some kind of euphoria about having placed at all. Instead, there was only a hollow, dissatisfied space within her that she could not fill.

Her childhood was gone. Her teen years were gone. Soon she would go away to college. Which college? Should she make running her life and accept the many offers she had to pursue that course? The only other option was agricultural college.

Elena shook her head in aggravation. She had hated those boring agricultural classes, but had diligently applied herself to learn everything well. She knew this was the only way she could continue the love of her life—running. So she had earned high marks in all her exams.

The sun began to cast long shadows down the hill. A herd of goats on the opposite hill was running down toward the village, followed by the fleet goat herder.

Elena tossed her dark hair back. If only she could be as free as the goats. Leaping about, nimble and free on the path chosen for them. But Elena's own path into the future looked dark and gloomy, without purpose.

Where was the God of her childhood? The God that her father, her grandfather, and her grandmother had worshiped? The God that Mama still served?

Wrapping her arms around her knees, Elena let her tears flow again. What did life have to offer? It all seemed so aimless! So hopeless!

11

Reason to Live

Come unto me, all ye that labour and are heavy laden, and I will give you rest. Take my yoke upon you, and learn of me; for I am meek and lowly in heart: and ye shall find rest unto your souls. For my yoke is easy, and my burden is light.

Matthew 11:28-30

"Come on, Elena! Come with us!" The three girls paused before leaving the student apartment.

Elena looked up from her books. She heard the chatter of the university students in the halls. She shook her head.

"All you do is study!" the girls protested. "You get good marks already, so you wouldn't have to study so hard. You need to have fun too!"

"No, thank-you," Elena protested. "I—I don't really want to go."

"Well, then. At least we invited you. Come on girls, let's go. I saw the boys leave their building."

With a clatter of heels in the corridor, the three left.

Elena sighed, then got up and walked to the window. She checked her laundry hanging just outside the window. At first, she had been embarrassed to hang out her laundry, but recently she had joined the scores of other students who made makeshift clotheslines and dried their clothes outside.

The Agronomical Institute was bordered by a broad, attractive avenue, and sat next to the lovely, expansive Botanical Gardens. Many of the campus buildings were shaded by huge chestnut trees. Her surroundings were not dismal.

But as Elena stood by the window and watched the comings and goings of the university students, she did indeed feel alone. The first several months of getting adjusted to the classes and schedules had not been easy for the shy girl. *Iasi* was a big bustling city and the university campus covered many city blocks. The professors usually did their jobs diligently, but most of them had little time to really connect with the students—there simply were too many. Besides, their goal was to cram as much information as possible into the young, developing minds.

"Agriculture! Why am I stuck studying a subject that I abhor?" Elena asked herself, as she had countless times before. "I don't want to pursue a career in agriculture. But here I am, learning how to make dairy cows yield top milk production! I hate it!"

But Elena knew why she was in this university. Mama's question last summer had made her think hard about pursuing running. She had the talent and ability to go far, she knew. But she had seen enough of the lifestyle that accompanied much of the sports world that she had stopped and reconsidered. Did she really want to be a part of the partying, the worldliness, and immorality she had seen while traveling in the competitions? Did she really want to cut church out of her life in favor of the track meets that were usually held on Saturdays and Sundays? Did she really want to throw away all she had been taught? Although she did not yet know Christ in a personal way, she knew that making running her life was not what she truly wanted.

So, she had chosen to turn down the many offers from other universities, and decided to attend the Agronomical Institute in Iasi. The school had specialized in agriculture during her boarding school years. Her high school emphasized the same subject, and her strong background in these subjects made it easy for her to pass the entrance exams and be accepted by the university.

"Cows!" Elena said bitterly. She returned to her books.

Elena had made no friends in college. Her days were spent between her room, the classrooms, and the dining hall—rare visits to the stores were her only outings. Her roommates were not unfriendly; they simply did not understand a girl who was not interested in partying and having "fun."

Even Elena was not always sure what it was, but something kept her from wanting to experience life on the campus. Something kept her from running with the crowd, even when she was invited.

Elena sighed again and opened her notebook. Her pen moved rapidly across the page as she prepared for the next day's classes.

"Elena! Wait!"

Elena turned quickly to see who was calling her. It was not often she heard her name being called.

"Elena!" A short, vivacious girl pushed toward her in the crowded hall. "I want to talk to you!"

Eugenia fell into step alongside Elena, and the two girls headed down the stairs.

Whatever could Eugenia want with me? Elena wondered. She had hardly ever spoken to her before.

"Come, let's walk toward the park," Eugenia suggested as they exited the building. "I know we hardly know each other, but I want to ask you something." She looked up and down the street and then spoke again.

"I have noticed that you're different from many of the students here," the lively girl chattered. "You don't go out and party like the rest of the girls do. You don't go out with boys and stuff like that."

Elena did not respond. Whatever was Eugenia leading up to?

"Elena, I wondered if you would like to come with me to a special program. There will be singing and poetry reciting. I think you would enjoy it."

There was silence as the two girls walked side by side through the park. The early green of spring spread over the trees and a few daffodils nodded cheerfully beside their path.

"What kind of meeting?" Elena asked.

"Well," Eugenia lowered her voice. "It's at church."

Both girls knew the danger Eugenia had placed herself in. Students could be expelled from school for inviting other students to religious meetings.

Elena felt a yearning inside of her—a yearning to return to the secure world she had known as a child, when she attended services with her family.

"Well!" She gave a little laugh. "I—I don't know! I won't know anyone there. Except you!" She looked at Eugenia.

"That's OK. We're hoping people who really want to know more about—about God, will feel welcome. That's why we're having this special program. Our pastor told us we should invite our friends."

"When is it?"

"Next Sunday morning at nine o'clock."

With a sudden resolve, Elena said, "I'll come."

"Great! I'll be outside your building at eight o'clock. That will give us plenty of time to catch a bus and get to church on time."

Elena drew a quick breath and smiled at Eugenia. "Thank-you for inviting me. I—" she hesitated. "I don't have many friends."

"Now you have one," Eugenia smiled warmly. They retraced their footsteps toward the avenue.

"Bye, Elena! See you on Sunday!"

"Bye," Elena echoed with another smile.

Oh, yes, He cares, I know He cares!
His heart is touched with my grief;
When the days are weary, the long nights dreary,
I know my Saviour cares!

Elena brushed away a tear. It was so good to be in church again. She had not realized how her heart hungered for spiritual food until she was once more in a place where people spoke about God. Not only spoke about Him, but sang about Him and prayed to Him.

Eugenia smiled warmly at her. The two girls sat side by side until Eugenia left to sing with the choir.

An earnest-looking young man stood up. He cleared his throat and then began reciting the Prodigal Son's poem in a clear, vibrant voice:

Oh come home, my lost son
Why don't you get up and come?
Don't you hear the Father's call
Why don't you come?
He's waiting for you at home
His arms are open wide
For you to come and fall
Into His bosom
Why don't you come?
Oh, come!

A profound feeling of having come home reached deep inside the lonely girl's heart. The same words she had known since her childhood came back and found a resting place in Elena's heart. She listened intently, hungrily, to everything that was shared.

The congregation stood for the last song and the benediction. Elena closed her eyes tightly and held her arms at her sides during the prayer. Then the service was over.

In the buzz of conversation that surrounded her, Elena suddenly felt alone. She looked around for Eugenia, but she could not see her new friend. She knew no one else.

Timidly, she made for the door. Most of the others were moving toward the side, visiting. Elena felt too shy to join them. She escaped out into the spring sunlight and went down the steps. Once, she glanced over her shoulder but she didn't see anyone she knew. She continued on her way back to her room.

"Elena! Wait!" Eugenia detached herself from a group of girls and hurried down the hall.

"You didn't stay long after the church service! I suddenly remembered you and tried to find you, but you were gone!"

"That's all right."

"So did you enjoy the program?"

"Yes! It reminded me of going to church with my family when I was little."

"Ahh! So that's what makes you different! You were raised in a Christian family."

Elena nodded. "I had wonderful Christian grandparents. My father was a strong Christian too. They all three passed away and my mother is left a widow. She tried to raise us the best she knew, but four of us spent all our school years in a boarding school. I guess we just kind of drifted away from what we were taught as children."

"I have always gone to church with my parents," Eugenia said briskly. "Even now, I live with my parents. I kind of envy you, living in one of the dorms."

Elena gave her a look of consternation. "Oh, no! You are very privileged to live with your family! I have lived away from home since I was eleven."

"Oh, well," Eugenia laughed. "I'm glad you liked our service. Will you come again?"

"I want to," Elena replied. "Maybe I can find answers to some of my questions."

Sunday after Sunday Elena attended the church services. She joined in singing the familiar songs and tried to learn the new ones. She paid close attention to the sermons. The pastor spoke simply and encouraged his listeners to draw close to God. He read many scriptures that spoke directly to Elena's heart.

At first, Eugenia tried to be friendly to the lonely, shy Elena. But after awhile, Elena saw less and less of her. Many Sundays she could not even find her among the crowd of about two hundred worshipers.

At the university, their paths crossed occasionally, but many times Eugenia hardly did more than wave to Elena. She was usually with a noisy group of girls, laughing and talking merrily.

But Elena continued attending church. After every service, she quietly slipped from her seat and made her way outside. An occasional smile was sent her way, but no one spoke to her.

She attended faithfully for a year. During that time, Eugenia quit going altogether and rumors circulated on the campus of the popular girl's shameful activities. Eugenia no longer even acknowledged Elena when the two met. The girl who had started Elena on her journey back to God was no longer interested in Him.

Still, something within Elena drew her back to hear more from the Word of God. She wanted to hear more about what God wanted from people. She wanted to know what God wanted for her. This deep desire kept her going back week after week, in spite of her loneliness.

Praise God from whom all blessings flow,
Praise Him, all creatures here below,
Praise Him above, ye heavenly host,
Praise Father, Son, and Holy Ghost. Amen.

As the congregation sang the Doxology, Elena stood with the rest. She had felt moved by the service. God's Word was a comfort to her, as were the songs and sermons.

When the benediction was over, she noticed a middle-aged woman making her way toward her. Elena smiled hesitantly.

The woman stopped in front of her. Her eyes traveled up and down Elena's figure.

"Don't you have a longer dress to wear for church?" the woman asked bluntly.

"What?" Elena stammered.

"You should wear a longer skirt for church. You have been coming for quite awhile now, and you ought to know it is not proper to wear short skirts to church." Her dark brown eyes bored into Elena's.

"I'm sorry!" Elena could hardly speak. "I just didn't think about it."

"Well, now you know." The woman turned and left. Elena watched her exit the sanctuary.

Tugging at the hem of her skirt, Elena slipped outside. She rushed past the group of lingering church attenders.

Cheeks burning with humiliation, the lonely girl fled to her room. Her chest heaved. Her throat hurt and her vision blurred with tears.

"Finally, I thought someone was going to speak to me!" Tears began rolling down her cheeks. "After a whole year of attending, I thought someone had finally noticed me! But all she saw was my dress." A sob escaped her constricted throat. "How could she? I know she meant well, but I'm sure she never realized what she has done!

"I feel so alone! Lord, You can't imagine how I feel! Not one friend to care about me! No one to ask me how I am! No one in school to care! No one in church to care!"

She lay on her cot and cried. Her shoulders heaved as bewilderment and loneliness swept over her.

"I won't go back again! If no one cares enough about me to make friends, I won't go back. I know I'm shy and not very friendly myself, but I thought maybe at least the young people would be friendly. No, I won't go back!"

"Elena, would you like to come to church with me?" Sonia smiled. "We're having a Harvest Day service and I hope you can come!"

Elena looked at Sonia for a moment. She had noticed the quiet girl in some of her classes, but had never had an occasion to speak to her.

Was this another invitation to the church she had just quit attending? Elena did not remember seeing Sonia there, but she wanted to make sure. "Where is your church?"

"On *Sarariei* Street," Sonia replied.

It was not the same church. Elena considered a moment. "I'll come and try it," she promised.

The trolley was not crowded on Sunday morning. Elena found an empty seat beside the window, and idly watched the pedestrians and the few cars that motored down the wide avenue. A small line furrowed her forehead. What kind of church would this be? Would she be welcome? Would anyone talk to her?

She easily found the address. The church yard was enclosed by a fence, but the gate stood open. Elena followed several other people into the yard. Strains of song reached her ears.

. . . thank we all our God
With heart, and hands, and voices,
Who wondrous things hath done,
In whom His world rejoices . . .

The singing was beautiful! Through the open door, Elena heard the voices of the singers, lifting the words into the autumn air, thanking God for the bountiful harvest of the summer.

The music and the words drew Elena inside. A friendly man, singing lustily, ushered her into a pew beside a woman who welcomed her with a smile. The entire church building was filled with praise.

Elena allowed the beauty of the song to wrap around her. The air was vibrant with worship.

Next came a period of prayer and praise. All around Elena, men, women, and children poured out their thankful hearts in adoration to God.

The earnestness, the sincerity, and the fervency of these people moved Elena to tears. This—this was what she had been longing for! This was how Bunica had prayed! These people spoke to God because they believed in Him! They *knew* Him!

"Dear people," the pastor's clear voice reached Elena's ears. "We have come together to give thanks to God for His wonderful provisions. Winter will soon be here, but we are so grateful that our gardens and orchards have produced good crops for us.

"But we are grateful for more than a good harvest. We are thankful for the gift of Jesus Christ as our Saviour! We rejoice that our names are written in the Book of Life!"

Elena drank in every word. Her hungry heart feasted on the message the godly man delivered.

Clearly and lovingly, he preached a message of an abundant life in Christ.

Point by point, he brought out the hopelessness of life without Jesus, then, in contrast, told of life changed by the power of Jesus.

Throughout the service, a chorus of "Amens" filled the auditorium.

Elena felt her heart beat faster. A yearning came from deep within her. *I want what he is talking about!* she thought to herself. *I want a changed life in Christ! A reason to live!*

"Perhaps," the pastor went on, "there is someone here who has not experienced the life-changing experience of believing in Jesus Christ. Think deeply about your life! Have you been searching for answers to life? Have you been looking for a reason to live?

"I invite you to repent from your sins and call on the name of Jesus Christ to be saved. It does not matter if you have been raised in a home where you did not get any teaching about God and His Son, Jesus Christ. The invitation is for you.

"Nor does it matter if you have been raised in a home where Jesus Christ was a welcome guest. Each person needs to make his own personal choice to accept or reject Christ. 'For all have sinned and come short of the glory of God.' Everyone of us needs to know the Saviour personally.

"Let the Spirit speak to your heart. If you hear Him calling, do not push Him away. Open your heart to the loving Son of God."

Softly, the choir began to sing:

Just as I am, without one plea,
But that Thy blood was shed for me,
And that Thou bidd'st me come to Thee,
O Lamb of God, I come! I come!

Elena felt something break away and melt inside her heart. The longing for perfect peace overwhelmed her. Tears began trickling down her face.

Throughout the song, Elena wept. She wanted Jesus as her Friend! Her Saviour!

Just as I am, Thy love unknown
Hath broken ev'ry barrier down;
Now, to be Thine, yea, Thine alone,
O Lamb of God, I come! I come!

"If you have felt the Lord calling you, share it with us! Let us rejoice with you and pray with you!" the pastor said, looking over the crowd. "Make it a day of thanksgiving for the harvest of souls!"

Elena stood up. Her deep longing for peace gave her the courage to rise to her feet and voice what was happening inside.

"I want to accept Jesus Christ as my Lord and Saviour! I repent of my sins and invite Him into my life! I want to be obedient to His Word and be baptized!"

Then her legs nearly gave way, and she sat down.

"Glory be to God!" "Thank-you, Jesus!" "Praise the Lord!"

A chorus of voices rang out in joy! The woman next to Elena reached over and pressed her hand warmly.

After the benediction, a middle-aged man and his wife approached Elena. "Hello!" he greeted her enthusiastically. "I am *Nicolae Sfatcu*, and this is my wife, Maria. We are so glad you are with us today! God bless you for your testimony. What is your name?"

"Elena." The answer came quickly.

He smiled warmly. "Are you a student here in Iasi, Elena?"

She nodded.

"Where are you studying?" Maria asked with interest.

Elena cleared her throat and looked at the friendly couple. "At the Agronomical Institute."

"Elena, do you have a Bible?" Elena held up her Bible in reply.

"That's good. Come, you must meet our daughter, Genovieva. She, too, is a student."

They led her to a dark-haired girl who detached herself from an animated group of girls. She smiled and shook Elena's hand.

"Hi!" she greeted warmly. "My name is Genovieva. I'm so glad you came to visit us. I appreciated your testimony!" She smiled again. "God will surely give you your heart's desire. Now come! You must meet several more of the girls. Silvia! Come meet Elena! *Valerica!* Come, this is Elena!"

Beaming faces shone on the shy visitor. Elena smiled back at all the greetings and welcomes. Never before had she been so warmly welcomed anywhere.

"Sister, I welcome you." With an outstretched hand the pastor approached the group of girls. "What is your name?"

"Elena. Elena Boghian."

"Elena, my name is *Radu Cruceru.* We are meeting in the next room with the applicants for baptism. Would you like to join us? You're welcome! Perhaps afterwards, you can share your testimony with my wife and me."

Elena nodded gratefully. Yes! She wanted to attend the class! She wanted to share her testimony with the pastor!

Her heart overflowed as she followed the pastor down the stairs. These people understood what she was longing for! They were ready to help her in any way they could. Already she felt a wonderful change in her heart. Her life would be different now. She knew it! Now she felt eager and ready to do anything the Lord wanted her to do. Life was no longer hopeless and without purpose! She had a reason to live!

12

A New Life!

Therefore if any man be in Christ, he is a new creature: old things are passed away; behold, all things are become new.

II Corinthians 5:17

"Valerica, I feel so useless! I want to do something for the Lord! I love Him so much because He saved me. I need to do something—something to show how much I love Him!" Elena poured out her heart to her friend.

Valerica smiled. "Have you told the Lord how much you love Him? He delights to hear of the love in the hearts of His children."

"Yes! I tell Him every day that I love Him! But I guess I want to show it too."

Valerica nodded and tucked back a strand of hair. The noise of the traffic outside Valerica's apartment went unheeded by the two friends.

"Elena, the desire to be of service to God comes from the Lord Himself. It is a good thing. Many new converts have that longing, and there really is something for everyone to do. Why don't we pray and ask the Lord to give you direction."

Side by side, the two girls knelt. Both prayed simultaneously, asking for guidance for Elena. Full of gratitude for her salvation, Elena knew she was willing to do anything the Lord would show her to do.

"One thing you can do, my friend," Valerica said when they rose from their knees, "is go with me to visit dear Brother *Pavel.* He is old and weak and I know he would be glad to see us. We can read to him from the Bible and pray with him."

"Of course!" Elena agreed. "I want to be useful."

"I think one of the first lessons we can learn is that there are many things to do for Christ, right where we are. Those things might not seem very important or grand, but that is not what God asks of us. He wants us to do the so-called small things, ministering wherever we can."

"Does Pavel live here in Iasi?" Elena wondered.

"Yes, but it's on the other side of the city. We have to take the trolley. Let's go see what I have in the kitchen. We can take some food along for him."

Elena's longing to serve the Lord found an outlet in more than one way. Even though her studies at the university kept her very busy, she gathered with the believers every weekend and sought for ways to serve her Lord. One evening, the Lord interrupted Elena's studies.

"Go visit Pavel again," the voice came clearly. "Bring cheer and comfort to My child in his last years."

"Yes, Lord!" Elena answered. "Yes, I will gladly obey."

She had never gone to Pavel's house alone. Twice before she had accompanied Valerica, so she knew the way. But this time she would have to go alone since she knew Valerica was busy with other activities.

"Lord, I will go. You know I'm scared of the dogs in that neighborhood, but—but I will go anyway. I will take my Bible and read to him."

Getting off the trolley and walking up the alley to Pavel's house took courage for Elena. She clasped the packet of food tightly to her chest.

"Maybe I should have left the food at home," she muttered to herself. "What if the dogs smell the food and try to get it!" She looked apprehensively over her shoulder for the pack of half-starved dogs that had frightened her so on the earlier trips.

"Lord, help me," she breathed. "Just give me courage to walk right up there and get to Pavel's house."

It was still early evening and the streets in the neighborhood were nearly empty. The houses were small and the people poor. Garbage littered the streets and gates sagged on broken fences.

Elena breathed a sigh of relief as she entered Pavel's gate. She quickly walked toward the front door.

A loud shout from inside the house stopped her momentarily. She knew other boarders lived in the house, too, but she did not like the noise and the men's voices coming from inside. Timidly, yet with firm resolve, Elena opened the front door and stepped into the central hall. Pavel's room was the first one on the left, adjoining a larger room that was used as a gathering place for the boarders.

"Brother Pavel! It's Elena!" Pushing the door open into the old man's room, Elena almost scurried inside.

"Oh, Sister Elena!" The old man stirred feebly on his cot. "It's so good to see you! I was praying that someone would come visit me today! I have not been feeling too well and I'm very lonely." Tears spilled out of the old man's eyes and ran down his furrowed cheeks.

"Yes! God moved me to come tonight!" Elena replied graciously. "I have brought you some food! Would you like some now? Some bread? An apple?"

"No," Pavel shook his head. "I am not hungry tonight. I need spiritual food."

A burst of shouting from the group of men in the next room caused Pavel to wince. Only an open doorway separated the rooms.

"Do you want me to read something from the Bible?" Elena asked above the noise.

A feeble nod from Pavel indicated that was indeed what he wanted. "Pull the chair up to this lamp, and turn up the lamp so you can see."

Elena lifted a stack of books off a wooden chair and placed the chair beside the cot. She carefully adjusted the kerosene lamp that stood on the bedside table. She opened her Bible to Psalm 31 and began to read.

" 'In thee, O Lord, do I put my trust; let me never be ashamed: deliver me in thy righteousness.' "

The shouting, laughing men in the next room made it difficult for Elena to concentrate. She raised her voice and read louder.

" 'Bow down thine ear to me; deliver me speedily: be thou my strong rock, for an house of defence to save me.' " Her voice grew stronger.

" 'For thou art my rock and my fortress; therefore for thy name's sake lead me, and guide me.' " She read clearly and distinctly.

In the next room, there was sudden silence.

Elena read on. " 'Pull me out of the net that they have laid privily for me: for thou art my strength. Into thine hand I commit my spirit: thou hast redeemed me, O Lord God of truth.' "

"Yes, Lord! Amen!" Brother Pavel's voice was now easily heard. " 'Into your hands I commend my spirit.' The words of Jesus Himself."

Elena continued. " 'I have hated them that regard lying vanities: but I trust in the Lord.' "

"Trust in the Lord," the old man's voice echoed feebly and yet with thankfulness.

As Elena continued reading, she occasionally heard movements from the other room, but a respectful silence prevailed.

"God bless you for coming," Pavel said sincerely as Elena prepared to leave. "You have been an angel of mercy for my soul this evening. An answer to my prayer."

Elena grasped his bony hand in farewell. "God bless you, brother! I trust you will have a good night!"

"And a good morning! My morning will be when I wake up in the presence of Jesus, my Lord! My Saviour!"

With light steps Elena retraced her earlier route to the trolley, humming a tune under her breath. Not until she was in the trolley did she realize that she had forgotten to be afraid of the dogs! The Lord had given her better things to occupy her mind!

"If I don't see you Wednesday night, I will see you next Sunday!" Valerica said as she embraced Elena good-bye. "I must go. Andrei is waiting for me."

Elena watched as her friend joined the smiling man who stood patiently with a raised umbrella. The two went out the church door into the dark, rainy evening.

Things would not be the same anymore. Valerica and Andrei were getting married soon. Though Valerica was as kind and generous as ever, Elena knew their friendship would change. It had, indeed, already changed.

"What a mess in here!"

Elena looked at the speaker. It was Genovieva.

They were the last ones in the auditorium. Wet puddles and muddy footprints tracked up the entry. The floor of the auditorium was wet.

"Who cleans up in here?" Elena wondered.

Genovieva looked up. "I do," she smiled.

"Do you need help?" Elena wondered.

"Now I can't refuse an offer like that!" With a friendly grin, Genovieva looked at Elena. "But you won't want to mop in your good dress. Here, take this apron to cover up and I'll get another one."

"So, are you always responsible for cleaning the church house?" Elena started mopping up the wet footprints.

"Yes," Genovieva laughed. "Since I've been expelled from college, I work wherever I can."

Elena straightened her back and stared at the dark-haired girl busy at work. "You were expelled! Why?"

Genovieva did not reply right away. Then she said lightly, "Well, the secret police found out too much about me." She glanced toward the door as though she was almost expecting someone to appear.

Elena followed Genovieva's look. The door was still closed.

"What did they find out?" she almost whispered.

"Later. I'll tell you later."

Side by side the two girls cleaned up the floor. Elena's mind whirled. Whatever had Genovieva done that had caused her to be expelled from college? The secret police? She shuddered.

"There! That's done!" Genovieva wrung out the mop and put it upside down in the closet. "Come with me to my room."

Even though it was late, Elena followed Genovieva. They entered a small room at the back of the church.

"Here is where I often stay if it gets late," Genovieva said, moving some books from the cot. "Sit down and we'll talk."

Elena looked around the tiny room. She sat on the cot and gathered her legs under her.

"You asked why I was expelled," Genovieva said slowly and softly. "I'll tell you why.

"I was going to college to get a diploma in linguistics. So, I studied English as a foreign language. I've learned it quite well.

"Sometimes we have English-speaking foreigners come to visit our church. Since I know English, I translate for them. The visitors have been interested in us Christians in Romania and what life is like for us. So, I am often with the foreigners.

"There are secret infiltrators from the *Securitate* who come to church meetings, especially when they know we have foreign visitors."

"How do the police know when foreigners come?" Elena wondered. Her heart beat rapidly.

"They know," Genovieva said soberly. "The visitors must register when they enter the country and fill out forms where they will be staying while in Romania. They are followed by the secret police all the time. They know the visitors come to our church to speak. Elena, they know a lot about us." She looked keenly at the girl in front of her.

"But why did that make them expel you from school?" Elena was bewildered. There were many things about her own country she did not understand.

"Simply because they suspect that I am a spy for the foreigners. They have decided that since I can speak English with the foreigners, I am passing on secret information to them. Although I have told them over and over that I'm not guilty of passing any information to our visitors that is not common knowledge, they refuse to accept my word and had me expelled from school. So now I clean the church house and do whatever else I can to support myself."

Elena was silent. She was trying to understand what this was all about. She knew there was great conflict between believers and the Communist government of her country. She remembered the personal stories of persecution and harassment her own family had related, but now it came a lot closer to her.

"Did—did they beat you?" Elena stammered.

"No," Genovieva sighed. "But mentally and psychologically I have been persecuted."

Then she straightened her shoulders and smiled at Elena's troubled look. "But the Lord has been very faithful to me. I have not suffered nearly as much as many others. I claim by faith the promise that God will not give me more than I can bear. So, Elena, do not worry."

Elena smiled back. She liked this lively girl who was willing to serve the Lord, even if it meant mopping the church house floors.

"Well, I have asked God what I can do to serve Him, and now He has given me something else to do. I will help you with the cleaning whenever I can." Elena said simply. "I want to help with the work of the Lord."

"I know God will reward you for your willing heart," Genovieva said gratefully. "There is a lot of work to keep this building clean."

Genovieva shifted some papers on a table. "Listen to this, Elena." She began singing softly:

Thank-you, Jesus, for saving me;
In You I found all I need,
No ocean, no big waves
Will be able to separate my love from Yours!

Refrain:
O! I want to glorify Your Name
And your commandments to obey.

I want to do only your will
And to sing Your Love,
And to sing Your Love!

Thank-you, Lord Jesus,
For your Holy Ghost;
Your love and the Holy Ghost
Are all that I desire."

"Who wrote that?" Elena asked in wonder. "That is beautiful!"

Genovieva beamed, a little self-consciously. "I wrote it! At least part of it."

"You did! How wonderful! Did you write these too?" Elena looked at the other pages Genovieva was holding.

"Some I wrote and some I copied from other sources. My brother *Teodor*, Silvia *Tarniceriu*, and I are working with the children's choir and preparing for programs. I have some cassettes with English songs. I'm not supposed to have them, but I listen to a song until I know the melody, and then I translate the words into our language. That way we can teach the song to the children. My goal is to teach them one new song each Sunday."

Elena listened as Genovieva softly sang song after song. Time crept on.

"Why don't you stay here with me tonight?" Genovieva offered. "It's too late for you to go to the dormitory. You can go to college from here in the morning." Elena accepted gladly.

Together, the two girls knelt and prayed. Elena poured out her gratefulness to God for providing another Christian friend. Perhaps she would not feel the loss of Valerica's friendship as much. Also, she was struck with the thought that God was opening doors for her to serve Him in the church. She saw many opportunities to help Genovieva.

"Thank-you, God, for showing me that there is something I can do for You! I don't care if no one else notices it, I want to do it all for You! Thank-you, Jesus!"

"OK children, let's try that one more time. You sopranos did especially well in that second line. Your voices are more confident now that you know the song well." Elena watched as Genovieva directed the singing.

More than twenty children stood at attention on the platform in front of the church. With eager eyes they followed Genovieva's conducting.

Genovieva nodded at her brother, Teodor, and he gave the key at the organ. With a swift movement of her arms, Genovieva led the children into the opening bars of the song.

Silvia glanced in Elena's direction and smiled warmly.

She smiled back.

This was so wonderful! Being with friends who love the Lord and were busily occupied in His work. Friends who were warm and friendly and smiled and laughed. This was like heaven! Elena's heart sang with joy. "Thank-you so much for bringing me here, Lord. I never knew such joy before! This is what Bunica often talked to me about on our walks through the forest. Now I understand!"

"I think we are ready to record! Don't you, Silvia?" Genovieva smiled as the song ended.

"Oh, yes," Silvia smiled. "You children are doing so well! Elena, would you like to run the tape recorder?"

Elena looked at the unfamiliar machine. Could she?

"Here, I'll show you how." Silvia stepped up to the recorder. "The tape is in the machine, here, and everything is set. See? When you see Genovieva about to begin the song, push this button down. Then there is nothing to do except wait until the song is finished. Push this button, and it will stop. OK?"

It was quite easy. After that, Elena faithfully operated the recorder during choir practice. Every bit of work she could do brought a deep satisfaction. As time went on, she gained confidence in her own abilities and enjoyed her work more and more.

She especially enjoyed traveling with the choir to other cities. Although they attracted a lot of attention on the trains as they rehearsed and sang, the authorities miraculously left them alone. Surely the hand of the Lord protected them and opened up unheard-of doors. That such an obviously Christian activity could flourish in a communist country was indeed a miracle.

"Don't look now, but someone is watching us," Silvia told Elena on one such train trip. "We are being observed."

Elena froze in fear. Whatever would happen? They were surrounded by children; in fact, the children took up half the train car.

Trying to appear casual, Elena turned her head around, nonchalantly scanning the car. Instantly, she saw him.

With keen eyes that sharply took in everything, the man in civilian clothes sat at the extreme rear of the train car. A pompous air held him aloof from the other passengers. He looked directly at Elena.

Elena turned back. "I saw him," she said breathlessly.

But Silvia was not easily intimidated. "Children," she cried, standing and facing them. "Let's sing our new song one more time. Then we'll be ready when we arrive!"

Elena shook her head slightly and stared straight ahead. How could Silvia do this? She was so brave, knowing they were being watched.

The train car filled with music. The words skipped lightly from ear to ear of the passengers. Faces relaxed; warm smiles were sent toward the choir. A happy atmosphere spread through the entire car.

Elena risked another glance toward the rear. The man was gone!

"How could you do that?" Elena asked Silvia as the three girls left the church house that evening. They were back in Iasi after their trip with the choir. "Weren't you afraid we'd be arrested?"

Genovieva looked at Silvia significantly. Silvia looked serious.

"Elena, that is what the secret police want from us. Fear. They want to intimidate us to the point that we stop doing any work in the church. But we cannot do that! We must be bold for God." Silvia spoke in a low, passionate voice.

Genovieva nodded in agreement. "We must be willing to take many risks. For instance, we know that it is considered illegal for us to work with the children in church. But we have a higher command from God to teach and to train the children about the Bible. It's because of our love for God that we can be bold!"

As their footsteps sounded in unison on the sidewalk, Elena thought about what her friends had said. It was true, she herself was willing to do things she had never done before. Like going to visit Pavel by herself. Or, even going home alone after church. God had indeed given her a braver heart.

"Do you know what was in the parcel that we asked you to carry today?" Genovieva asked, looking at Elena.

Elena shook her head. She had not given much thought to the bag she had taken along to the church where the children had sung earlier that day. "What?" she asked innocently.

"Bibles," Silvia told her. Both girls watched for Elena's reaction.

"Bibles? That's good," Elena said simply.

"Well, you know if we would have been caught taking Bibles anywhere, there could have been some serious consequences," Silvia said bluntly. "Like prison!"

Elena gasped. Prison!

All the terrors and fears of her childhood swarmed into her mind. The fear of being locked up, the fear of being beaten, the fear of all the horrible uncertainties and unknowns of prison threatened to overwhelm her.

Then a voice seemed to speak directly to her heart. "Think of the price I have paid for your soul! Think of what I have gone through for you, Elena. Surely, it should not be too much to ask that you, My child, should be willing to suffer for Me."

Taking a deep breath, Elena looked at her friends. "Jesus did so much for me, I am willing to do anything for Him. Anything! 'For to me to live is Christ, and to die is gain' (Philippians 1:21). He gives me courage." She smiled. "If you can be involved in this work, I will gladly do all I can to help!"

"Good!" Silvia exulted. She laughed as she said to Genovieva, "God truly has put a new heart in Elena! She is willing to put her fears aside and work for the Lord!"

The three girls boarded the trolley. Headed for a future unknown to them, they were confident through their trust in the Lord Jesus Christ.

13

Shadowed

FEAR THOU NOT; FOR I AM WITH THEE: BE NOT DISMAYED;
FOR I AM THY GOD: I WILL STRENGTHEN THEE; YEA, I WILL HELP THEE;
YEA, I WILL UPHOLD THEE WITH THE RIGHT HAND OF MY RIGHTEOUSNESS.

ISAIAH 41:10

"I'll race you to the top!" Teodor shouted. He sprinted up the slope of the mountain, the picnic hamper bumping wildly against his legs.

"Be careful with our lunch!" Silvia cried, laughing as she scampered after him. Genovieva and Elena saw what was happening and, with squeals of laughter, raced after them.

The tall man whom the group called *Simeon* stood still for a moment, watching his friends run up the steep slope.

"So they do take time to relax and enjoy themselves," he murmured, smiling, and followed them more leisurely.

Even though Teodor had a head start, he was slowed down by the basket. The three girls reached the summit before he did.

Elena sank to the ground. She flung back her head and breathed deeply of the mountain air. It was wonderful to be in the country again!

She watched as Simeon came closer. "I hope our friend from Denmark doesn't think we're giddy!" she said to the rest of the group.

"Hey, he knows we're having a wonderful time here in the mountains!" Silvia said with a laugh.

When Simeon joined them on the grassy meadow, Genovieva spoke to him in English. Simeon responded and then Genovieva turned to the others.

"He said it is good to see us run and laugh together. People from the West often think of us Christians as being quiet, repressed people. Now he can see that we are like everyone else, enjoying ourselves whenever we can."

"Well, we still have our faithful 'shadows,' I see," Teodor announced quietly. "Down there by that little brook."

Elena felt a stab of fear. They were being followed.

"The same two," Silvia said as she stood up and looked intently down the mountain slope. "They're wearing different clothes this time."

Genovieva interpreted for their visitor. A rapid exchange in English followed. Simeon reached for his backpack and went down the opposite slope.

"He says he will sleep under the open sky tonight," Genovieva said, her voice subdued. "He doesn't want to endanger anyone by staying in their home."

Elena looked at the two young men beside the stream. With elaborate preparations, they were baiting hooks and throwing them into the little creek.

"If they think they can fool us by looking like sportsmen, they have failed," Silvia said, shaking her head. "A pair of amateurs, I'd say."

"What about this evening?" Elena asked tensely. "Will Simeon come to the meeting?"

Genovieva nodded. "He said he will come late. If our two 'shadows' are there, he will only stay a short while. He feels it best not to jeopardize anyone."

The little group was silent as they thought about their danger.

Simeon had arrived in Romania as a tourist and visited their group in Iasi. He had told Genovieva that he wanted to see how believers in the villages were faring. They had arranged to bring him on this excursion into the mountains to meet the local Christian villagers. On the bus, their little group had first noticed the two well-dressed young men who seemed to take a keen interest in the foreigner and the church young people. When they left the bus at the edge of the village to which they were traveling, the two shadows had mingled with the crowd getting off. They had quickly decided not to go to any of the believers' homes, but to take their lunch and hike up the mountainside.

Elena plucked at the grass beside her. "Could we pray?" she said in a low voice.

The four bowed their heads and each one began praying. A holy hush settled over them.

The rumbling bus slowly sputtered and smoked its way back to Iasi. The crowded seats could scarcely hold all the passengers.

Elena was squeezed in tightly between Silvia and Genovieva. Genovieva sat at the end, next to the aisle. Teodor sat beside two men directly in front of them, and Simeon occupied a third of the seat behind them. The two grandmothers sharing the seat with Simeon babbled excitedly to each other. Everyone on the bus kept glancing at the visitor, so obviously from the West, then quickly averted their eyes if they saw him look at them. The two faithful shadows sat toward the back of the bus.

"What a contrast to the pure mountain air," Silvia chuckled ruefully. "All we smell now is what everyone else had for their latest meal!"

Genovieva smiled briefly, but she was obviously thinking hard. She leaned toward the other two girls. "I have a plan. Since we are close to the front of the bus, let's pay the driver to stop at *Castanilor* Street, and we'll all quickly get off. No one else expects the bus to stop there, so even our 'shadows' will be taken by surprise."

"Send Teodor up to talk to the driver," Silvia immediately agreed. "It's worth a try."

Genovieva leaned forward and conveyed the plan to her brother.

"I'll write a note to Simeon so he will be ready," Genovieva said.

Elena began praying. Her heart beat faster. Perhaps this would be a way to shake the two men who had shadowed them for the last two days. No matter where they went in the mountain village, the two men could always be seen hovering in the distance, trying vainly to look like vacationers. Once the men had attended a church meeting. The other evenings, they had lurked nearby. Simeon had made himself scarce, spending most of his days on strenuous mountain hikes and only coming into the village in the evenings. Nights he had spent outside, sleeping by himself.

"Dear Lord," Elena prayed. "Please move the driver's heart to accommodate us! Don't let any harm come to Simeon! And please keep us out of the enemy's hand!"

Teodor had come back to his seat. He nodded his head slightly and settled himself down. Genovieva passed the note back to Simeon.

Would their plan work? Elena grew nervous. At least if the shadows also got off, they would know for certain the men were following them.

A part of Elena wanted to know for sure, but another part did not. Just how much did the secret police know about all of them? About her? Were they truly being watched and marked because of their work with the children's choir? Or was it because of their involvement in distributing Bibles?

Not for a moment had Elena regretted her decision to help smuggle Bibles. Without question, she helped unload packages from cars with foreign license plates. Many times she barely saw the driver of the car, so quickly did they unload the packages and transfer them to one of their own vehicles. Then, with quiet speed, she helped place the precious, dangerous cargo in a designated hiding place.

"We're close," Silvia nudged Elena with her knee.

Elena's mind snapped out of her reverie. The bus was slowing down at an intersection.

Teodor was still sitting at ease in front of them. Would the bus driver really stop? Had he taken Teodor's money and pocketed it, knowing they could not ask for a refund if he refused to stop? Would the two men see what was happening in time to follow them?

The bus stopped.

"Now!" Genovieva whispered to the girls.

In a flash, Teodor strode forward. Simeon darted past the girls as the three of them crowded into the aisle. The door of the bus opened and all five piled out onto the sidewalk.

The door closed behind them and the bus lurched into motion again. Elena looked back and saw the two men hurry up the aisle to the front. She saw them talking to the driver.

The driver shook his head as the bus moved forward. The frustrated men stared out the window at the little group. Smiling broadly, Silvia waved her hand gaily at them as the moving bus gained speed.

"Silvia! How can you?" Elena gasped. The rest laughed in relief.

Simeon spoke to Genovieva and then shook hands with them all in farewell. "God bless you and protect you!"

They watched as he turned and walked away.

"Over here in the corner is a table available for us," Silvia suggested. Genovieva, Elena, Anne and Tim, and Ruth and Jeff followed Silvia to the corner of the café.

"Good! Very good!" Tim said in English.

It was easy for Elena to understand that their foreign guests were pleased with the decision to sit and rest. The long hours of travel from the West to

Iasi were etched on the American visitors' faces.

"Elena, do you mind if I sit there?" Genovieva asked. "I will sit next to Anne and interpret for her."

Elena sat in a chair facing the street.

A waiter came up to them. "Seven coffees, please." Silvia ordered for everyone.

"Do you have some cakes?" Genovieva asked politely.

"Chocolate or white?"

"I'll have chocolate," Silvia ordered for herself. "Elena, what would you like?"

Elena hesitated, then said, "I think I'll take white."

"Do you want to ask—?" Silvia turned to Genovieva.

"Three more chocolates and two whites," Genovieva hastily interrupted Silvia.

After the waiter left, Genovieva frowned slightly at Silvia. "I think it's better not to draw attention to our guests. It's safer that way."

"But everyone can see they are foreigners!" Silvia protested. "The waiter was looking at them curiously all the time he was here."

"Still, it is better they don't speak," Genovieva said somberly. "We can't be too careful."

She turned and spoke softly to the couples. They nodded their heads.

"But what if they don't like chocolate?" Silvia teased.

"Then I will trade with them." Elena said. "I don't mind—"

Elena's throat went dry.

A man was circling the outside patio, sending quick but piercing glances toward them. He especially scrutinized the foreign couples.

"Here is your coffee and cake," the waiter slid the cups and plates in front of them. He placed a fork beside each dessert plate.

"Someone is watching us," Silvia said in a low voice, confirming Elena's suspicions. Genovieva said something in English to the visitors, who again nodded.

"You like the coffee?" Silvia asked in English.

Anne took a sip and raised her eyebrows. She laughed and waved her hand slightly in front of her mouth. She looked at Tim and said something. He tasted his and made a wry face.

Genovieva spoke to them in English. They laughed and responded.

"They are not used to such strong coffee," Genovieva interpreted. "They said American coffee is much milder."

"Coffee, *foarte buna!* "

The three girls smiled in delight at Ruth's approval of the beverage and her attempt to speak their language.

Another man had joined the first one on the patio. The two now openly stared at them and conferred with each other. Elena could hardly eat her cake.

The others pretended they had not noticed anything. They continued to eat and enjoy the treat.

The door to the café opened and footsteps approached their table.

"All of you, come with us." The command came with authority, yet the tone was low. Elena turned quickly to look at the speaker and his companion.

"Come," the man said again. "You must come to the police station."

"But why?" Genovieva asked mildly. "What are we doing that warrants this?"

"You will find out at the police station. You must come immediately." The second man stepped closer.

"Let us finish our cake and coffee first," Silvia objected. "Our guests have insisted on treating us to dessert. It would be impolite to leave them."

"They must come too," the speaker said impatiently. "You must all come. Immediately!" He pulled on the back of Silvia's chair.

"Why?" Genovieva's voice rang out with dismay. The other patrons of the café stared at the unfolding drama.

"Shh!" the speaker warned. "There must not be any commotion! Now *come!*" He clenched his teeth and dragged Silvia's chair from the table.

The two American couples had risen from the table. Ruth's face was drawn and white. She nervously entwined her fingers with her husband's.

Elena followed their example and stood. Genovieva and Silvia took their time. Silvia swallowed the last of her coffee before slowly standing up.

Eyes followed them as they left the café, one of the plainclothesmen leading them to the police cars parked in front of the coffee shop, and the other bringing up the rear.

The ride to the station took only a few minutes. They were all taken into a room where the officer who had spoken to them at the café sat at his desk.

"Where are you from?" He looked directly at Anne and Tim.

The two visitors shrugged their shoulders and looked to Genovieva for help.

"Sir, they—" Genovieva began.

"Quiet!" the officer roared. "I am speaking to them, not to you."

Turning once more to the couple, he asked in a louder tone. "Where are you from? Where are your passports?"

"Ahh!" Tim said in relief, "passports!" He withdrew two dark blue passports from his briefcase and handed them to the officer.

"Humph!" the officer sniffed. "Americans! What are you doing here?"

Tim smiled helplessly and looked at Genovieva. He replied to the officer in English. Again, he looked at Genovieva.

"What?" the officer raised his voice. "Speak in our language."

Again Tim said something. Anne said timidly, "*Nu inteleg.*"

"Well, who in here can translate for them?" He glared at the three girls.

"Sir, I can," Genovieva said simply.

"How did you learn to speak English?" He looked suspiciously at her.

"I learned at the university."

"Where are these people from and what are they doing here?"

Genovieva cleared her throat. "They are from America. They are guests in our country."

Then followed a lengthy exchange, with the officer asking for all four of the visitors' passports and purpose for their visit. He wrote down all the information carefully.

"Why did the officer want all that information?" Elena asked nervously. The two hours spent in the police station had given her indigestion.

Genovieva turned her head once more to see if their guests were still in sight. She watched them disappear through the front doors of their hotel.

"They want to know everything," Silvia answered. "Plus, they want to constantly remind us that they are watching all our activities. I'm sure they expect us to slow down or even stop our activities if they constantly shadow and harass us."

"Are you ever tempted to stop with the—the 'work'?" Elena asked.

Genovieva looked at her. "Are you?"

Elena drew a deep breath to still her quivering insides. "No, not really. Like I said earlier, I want to do anything for the Lord. I want to show Him that I really love Him!"

"Amen!" Silvia responded with quiet joy. "That's the way we all feel, I'm sure. As long as we can be but one small link in the work of the church, we will continue."

"Did—our guests bring any 'luggage'?" Elena asked.

"So far, no. This incident today at the café may keep them from being able to deliver any goods. We will see what the Lord will do. If they can't pass the luggage on to us, they may be able to give it to other believers. We are only one small contact, and nothing can ever be depended on to work every time."

"But God is the One we can always depend on," Genovieva said softly. "He has never failed us in any way."

"Have you ever thought of responding to the invitation from abroad?" Silvia asked her friend.

The girls walked on into the shadows of early evening. Genovieva did not reply immediately.

Elena pondered her friend's situation. She knew the problems Genovieva had since she was dismissed from the university. She had not been able to get a job and had difficulties with the police. They shadowed her almost everywhere she went, clearly suspicious that she was somehow working as a spy for the West. Her command of English made her a prime suspect, as well as her work as an interpreter for foreign guests who visited their church. Elena knew her friend lived under an ever-increasing strain.

"Will you pray with me concerning that question?" Genovieva finally responded. "I don't want to flee Romania just because of the pressures, and yet . . . yet I feel the net getting tighter all the time. Like today. This is one more item they'll add to their files about me." She stopped talking as two men dressed in business suits passed them. Even after they had passed, she remained silent.

Silvia turned around and backed up the sidewalk in front of the other two girls. She watched the two men walk farther and farther away. Then, she turned around and fell into step beside Genovieva. She linked her arm companionably with her friend.

Genovieva smiled at her and then took Elena's arm. "Whatever happens, we will never forget our times of fellowship and friendship. It means so much to me to have sisters who pray with me, support me, and understand me.

"Regarding the invitation, I must tell you I'm really considering it. Like I said, they seem to be shadowing me more and more. I am willing to do the work of the Lord, but sometimes I don't know how effective I am anymore. Especially when I think of being arrested and spending years in prison. How could I ever be useful there, shut away from society?"

Prison! Elena heard the word with dread. Her heart pounded faster again.

14

A Life by Day, A Life by Night

But thanks be to God, which giveth us the victory through our Lord Jesus Christ. Therefore, my beloved brethren, be ye stedfast, unmoveable, always abounding in the work of the Lord, forasmuch as ye know that your labour is not in vain in the Lord.

I Corinthians 15:57-58

"We come at dark," the man concluded in broken Romanian. "Be ready." Then he drove away in a small white van.

Elena hurried after Silvia into the church house. "Many," the foreigner had said. "Many, many packages."

"Elena, I think we will store as much as we can in the attic," Silvia planned. "They will just have to stay there for several days until we can move them on their way." The two headed for Genovieva's little room.

"Genovieva," Elena announced, "a vehicle will come at dark tonight with many parcels. We have just been told by a foreigner who spoke a little Romanian.

"Come, let's pray about it. So many things have been happening recently and I feel we need the Lord's protection for this delivery." Elena knelt beside Genovieva's cot and her two friends joined her.

With intense prayers, the three pleaded with God to watch over the activities of the evening. They asked God to bless the Christian brethren in other countries who cared enough about the plight of Romanian Christians to risk their lives to send them Bibles.

God answered the three girls by sending His Spirit to give them rest in His divine providence. They prayed until the evening shadows darkened the room, reminding them that it was time to prepare for the arrival of the Bibles.

"I hope it's not too large a vehicle," Genovieva worried. "He'll have to drive between the church house and the fence to get all the way around to the back. Otherwise, the police could easily see someone is parked here and get suspicious."

"I have an idea," Elena volunteered. "I'll climb up the big tree by the street and watch for the vehicle. I'll be able to see all the way down the street, and I'll motion to Silvia when to open the gate. Then he can drive right in without having to stop on the street. Do you think that will help?"

Both girls agreed enthusiastically. "That way," Silvia said, "if someone is watching, I won't open the gate and he will have to drive on. Elena, you make sure the street is clear of anyone who looks as though they were spying on us."

The huge maple was covered in green, summer-clad leaves. Elena looked up and down the street before grabbing the big, horizontal limb that grew conveniently low to the ground. She swung her lithe body up into the tree and quickly climbed higher until she was hidden among the branches. Then she carefully worked her way out from the trunk until she could see through the foliage and find a clear view both of the street and the double gate to the church house.

Silvia stood beside the church house, watching her. Elena waved and Silvia waved back. Genovieva's brothers, *Costica* and Teodor, arrived and waited behind the church house with Genovieva.

Elena waited. A teen-aged boy walked down the street and under the tree, keeping a tight leash on his dog. The dog stopped and sniffed at the base of the tree.

Would the dog bark and betray her presence above him? "Please, Lord," Elena prayed, "don't let him bark!"

"Come on," the boy said impatiently. He pulled the dog after him.

Now the street was almost deserted. No cars rumbled up the cobblestone street. Only an occasional pedestrian crossed the street.

"Now! Oh, Lord, let him come now! This would be the perfect time!"

She heard the sound of a motor! Elena peered down the street as far as she could see.

A vehicle was coming! Elena pushed away a small branch to see better. She gasped!

It was a panel truck! Never before had she helped unload parcels from a truck that big! Would he even be able to fit through the gates and drive behind the church house?

The truck came closer. Quickly Elena scanned the streets for a sign of anyone watching. She could see nothing. Not a single person! Frantically, she signaled to Silvia.

Silvia darted out from her hiding place and swung the metal gates wide open. The truck roared up the hill and swung into the church yard. He followed Costica's beckoning arms and drove into the narrow alley beside the church. The truck just fit between the fence and the building!

Silvia closed the gates and barred them. Even before Elena could get out of the tree, the engine in the truck was shut off. The summer evening peacefulness settled over the street once again.

The driver, the three girls, Costica, and Teodor knelt in the open space behind the church house. They thanked God for the protection He had already given them and for safely delivering the packages this far. They asked Him to protect them the remainder of the night. Then the driver opened the back doors, and they began unloading the precious cargo.

It was long after midnight before the truck was completely unloaded. The driver, clearly in a hurry to leave, shook hands with everyone, crawled into the driver's seat, and started the motor. In the quiet of the night, it seemed so loud Elena wondered how many of the neighbors were awakened out of their sleep.

Cautiously, the driver steered the truck back through the narrow passage. A tree growing right on the property line made it difficult to maneuver the big vehicle past the tight spot. They all held their breath, as the cab of the truck cleared the tree. But just as the rear dual wheels came even with the tree, the entire truck shifted toward it. The large tires bounced against the trunk and stopped. The outside wheel was wedged tightly between the tree and the edge of the sidewalk.

The truck was stuck! The driver revved his motor and tried to pull forward. The back wheels rotated swiftly in a helpless, complaining whine. Desperately he tried to back up. Again, the tires merely spun helplessly.

Cutting off the engine, the driver hopped out and peered anxiously at his predicament.

"Try again," Costica encouraged. "We'll all push and see if we can move the truck sideways enough for the wheel to get around the tree."

Once more, the engine roared into the quiet night. Everyone crowded against the side of the now empty truck and pushed.

It was useless. The truck stayed stuck.

They prayed. In desperation, they begged God for help. Beads of sweat wet the driver's forehead. He kept glancing at his watch as he paced back and forth.

He kicked at the offending outside tire, but it remained firmly lodged in its prison of concrete and wood. The inside tire was still on the sidewalk.

All at once, he was seized with an inspiration. He bent over and unscrewed the cap from the valve. He pushed the valve in and everyone could hear the hissing sound of escaping air. It took only a moment or two for the tire to deflate enough that it no longer bulged against the side of the tree.

With renewed hope, the driver hopped in and started the motor. Again, everyone pushed from the rear. The truck moved forward!

The outside tire scraped against the tree trunk, but slid right past! Teodor opened the gate, and with a relieved wave of his hand, the driver maneuvered the truck into the street.

Rejoicing, the five young people watched the truck rumble down the street. Then, closing the gate, they hurried back inside to stash the packages in the attic and under the elevated platform at the front of the church and in any other safe hiding place they could think of. As they worked, Elena noticed that the sky was already turning pink in the east. Morning was near, but they had the packages inside and the driver had been able to get his truck free. What did it matter that the night had been long and hard? It was a satisfying feeling to have helped bring God's Word into their country.

Elena and her companion, *Lili*, stepped off the public bus and into the grass beside the country road. As the creaking vehicle continued on its journey, the two stood silently surveying their surroundings.

The rolling hillsides of northeastern Romania were green with spring wheat. Trees covered some of the ridges, but for the most part, huge fields stretched into the horizon for miles. A rutted dirt road stretched away from the highway and disappeared around a curve on a hill.

Lili lovingly drew Elena close to her. "Dear Elena," she said in a voice husky with emotion, "we will kneel down and ask God to give us direction for this important step for your future. He knows what is best."

There was no traffic on the highway—no cars, no horse-drawn wagons, not even anyone on foot. In all the vast landscape, they were the only two people in sight. Elena felt as though they had been dropped into the center of an alien world. Nothing was familiar. Nothing except God and her dear sister in Christ, Lili.

It was in the Agronomical Institute lab that Elena had first met Lili, the science teacher. There was a softness, a gentleness in this teacher that set her apart from most of the other instructors. Even before Elena had surrendered her life to Jesus, she had been drawn to her. Strict she was, yes, but along with the strictness accompanying her professional life, there was a kindness in Lili that had touched Elena's lonely heart.

Thus their friendship had flourished and grown, especially after Elena had become a Christian. It was not uncommon for her to slip into Lili's lab and pour out her heart to sympathetic ears. Almost always, Lili prayed with Elena before they parted. To have found such a wonderful mentor among the many calloused instructors in the university was truly Providence.

Now here they were, out in the spring sunshine, kneeling together in the grassy ditch. The two women pled with the Lord for further direction.

"Lord," Lili prayed, "give dear sister Elena much courage for her new job. Open the way for us to find a place where she can stay with someone who is kind and considerate. Look upon this sister—she needs Your direction for her life. Guide her every footstep, and make her very conscious that You are holding her in the center of Your hand."

"Yes, God," Elena prayed with a trembling voice, "I need You very much. You have proved Yourself faithful to me ever since I have given my life to You. Never have You forsaken me. Now I ask again for Your guidance to find a place to live and for direction for my job. You know the only reason I chose this place is because it's not as far away from my sisters and brothers in Iasi as the other job openings were. Lord, I need the strength from my church family! I don't want to be here, but I had to come! Please be with me, Lord!"

Lili gently placed her arm around Elena's narrow shoulders and hugged the trembling girl.

"I have come under orders from the Agricultural Division in Iasi," Elena said, handing her document to the head of the collective farm. The headquarters, housed in a small, unpretentious building, sat on a knoll facing the dirt road they had just walked on.

The walk had taken them over an hour. Although Elena was tired, nervousness kept her on edge and tensely alert.

"Welcome to our farm."

Elena thought the man's words sounded nice but rather forced. She returned the gaze and tried to read the language his eyes were speaking.

"Do you have a place to stay?"

This was the very question that had plagued Elena ever since she had known she was coming to *Bratulesti*. She shook her head. "No, sir."

"There is an empty house here on the farm, but the last people living there left it a mess. You may live in it, but it will take a lot of work to make it habitable." Again, the man sounded pleasant, but Elena felt that he was not sure she had what it took to do the job. He was probably wondering if such a young woman could even begin to manage a farm with more than thirty workers, most of them unlearned village men.

"However, you may want to check with the *Enache* family here in the village. They are a childless couple and they may have an extra room. You would be more comfortable there."

Elena looked at Lili and smiled. Perhaps this was an answer to their prayers!

From the outside, the Enache house looked neat and well-cared-for. Carved woodwork decorated the front porch. Flowers bloomed cheerfully along the walk that led from the yard gate to the house. Verdant grape leaves cast a pleasant green shade over the arbor.

"Please, God, let these people be nice and willing to accept a boarder," Elena prayed under her breath. "Soften their hearts toward me!" She knocked on the door and waited as footsteps neared in response. She smiled at the small, cheerful woman who opened the door.

"Hello! My name is Elena Boghian and I will be working at the collective farm here in the village. The president of the farm recommended that I check with you about renting a room."

The woman stepped onto the front porch and studied the two visitors. "I don't know for sure," she said hesitantly. "We were planning on doing some renovations in the house soon."

Her husband pushed the door open and joined them. He, too, looked curiously at their visitors as the woman turned to him and explained their mission. It was obvious that they hardly ever saw people from outside their own village.

"Ahh!" he said slowly. "The young lady needs a place to board." He con-

1958
(left to right)
Back: Mosu *(Grandpa)* Costache, Gheorghita *(Elena's dad)*
Middle row: Vasile, Bunica *(Grandma)* Raveca, Mama Viorica with baby Lucia, Lidia
Front: Rodica, Dan, Elena

Gheorghita (Elena's dad) when he was a guard for the king of Romania in 1941, at the Sinaia palace (visitors can still see the palace today).

Her Bunica was very special to Elena. (Photo taken around 1965).

This photo was taken the year Elena's dad (standing in center) died. After he died, the family had only one brief look at his body (photo at right).

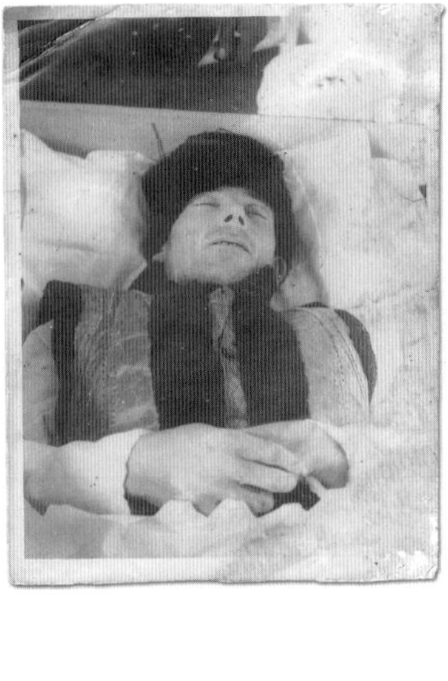

1965
(left to right)
Back: Elena (12 years old), Mama Viorica, Lidia, Rodica
Front: Nicu, George (born soon after Daddy Gheorghita died), Mari, Lucia

In 1995, Elena visited the boarding school where she spent some of her childhood years.

This spot brings back memories of sitting at the low tables in the boarding school's dining room to eat meager meals. If privileged to sit close to the food serving opening, the children would dash up to beg for more food to satisfy their hunger.

Elena remembers peeking out through this fence surrounding the boarding school, hoping for glimpses of normal life such as a child with its mother. But such peeking was quickly stopped if her educator caught her. The yard inside did not have nice, soft grass — only gravel stones.

The boarding school's courtyard shows more of its cold, impersonal atmosphere. Here Elena lined up many a time to quickly wash hands at the water trough on the right, or to go inside for classes, etc. Dorms were above, off the balconies.

Elena spent many lonely, tearful nights in her bed by the window. Scared and friendless, the 12-year-old girl struggled to cope with life at the boarding school.

Elena's brother Vasile, 14 years old and also at the boarding school, proved to be a protector to young Elena when others bullied her.

1970
At 17 years old, Elena threw her energies into sports. Here she had just won a county race, running 800 meters in 2 minutes, 24 seconds (see diploma at right). Sports filled her lonely life with purpose, took her away from the hated boarding school on weekends, and won her gifts (which she did not get at home while growing up). Later, at about 20 years old, Elena left her dreams of being the best runner in Romania and participating in World Olympics, choosing to follow Jesus instead.

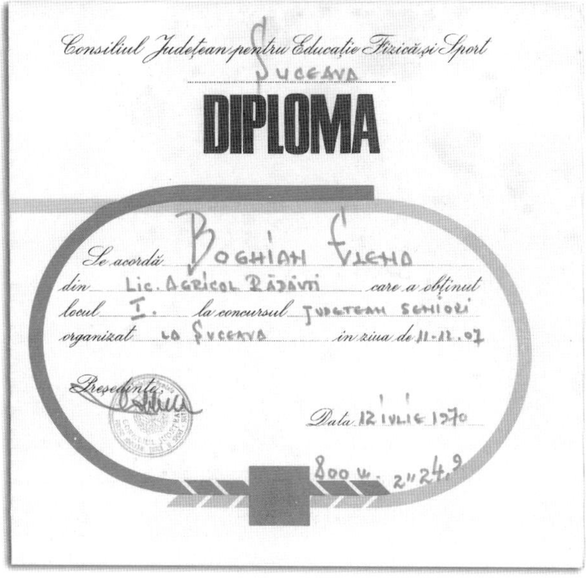

Consiliul Județean pentru Educație Fizică și Sport SUCEAVA

DIPLOMA

Se acordă BOGHIAN ELENA
din LIC. AGRICOL RĂDĂUȚI *care a obținut*
locul I. *la concursul* JUDEȚEAN SENIORI
organizat LA SUCEAVA *în ziua de* 11-12.07

Președinte,

Data 12 IULIE 1970

800 m. 2"24.9

Her baptism marked a very important day for 23-year-old Elena.
Special care was given to her dress, like for a wedding.

Costica and Alexandrina Enache were Orthodox but treated Elena like a daughter when she stayed at their house while working at the collective farm. This home in Bratulesti was a great blessing to Elena during a difficult time of her life.

The children's choir supervised by Teodor, Genovieva, Silvia, and Elena.

Dreaded prison life became a reality here for Elena. Tears were shed in the partly-underground prison cells where Elena was first held for about one month. Only a small window sometimes let in rays of light. (Photo taken during a 2002 visit.)

Elena, Daniela Branzai, Silvia, and Daniel Branzai (L to R) on August 27, 1981, the day the two girls were released from prison.

In Iasi, faithful friends welcomed Elena and Silvia the day after they were released, quieting their fears that no one would love them after they had the stigma of being in prison.

In 1982, Elena walked many miles to gather addresses of poor Romanian families who then receive aid from Christian Aid Ministries (then *Christian Aid for Romania*). She found this work very fulfilling. Here she crosses a rickety hanging bridge.

1983
Just before Elena came to America, her youth friends climbed the hill behind her beloved home village Patrauti, to be together one more time. These friends also made memories by singing Easter songs in the nearby monastery (see nun seated in center of photo at left).

A large group of friends traveled more than three hours to come say good-bye to Elena before she left for America.

Leaning from the train window, Elena waves farewell to family and friends, thinking she might never see them again on earth.

1984
Elena and Silvia in the USA, serving God in a new, free country.

2000

Elena, now married to Cornel Marza, visited the prison where she was held for three months. Her brother George is on the right (above). The purpose of this visit was to start a sewing center there, with the help of Christian Aid Ministries staff (below).

2003
Elena with six (out of eight) of her sisters and brothers.
Left to right: Nicu, Rodica, Elena, Vasile, Mari, Lidia, and Dan.

Elena's family house, before it gave place to
Christian Aid Ministries' distribution warehouse.

The hill overlooking the village of Patrauti (girl is Monica, Elena's niece).
Christian Aid Ministries' warehouse now stands where Elena's family house used to be.

sidered their request thoughtfully.

"What beautiful flowers you have!" Lili couldn't help herself. She bent to examine the colorful border of flowers along the path. "Isn't it wonderful how the Lord has given us so much beauty? You obviously have a special touch with flowers."

"Yes, my wife enjoys flowers very much." The elderly man smiled at Lili's enthusiasm. "She spends a lot of time weeding and watering the flowers every day."

"Perhaps you would consider renting a room to me for a while," Elena returned to her mission. "At least until I can find another place?" She could not help pleading. She wanted to live here in this peaceful house with this gentle couple.

"Well, that might work," Mr. Enache said. "Would you like to see the room?"

With high hopes, Elena and Lili followed the couple into the hall. Directly opposite, a doorway opened into a room with several cots. Off this room was a smaller room with a cot along one wall. A table stood in the corner, and a window opened into the side yard.

"What a beautiful room!" Elena exclaimed. She added impulsively, "Oh, I could be so happy here!"

The couple looked at each other and smiled. "Then I guess it's settled. Why don't you join us for tea and we will settle on a fair rent?"

"Please, could we pray right now?" Lili asked with a smile. "You see, Elena and I both prayed and asked God to show us the right place for her to stay. And see how God has answered our prayers! We would like to thank Him!"

The Enache couple knelt respectfully while Lili and Elena prayed. A look of awe rested on their elderly faces as they listened to these two strange women talking to God. They had never heard of anyone talk directly to God, praying as though He were someone who cared about everyday needs like this. Yes, they could tell that these women believed God was listening!

"How is your job going, Elena?" Silvia asked as the two settled down on the cot in what used to be Genovieva's room. Since Genovieva had been expelled from Romania for her "subversive" activities, it was a good place for the two girls to meet after choir practice and catch up with each others' lives.

"Actually, it's not going too bad," Elena answered. "Since I've only been there two weeks, it is too early to tell, but I thank God daily for guiding me to stay with Mr. and Mrs. Enache. They are so sweet and kind to me. After I come home from work, they often invite me to eat with them, and they seem to care about what happens to me."

"Sometime I'll come out with you and meet them," Silvia said impulsively. "I could use one of my days off to visit you!"

"I'd like that, Silvia," Elena said gratefully. "Since Genovieva left, I'm even more keenly aware of how good it is to have close Christian friends. I wonder how she likes it in America."

"Since she speaks English so well, it probably won't be too difficult. But I think the cultures are quite different." Silvia paused. "I can't really imagine life in the United States."

Both girls were silent as they thought about Genovieva's departure. It had been extremely painful to see their dear friend leave. Nevertheless, they were glad to know that Genovieva no longer faced the daily scrutiny and constant threat from the secret police.

"Anyway, what do you do at the farm?" Silvia queried, taking a sip of coffee.

"Well, at first, I studied the records of the farm. At least, what records were available. I must say, things have been going rather haphazardly there for a long time. The milk production records must have been falsified—for I can't see how they ever got as much milk from those poor cows as the records indicate! Silvia, those cows are so skinny, I almost can't bear it! How can anyone expect cows to give milk if they are not fed? The feed allotted for the cows this month ran out before the new shipment came in, and the cows were constantly bawling because they were so hungry! It was terrible! Yet we're supposed to meet our quota of milk production! I know I have a difficult job ahead of me."

"It sounds like it," Silvia sympathized. "I face similar situations at the factory. Too many orders coming from people who don't understand what's actually happening." Abruptly she covered her mouth and rolled her eyes.

The two grimaced. Genovieva had told them she suspected the police had bugged her room, for they knew information that surprised her.

"You know, Silvia," Elena continued in a whisper, "I live for the weekends when I can come here and be with the church. The job I have is definitely necessary, but I just love my work with the church. It's as though I have two lives: my life at work and my life with the church. I thank God every day for making it possible for me to have a job so close to Iasi, even if I sometimes get back late Sunday evening or early Monday morning."

Many thoughts lay unspoken between them. It had been difficult to say farewell to Genovieva, not knowing if they would ever see her again. But the noose that had been drawing tighter and tighter around their friend had not disappeared. It had merely enlarged to include them. For the two had continued with the children's choir, teaching the children about the Bible and God through song after song. Children from non-Christian families attended, eager to be a part of the trained singers. This brought great joy to the church, but their activities were not unnoticed by the secret police. Even though they could not share their fears openly with each other, both Silvia and Elena lived under the shadow of constant surveillance by the police. More than once at a program, Elena felt the cold fingers of fear clutch at her heart as she realized that someone in the audience was secretly observing the children's choir directors and other workers.

As though sensing Elena's thoughts, Silvia reached out and took her hand. "Let's pray and ask the Lord for His daily guidance. For His protection."

The two friends knelt side by side in the small room, lifting up their voiced and unvoiced petitions to the One who had ever proved Himself faithful to them.

15
Running Uphill

I WILL LIFT UP MINE EYES UNTO THE HILLS,
FROM WHENCE COMETH MY HELP.

PSALM 121:1

Elena knew immediately that something was wrong. *Ioan*, the dairy barn manager, was waiting for her when she entered the office on Monday morning.

"The milk man has not come to pick up the milk," Ioan reported in a dull and dispassionate voice. "We have three days' worth of milk here and nowhere to put it anymore. All the cans are full. We even washed out all the barrels we could find and filled them."

"What?" Elena could not believe her ears. "Where has he been?"

Ioan shrugged his shoulders. A smile hovered about his lips. Just as he figured. This young woman couldn't handle a crisis. Now perhaps she would be brought before her superiors in Iasi and fired. It took very little to topple those in authority if they did not meet the demands mandated to them. It wouldn't matter to them that she had been away from the farm over the weekend and thus was not responsible for what happened in her absence.

Elena's mind whirled. She had to think of something. She, too, knew that her job was at stake. Even worse, she could be investigated and tried in court. What if they found out about her involvement with the Bible work? Or did they already know and were just waiting for something like this to trump up charges and destroy her career?

"Lord! Please help me to know what to do!" She went into the storage room where can after can full of milk stared at her. She lifted the lid of one can and dipped her finger into the milk. The top was smooth and creamy. She bent over and sniffed.

The slightly sour smell gave her an idea.

"Ioan!" she called to her co-worker, "we can skim all the milk and sell the sour cream! We will take the jars of sour cream to the market in *Mircesti*. There is always a demand for sour cream!

"And cheese! With the milk we will make soft cheese and sell that too! This is Monday. By Wednesday, we will have it all ready for market. Call the other dairy workers. Quickly! And fetch me all the glass liter jars we have and I'll start washing them!"

Ioan scratched his head as he stared at Elena. Could this crazy scheme work? "OK," he shrugged. "If you say so. I don't know that much about making cheese, but you're the boss."

All day long and into the night, Elena supervised the work with the cheese. The milk had already set up and was ready to be heated. Batch by batch, the workers heated it and cut it into squares. Then they strained off the whey and tied the curds together in squares of muslin. Bag after bag, dripping with whey, hung from the ceiling.

The bleary-eyed milk driver who showed up on Monday evening blinked in astonishment at the activity. Elena wasted little time with him, hardly hearing his spluttering excuses for not showing up at regular time. She already knew his problem—alcohol. Daily, she had to cope with farm workers who showed up late, struggling with hangovers. But right then, she was too busy to even reprimand him.

On Tuesday, the dairy workers carefully spooned the soft cheese into containers. By evening, rows of sour cream jars and scores of cheese containers were ready for the market.

"All sold!" Ioan exclaimed in wonder on Wednesday evening. "I couldn't believe how quickly the word spread that we had sour cream and cheese to sell. In fact, I sold the last cheese by early afternoon. We should do this every week!" He pulled a wad of bills out of his pocket. "Here is the money."

Elena took the money and counted it. There was much more than what the milk would have brought the State! More than three times as much, in fact!

"Ioan! I will take the money to the director in Iasi. Then, I will tell him what we did and suggest that we do it all the time. That would provide capital to buy more feed for the cows and boost their production." Elena was excited about the prospect.

"Comrade Boghian, we commend you for your ingenuity. We will look into the matter of the milk driver." The director took the envelope of money that Elena handed to him and opened it. He carefully counted the lei.

"Sir, I have a suggestion to make," Elena spoke boldly.

The director looked up at her. "Yes?" he said curiously.

"Let us keep the milk and sell the sour cream and cheese each Wednesday at the market. We could buy more feed for the cows and pay our workers better. With the increased production, we would still be able to supply you with our milk quota." She had carefully rehearsed her speech. "It would give our division a favorable showing in the national records."

The director looked at the young woman in front of his desk. Then he looked at the money. What she had accomplished astounded him. He had never expected anything so spectacular from Elena Boghian. When he had approved her for the position in Bratulesti, he had briefly wondered how long she would last. Now she had shown surprising resourcefulness. She had brought him the full amount of the money—he did not doubt that, both because of the amount of money and the look of integrity in this girl's eyes.

He considered her request. Then, almost in regret, he shook his head. "It would never work. We cannot have anything like this happening on our State farms. My superiors would never agree. We must keep on with the system." Then his eyes grew firm and he drew himself erect. "Someday the entire world will emulate our superior system! We will show everyone how wonderful and successful our communist society is!" With a scowl, he dismissed Elena.

"I should have known better," Elena said ruefully to Silvia the next weekend. She had told her friend the whole story. "They and their system! Can't they see it doesn't work? No more than their threat against Christians. It will not work!"

In spite of the cold winter weather, the two were walking in the Botanical Gardens of Iasi. The lonely paths winding around the sloping hillside were an excellent place to rendezvous without being spied upon.

"No," Silvia said soberly, "the system will never win. The gates of hell shall never prevail against the church. We have the promise in the Bible to remind us of that.

"But I must tell you that persecution against the church is raging anew. Pastors all over Romania are being arrested and imprisoned. We have to be more cautious with our 'work' than ever before. I'm not sure how long it will be before we'll be discovered. I know I'm constantly being watched. And I have been warned at work that someone is asking questions about me. Elena, we must pray! Satan is not pleased that children are being taught songs about Jesus and His Word."

The two walked on in silence. They had come from visiting Genovieva's family who lived on the edge of the gardens. They had read the letter Genovieva was able to smuggle to her family and friends.

"Come to America," she had urged Silvia and Elena. "There is work for you—work to help our people in Romania. The Christians here are very interested in the plight of the brothers and sisters at home, and they want to help. They invite me to come to their churches and speak of the suffering our people face. As you know, there are ways you can come. I miss my friends."

"Do you think we should consider applying for visas?" Elena asked slowly. "Will they expel us as they did Genovieva?" She was not sure how she should feel. Did she want to leave? Did God want her to leave? Her thoughts and emotions were in a turmoil.

"I don't know," Silvia answered slowly. "Sometimes I think we should stay to work with the children in the church and help with the 'work.' Other times I wonder how much longer it will be before we'll have to stop—I mean, be forced to stop."

Elena felt the old, familiar fear clutch her heart. How could she endure it if she were captured? Put into prison? Separated from all her friends? The mere thought of the fear and loneliness made her shiver inside her warm coat.

"Both of us are financially better off than we have ever been before," Silvia continued. "I never dreamed I would be able to have a salary as large as this. And I can tell your salary has made it possible for you to buy clothes you could never have afforded at one time. I guess on the outside, life must look pretty good for us."

"But we cannot stop our 'work' or the work with the children," Elena said passionately. "God has answered my prayers and given me a work to do. I love doing everything I can for Him! I won't stop just because I'm afraid of what could happen to me!"

"I feel the same way," Silvia said honestly. "We need to pray and seek the Lord for direction for our future. Meanwhile, we cast ourselves into God's hand as we do His work."

Elena pushed the gate open and stumbled up the walk toward the little village house. Tears streamed from her eyes and she felt faint. It was just too much. How much longer could she stand the strain?

"Elena! Whatever is the matter?" *Alexandrina* Enache asked in concern. She was on the front porch, tending her flowers.

Elena shook her head wordlessly. She felt completely drained. "It's no use," she replied faintly. "I fight against the waste, the thievery, the drinking, the apathy of the workers. And just when I seem to have gained some headway, I'm thwarted again."

"Oh, Elena, I'm so sorry," sympathized Alexandrina. "Come in and sit down." Gently she led Elena by the arm into her kitchen. "Have a piece of bread, fresh out of the oven! We'll put a little of Costica's honey on it and, with a cup of tea, it will make you feel better." Her soothing tones calmed the distraught girl. "I know you work too hard, dear. You must not try to change everything. It will not work."

Elena dabbed at her eyes. Already she felt better. The smell of the freshly baked bread stirred up the hunger she had pushed away all day.

Alexandrina poured the hot tea into a delicate porcelain cup. "Why don't you do what everyone else does? Everyone knows that the workers all take what they need from the farm. The system doesn't work any other way. Just look the other way when that happens."

Elena took a bite of the crusty bread. It was delicious.

"What happened today?" Alexandrina asked, sitting down on a chair and leaning her elbows on the table.

"Nothing so unusual, I guess. You remember, last year I gave all the workers a bonus because we actually had made more money than what our quota was. That worked for that year, and I remember how pleased I was with the cooperation of the workers. They knew I really cared for them and they responded by doing good work and showing up on time. Some even stopped their habitual drinking and became decent workers. Now this year, all at once the authorities docked their wages for no known reason, and most of the workers are back where they were before. Two men showed up late for work today, half drunk. They argued with me and wouldn't clean out the dairy barn. They said they didn't get much pay for their work, so they weren't going to work hard either. You know how they are when they drink—loud and quarrelsome. It was just a frustrating day and nothing seemed to go right."

Elena leaned back against the wooden chair and closed her eyes. "I don't know how I could take it all if the Lord did not give me strength to try again the next day. That, and the refuge and solace I find here with you and Costica. You take such good care of me and listen to all my problems. It surely was the Lord who led me here."

Alexandrina stood and put a comforting hand on Elena's shoulder. "We love you like a daughter, Elena. We, too, are glad you came. It has made our childlessness easier to bear."

More and more, Elena felt hopelessness settling over her life. During the week she did her job conscientiously and well, but found it difficult and frustrating. She noted with concern the continual stealing and dishonesty among the farm managers. Because she refused to take anything illegally, they resented her. She constantly felt their cold hostility.

It was always with relief that she boarded the bus and rode back to Iasi for the weekend. Back to her friends and the church she loved so well. Back to the secret work of meeting foreigners and helping to secrete packages containing Bibles and songbooks. She knew that at times the packages contained Russian Bibles and were smuggled across the Romanian border into the Soviet Union. She well knew the danger that accompanied the work. Yet, she always felt satisfied that this was God's work for her.

"Elena," Silvia told her in July on one of their walks in the Botanical Garden, "I can no longer do anything with the 'work.' I'm watched so continuously that it would be a danger to everyone else if I tried to help. Ever since Genovieva has asked us to join her in America, I have prayed and fasted about it. I have made up my mind to leave Romania. Will you go with me?"

The simple, calm *I have made up my mind to leave* rang in Elena's mind. *Will you go with me?* sent another host of emotions surging through her heart. Although they had talked about it before, Silvia's announcement came as a shock.

"But how?" Elena stammered. "How can you leave?"

Silvia looked cautiously all around them before answering. In a low voice, she said, "My brother *Costel* from *Timisoara* knows how we can do it. He has agreed to help."

Elena took a deep breath. "Silvia, I will need to pray about it. I know there is little I can do here in Iasi except on the weekends. And in Bratulesti, my life is miserable and getting worse. I think it's only a matter of time until someone will try to get me fired from my job. They know I won't cheat, and they are afraid I will inform on them. But, try to escape Romania?" She paused. "I have to pray about it."

"I won't pressure you, Elena. But from what Costel tells me, we can escape into Yugoslavia and then ask for political asylum as refugees. From there, we can apply to go to America." Silvia's voice was full of hope.

America! How would it be to live where believers could worship God as they pleased? How would it be to have a job where no one would expect you to overlook fraud and cheating? Could she learn the language? Could she adjust to the culture?

And what if they were caught trying to escape? What if they used dogs to track them down? If captured, could she take the beatings and imprisonment that other believers constantly endured? Elena felt the twin hands of fear and horror clutch at her throat.

"Please, Silvia, pray for me," she choked. "I want only to do the will of God."

"I will be praying," Silva lovingly assured her friend. "In fact, I have been praying for you as well as for me. I don't want to try this by myself, and I would love to have you accompany me. But it must be your decision."

The two girls walked among the beautiful flowers, but they did not see the lovely scenery around them. Their minds were far away on things they could not see.

The whole setting seemed unreal. Elena and Silvia had been waiting with eighteen other people for two days now, and still word had not come. Elena felt exhausted both emotionally and physically. She and Silvia had spent weeks in careful preparation for this moment.

Elena had sold most of her possessions and even borrowed money from her friends to come up with the amount that fleeing Romania would cost her. Fifty thousand lei was a lot of money to collect over just a period of weeks—nearly two years' salary. But she had done it.

The emotional part had been much harder. She and Silvia had agreed to tell only a few people what they were planning to do—both for their own sakes and for the sakes of their families. If they should succeed, their families could truthfully say they had not known anything about it. Elena had told only her sister Lidia during a recent visit to her home.

"Sister, I'm going with Silvia Tarniceriu to try to escape the country. I'm telling only you and your husband. If no one hears from me, you will know we have managed to escape." She wrung her hands together on her lap. Her voice was barely a whisper, even in her sister's house.

The two sisters embraced. "God go with you," Lidia breathed, tightening her arms around Elena. "If we never meet again here on earth, we will meet in heaven!"

The only thing Elena had told Alexandrina and Costica was that she was leaving for a vacation. She did not specify a return date.

Both girls had kept an option open to return to their jobs. They knew the venture they were getting ready to embark on was risky and considered extremely chancy. If the escape did not succeed, they wanted to be able to return to their work without creating an upheaval.

So here they were in Timisoara, still waiting. Costel Tarniceriu's little house was filled with people. No one dared venture outside, lest the neighbors see the presence of strangers. The rooms were crowded and stuffy, the air hot and stifling.

"Is he coming tonight for sure?" a man with piercing eyes asked Silvia's brother.

All attention turned toward Costel. He looked at the collection of people and said, "He has promised me he will come at ten o'clock."

"Did you give him the money?" asked a lady with short, cropped hair.

"Yes. He demanded the money before he went to get the truck." Costel tried to speak reassuringly.

An uneasy silence settled over the group.

Hope pushed away the weariness in Elena's heart. In spite of her weariness and apprehension, she felt her pulse quicken at the mere thought of getting out of Romania and going to America. Genovieva would be so happy to see them! And all the sponsors and friends from *Christian Aid for Romania!* Over and over, Genovieva had assured her Romanian friends that she was well taken care of and welcomed by her friends in Ohio.

A cough from the lady beside her jerked Elena back to the present. She looked around the room. *Where did all these people come from?* she wondered. *Why did they want to leave the country? Were any of them criminals?*

They were all strangers to her except Silvia.

Her thoughts went to the little she knew of their escape plans. They would cross the border in a truck, Silvia had told her. A man Costel knew had told him of a driver who frequently trucked cargo between Romania and Yugoslavia. Each time, an official sealed the doors on the truck before he crossed the border. It was not to be opened until the cargo had reached its destination. So often did the truck cross the border that the guards did not bother to open the truck anymore, they just checked the seal.

An official had been bribed to seal them inside the truck. No one was to move around whenever the truck stopped. There must be absolutely no noise. No coughs. No sneezes. Nothing. Their safety depended upon their strict adherence to the rules.

Elena shivered in spite of the stuffy room. Silvia opened her eyes and squeezed Elena's arm. She must have felt her shiver.

Pray! That was what Silvia was doing! Elena closed her own eyes and began to pray.

The wait seemed to go on forever. The clock on the wall ticked away the minutes and then the hours. Still there was no news of the driver's arrival.

At ten o'clock, a stir of anticipation swept through the waiting group. Anytime now, they should be going. After the long wait, Elena felt ready for some action, yet a part of her dreaded the danger it would bring.

Costel slipped silently out of the house. He was gone for fifteen minutes. When he came back into the dimly lit room, everyone looked expectantly at him. He silently shook his head.

One of the men muttered under his breath. People stirred restlessly. Several got up and stretched their tired backs.

But there was absolutely nothing else to do but wait. Time dragged on, but still no one came to tell them the truck had arrived.

A tall man was pacing the room, threading his way between those seated on chairs. He ran his hands through his hair. A scowl pulled his eyebrows into a sharp V above his nose.

Once more, Costel left. This time he was gone for more than thirty minutes. When he came back, his face was stricken. His chest rose and fell spasmodically. He dumbly shook his head again to the questions in their eyes.

Elena felt all hope fade away. Something must have happened. They were not going. She was sure of it.

A babble of voices broke out in the room. Elena covered her ears. This was terrible! The people were getting very angry!

"That rascal has taken our money and left without us," the tall man rasped out in an ugly voice. Enraged, he glared at Costel. "Or maybe you are in cahoots with him and took part of the money yourself!"

Their emotions had been stretched to the breaking point after all the careful planning and suspense. Now they found bitter words to vent their fears and darkest forebodings. And Costel bore the brunt of it.

"Stop!" Silvia suddenly cried loudly. "Costel has nothing to do with this. He has endangered his life by letting us stay in his house, and he was not even planning to escape. He just wanted to help us. So stop blaming him. Something may have happened to the driver. He may have been found out. It was a risk for us to try to leave, but it is a risk we all understood and took. It failed, so don't blame anyone."

"It failed all right," the tall man said bitterly. "And I will see to it that whoever was responsible for that failure will be exposed." He strode to the door and left.

The train ride back to Iasi was agonizing for Elena. She had tried to prepare herself for the possibility of failure before they left, yet she had not been able to really convince herself that their plan would fail. Now, she was trying to readjust.

"I sold almost everything I had to pay for the escape," Elena told Silvia. "Now I need to start all over again. I even gave away or sold most of my clothes!"

"I did the same," Silvia said soberly. "Even though I did not tell people I was leaving, I think some of them thought about it when I gave away my few possessions. How can I go back into such a life again? I know I will be shadowed and watched all the time!" Her voice was bleak and colorless.

Elena stared out the window unseeingly. Back to Bratulesti. Back to her work on the farm. Back to the fear of discovery and arrest.

Oh, God, why? Her question rose soundlessly from her weary heart. Why had God allowed this to happen to them? Was this His way of saying they shouldn't escape? They had prayed and felt sure God had wanted them to do this. But now, the door had slammed shut in their faces. Firmly. *"Why?"*

16

Across the Border!

IF IT HAD NOT BEEN THE LORD WHO WAS ON OUR SIDE, WHEN MEN ROSE UP AGAINST US: THEN THEY HAD SWALLOWED US UP QUICK, WHEN THEIR WRATH WAS KINDLED AGAINST US: THEN THE WATERS HAD OVERWHELMED US, THE STREAM HAD GONE OVER OUR SOUL.

PSALM 124:2-4

The linden trees stretched their bare branches overhead as Elena hesitantly started up the stairs toward the police headquarters. Fear made it a great effort to move her feet toward the front door, yet a greater fear propelled her forward.

You must report to our office on Sarariei Street on Monday, October 27, 1980, the official letter had read. Elena had quailed when she read the summons.

"They know about our attempted escape!" had been her gasping response. She could already imagine the yawning prison doors, gaping wide for her! Nothing terrified her more than the thought of prison. Deeply embedded in her memory were Bunica's stories of the terrors of incarceration. The lack of food, the unsanitary conditions, the foul language of the other inmates—over and over Elena and her siblings had recoiled in horror from their grandparents' experiences.

Trembling, Elena entered the cold, gray building.

"Follow me," the secretary barked as soon as Elena stepped inside. Their footsteps reverberated as they walked down the long, empty corridor. The secretary knocked on a steel door.

"Elena Boghian is here," she announced.

Inside the small, grim office, Elena found herself facing a man in military uniform. "Sit down," he said flatly.

Elena perched on the edge of the hard, wooden chair facing his desk. The secretary left, closing the door firmly behind her. Elena tried to slow her rapid breathing.

"Elena Boghian," the officer intoned, his voice cold and measured. He shuffled through the sheaf of papers in front of him. Then he leaned back in his chair and directed his gaze squarely at Elena. She tried not to flinch at the coldness in his eyes.

"In August, you were absent from your job for five days, two of which were vacation days you requested. Where did you go?"

"I—I went on vacation with a friend," Elena was surprised that she could speak.

"Where?" The voice was a little louder this time.

Elena gathered up courage. "I have the freedom to take my vacation wherever I choose." She tried to make her voice sound strong and sure.

"We know where you were. We know what you did." Now the officer's voice was hard and accusing. He looked at Elena contemptuously, then read from his report.

" 'The following people made an illegal attempt to cross the Romanian-Yugoslavian border from the city of Timisoara, on August 12, 1980. Each one paid a price of 50,000 lei for this unlawful endeavor.' Your name, Elena Boghian, is listed here."

There was a long moment of silence. Elena felt her heart pound unmercifully. She could not speak.

"So, young lady, you see we know all about your illegal activities. We know each one of you who were waiting for that truck to come and take you across the border in the sealed trailer. We know everyone who was involved." He lowered his voice to a menacing snarl. "You simple idiots, thinking you could escape! You will suffer for this!"

He stood abruptly. The legs from his chair scraped across the tile floor. Elena jumped nervously.

"Go!" He jerked his head toward the door. "You are dismissed, but we will see you again!"

Elena fled from the room and hurried down the corridor, past the watchful eyes of the secretary in the lobby. She tugged at the heavy front door and ran down the steps onto the sidewalk.

She walked as fast as she could, away from the cold stone building towering behind her. "Lord Jesus! Oh, I need You! Whatever is going to happen to me? To us?" she added, as she thought of Silvia. Then she remembered

Silvia's brother Costel. He had been under such a strain from the failed escape plan that he had lost his voice for several weeks afterwards.

Had the tall man carried out his threat? How did the police know everything about their plans? How did they know who had been involved? What about the driver of the truck? Had he been caught? Is that why he had not shown up? Was he the one who betrayed them?

Elena's thoughts tumbled riotously. Ever since her return from Timisoara, she had been nervous and jumpy. She had been able to go back to Alexandrina and Costica's house without answering many questions, and the people at the farm thought she had merely gone for a vacation. But to Elena, it seemed as though everyone surely knew about the incident. She had expected repercussions much earlier than this. But now that it had happened, she was shaken to the very core of her being.

"Lord, we seek Your will in this. You know how scared we are. You know the terrible emotions we went through the first time we tried to leave. We don't want to try again unless this is Your will." Elena's tears choked off her words. She could not pray anymore.

"Yes, Lord," Silvia continued the prayer. "We are two of Your children who want Your direction. Need Your direction, Lord. If we are not to go ahead with the plans, please firmly close the doors. You know our predicament. You know we are denied a normal life, and that our lives may even be in danger. Now money has come for another escape attempt. We thank You for it, for we don't know how it came. Thank-you for our missionary friends who have been able to visit and encourage us and give us clothes and food. Lord, You are good. Now, please direct us."

The two friends were spending the entire Saturday in prayer and fasting. There was very little talk between them. They spent time reading from the Bible, praying together, and praying alone, desperately asking God for direction.

The dark winter night had already blacked out all daylight when they went to bed in Silvia's apartment. Elena tried to sleep, but in spite of her confidence and trust in God, dark images floated through her consciousness. Questions hounded her mind.

What if they should try and fail again? Oh, but they must try to get out! Silvia, too, had been called to the police station and coldly told they knew all about her attempt to escape. She, too, had been told she would be called again.

Did the police know about their involvement in Bible smuggling? Or would they uncover this as they continued probing into their activities? How much did they already know? The unknown questions nipped and gnawed at her.

What if they did not try to escape? Elena shuddered. That thought, too, was unbearable. They would be shadowed, threatened, and, yes, surely imprisoned for attempting to cross the border illegally.

Prison!

"Lord, please help us get out of this mess! We are trapped!" Tears squeezed out of her closed eyes.

"Elena!" Silvia called softly. "Are you all right?"

"No, Silvia," Elena sobbed. "I am so afraid!"

Silvia came over and knelt beside Elena. She began to pray. "Lord, You see our need. I pray that You would give us Your Spirit to comfort and protect us. I pray for myself, and I pray for Elena. Send Your peace and Your love deep into our hearts. Lord, we know whatever You allow to come into our lives will be for our good. We put ourselves into Your care. We rejoice that our names are written in the Book of Life. Thank-you, Lord."

Sleep finally came for Elena. The Lord sent His sweet rest into her troubled soul.

The icy night wind blew over the low hills in southwestern Romania. Earlier, an unexpected thaw had swollen the river and swamps with melted snow and ice. Now the weather had turned colder again and the water standing in the swamps had frozen into thin layers of ice. The river, however, was still high and flowing swiftly.

Clouds scudded across the sky, completely hiding the moon and stars. In the nearby village, eight people silently filed out of a house and stole toward the river.

They tried to muffle the sound of their boots and shoes as they quickly, yet stealthily, walked over the frozen snow. Their crisp footsteps, sounding like breaking glass, thankfully were muted by the whining of the wind.

Elena held tightly onto Silvia's arm. Her other hand clutched a bag with a few clothes and her personal possessions. The two were in the middle of the group; the leader's wife and daughter walked just ahead of them, with the leader and his young son in the lead. The guide's son-in-law and a man who said he was from Bucuresti brought up the rear.

Eight people. Not as many as before, but still too many for Elena—way too many. After the first fiasco, she thought it would have been safer if there would only have been a few.

"Absolutely safe" was how this venture had been described. That, too, had bothered her. How could anyone be sure it was absolutely safe? It was not good to put too much confidence in anything.

Yet as they trod carefully, following their guide toward the river, Elena found herself thinking of the alternative. She was convinced that staying in Romania meant certain prison. She and Silvia had felt it much better to try to leave again rather than face incarceration.

So here they were again, far away from home, once more going through an experience that wreaked havoc with her nerves.

The original plan had been to walk across the frozen river, but the unexpected thaw had made it impossible. They had spent more time in waiting as the guide located a boat, smuggled it to a hiding place along the river, and arranged other details in order to make the escape successful.

If the escape failed this time, there would be no return. There was not enough time for the girls to return to their jobs and report for work after their allotted days off. This was final.

Elena was brought up short when she almost bumped into the two women ahead of them. They were at the river! The leader and his son were pulling a boat from a clump of alders.

"We will row across and keep one end of this rope with us." The leader gave instructions in a hoarse whisper. He handed the rope to the men. "Then you will pull the boat back with this end of the rope. Two of you will get in and we will pull you across. We'll repeat this until we're all on the other side." The plan sounded simple.

The son and son-in-law got in. They took the paddles and bravely pushed away from shore.

The swollen current caught the boat and pushed it broadside downstream. The son-in-law panicked and paddled madly.

From the shore, the watching group of people could hardly see anything in the dark. But they winced as a yell reached them from the distressed young man. Would anyone hear them?

Then there was a commotion in the water. The boat had capsized!

"Oh, Lord, have mercy," the old woman moaned. "*Petru* can't swim!" The leader went out to rescue the two young men.

Though it was only a matter of moments, time seemed to stand still before the group saw the three men coming back with the half-submerged boat.

Drenched completely, they were shivering in their wet clothes. Thankfully, their bags with extra clothes had not been in the boat, and they hurriedly changed. They emptied the freezing water out of the boat. This time, the leader got in by himself and rowed off into the night.

Elena closed her eyes and prayed desperately. She shivered in the icy wind, trembling not only from the cold but from the fear gnawing away at her reason. Suddenly the boat was back, empty, and she and Silvia were told to get in.

As they got in, the flimsy craft sank lower into the water, and Elena gave a soft moan. Silvia put her arm around Elena's shoulders. The man across the river pulled mightily on the rope. They clutched their bags as the boat began to move.

The dark waters surged against the side of the boat. They could feel the powerful current trying to push them downstream.

With trembling voices, the girls prayed. In her fear, Elena could say nothing but "Please, Lord! Please, Lord!"

The boat carried them through the dark night, across the icy waters, away from Romania. Away, away. Away from a life of shadow, a life of uncertainty, a life of restriction.

"Step right here," the leader's welcome voice came suddenly from the other shore. He helped them out. It was wonderful to feel solid ground under their feet.

The tiny craft made three more trips. The next arrivals were the mother and daughter. Then the man from Bucuresti and the son-in-law. Finally came the teen-aged son.

They pulled the boat into the tall marsh grasses and left it. The leader struck out through the swamp, the little band following closely in single file.

How could he possibly know the way? Elena felt her confidence wane as they stumbled over the uneven terrain. Time and again, they broke through the thin ice and got their feet soaking wet. To her, it seemed as though they were going in circles. Why was the noise of the river sometimes to her right and at other times to her left? The rough edges of the reeds brushed unexpectedly against her face and stung her cold cheeks.

"Stop! I lost my shoe!" The man from Bucuresti was behind them again. They could hear him groping frantically in the darkness.

Elena heard Silvia sigh behind her. "Maybe I could carry him," she muttered.

Stifling a wild impulse to laugh, Elena clapped her hand to her mouth. She could imagine Silvia picking up the slender man like a sack of potatoes and striding through the marsh with him. In fact, she wouldn't put it past her plucky friend.

Whether he found his shoe or not, Elena wasn't sure. They went on. Weariness made every step an effort. But on and on they tramped. Away from Romania. Toward Yugoslavia? Toward freedom?

They came to a sudden halt. The leader had stopped.

They were at the border and the dreaded trip wires. The wires that some people said were connected to land mines and would blow up anyone foolish enough to try to cross. The wires that others said would ring an alarm and bring soldiers on the run with their guns and dogs to hunt out the fugitives.

"Line up," the leader hissed. The eight made a line, standing shoulder to shoulder. "One, two, *step!* One, two, *step!*"

It was good they had rehearsed this part before they had ever started this venture. They obeyed their leader implicitly. At every "*step!*" they all moved in unison, lifting their feet to clear the hidden wires.

At last they were across! Relief flooding his voice, the leader told them to get back into a column. He led them up a small hill, away from the wide section of land that had been stripped of trees and tall grasses.

They were out of Romania! Elena felt a sensation she had never felt before. In spite of her physical exhaustion and her mental weariness in rehearsing what might happen if they were caught, she felt a lift in her spirit. They were free!

Not until now did she realize how heavy the cloud had been that hovered over her. Forgetting her weariness, she found herself praising God.

Now they were approaching a village. It was just a small cluster of houses, but it was a cluster of Yugoslavian houses! It looked very similar to a Romanian village, yet somehow, strangely different! It was in another country. Another communist country, true, but a country that allowed fugitives from Romania to move on into western Europe. From there they could fly to freedom in America! America, where Genovieva and her friends were waiting for them!

The leader tapped gently on the window of a cottage close to the road. Within minutes the door opened. As the warm air rushed out to greet them,

Elena suddenly felt all her strength flow from her. She slumped against Silvia and allowed her strong arms to steer her inside to a seat beside the mud-brick stove.

The babble of voices swirled around her, drifting through her foggy consciousness in bits and pieces. "They will help you . . ." ". . . no . . . must go on . . ." ". . . everybody does it that way . . ." But her weary brain could comprehend none of it. They were out of Romania, they had safely escaped, and they were free! That realization, and her complete fatigue, pushed away everything else.

"Elena!" Silvia's face was only inches away from hers, her voice urgent. "Elena! We have to get out of here! They are sending someone to let the police know we are here. Even though they tell us it is safe, I—I don't trust it!" Concern and fear tinged Silvia's voice.

Elena tried to rouse herself, but the blessed warmth in the cottage, with the heady relief of having successfully escaped, flooded her adrenalin-depleted body in welcoming waves. She had no more strength. She could not move. Could not think. Even Silvia's fears could not shake her now.

She closed her eyes again. All her tired brain could do was rest. All her tired body could do was rest. She sagged in her chair.

The next thing she knew, she woke to the sound of loud voices and a room filled with people. Someone gave her a cup of hot, sweet tea. The scalding liquid helped her focus her thoughts and eyes.

Police! Though she could tell by the uniforms that they were Yugoslavian police, Elena shrank from them.

The police spoke to their hosts and then, in broken Romanian, spoke assuringly to the refugees. No, they would not make them return to Romania. Yes, they needed to take them all to the station where they would ask them questions about who they were and where they were going. This was all a part of normal procedures. Yes, they realized that life in Romania was very difficult and many were willing to leave their careers behind and start all over in the West. They were sympathetic, they said. There was no reason to worry; all this was just procedure.

"Please give me your information. What is your name?" The man was almost friendly and spoke Romanian well.

Alone in the room with the police officer, Elena could not make herself relax. One by one, the members of their group were being ushered into this room to give vital information about themselves.

Elena answered each question as briefly as possible. The officer wrote everything down.

"What is the name of the person who helped you with your plans?"

"I don't know," Elena answered honestly. Why did he ask that? What did that have to do with giving her asylum?

"To whom did you give the money for bringing you here?"

Elena hesitated. "My friends took care of all that."

"Your friends? They would be the ones who helped Silvia Tarniceriu?" He looked at his papers.

Elena nodded. There should be no harm in agreeing. He already knew that.

"Do not be scared of us. We are trying to help you." The officer smiled at Elena. She tried to smile back, but could not force her lips to move.

"We will keep you for twenty days in order to clear your documents. Then you will be free to go to Belgrade and apply for help from any contacts you may have." He was actually trying to comfort her.

Again, Elena tried to relax. She settled against the back of the chair. But something bothered her. "Why do we need to stay here for twenty days?"

"Our government has decided on this policy because they feel there must be some form of detention for those who cross our border illegally." But then he hastily added, "It is merely a formality. That's all."

He stood and smiled, indicating the interview was over.

Elena gladly joined the waiting group. A guard stood at the door leading outside.

That evening, after the interviews were over, they were shown their rooms. The women were ushered into one room, the men into another. Three other women were already inside when Silvia, Elena, and the two women who had escaped with them came in. They all looked at each other curiously.

The twenty days stretched on. In spite of the good food they were served each day, Elena could hardly eat anything except bread. Soup, meat, potatoes, and fresh bread every day was much more than they had expected. In fact, they had not expected any of this.

They did not talk of their escape to each other. They spent their enforced stay mostly in silence, praying and sitting quietly on the beds. Elena sensed the uneasiness in her energetic friend as Silvia paced to and fro in the room.

At times they were called one by one out of the room for questioning. Some of the officers were blunt and to the point, others smiling and seemingly sympathetic.

For Elena, the questioning never got very far. Over and over she stated her name, her birthdate, and the place where she had worked. Time and again, she was asked question after question to which she could only answer, "I don't know."

They wanted to know who had introduced to her the idea of leaving, to which she replied that she had decided of herself to leave. They asked about her life as a child, her life at the Agronomical Institute, and her job on the farm. She answered as briefly as possible, trying never to give information about anyone else.

The strain began telling on all of them. They kept track of the days, and though each day dragged on excruciatingly, their twenty days were finally over!

This was the day they could leave their prison! For in spite of the good food, the warm place to stay, and the fairly comfortable beds, they were still in prison. Prison was the term used when you were kept somewhere against your will.

At times horror rose inside Elena as she remembered the stories her grandparents had told about prison life, and it was all Elena could do to keep from screaming in fear. She was learning to turn to God in her distress when those feelings came. Time and again, she committed herself into the loving care of her Saviour.

"OK, into the van!" The command was brisk, without emotion.

All eight of them had been brought out of their rooms and were now herded into the back of an enclosed van. The doors were closed and locked, and the vehicle moved forward.

The only light that illuminated the inside came through a vent in the roof. They braced themselves as the van picked up speed.

"They said we would be taken to Belgrade and released," the man from Bucuresti said nervously.

"Why did they ask us all those questions?" the teen-aged son asked in a strained voice.

No one answered. The leader, looking aged in the dim light, was preoccupied with watching the vent above him. A drawn look tightened his forehead into furrows.

Suddenly, he slumped forward. "We are headed back to Romania."

A stunned silence greeted his news. Elena closed her eyes as despair washed over her.

A moan of anguish rose from the lady sitting next to her husband. "How can you be sure?"

"I know which way we have turned every time since we started off. We are now going east." There was no hesitation in his voice. He was convinced.

They did not have to wonder long. Less than thirty minutes later, the van slowed, stopped, and after an exchange of voices outside, drove forward again, quite slowly.

"Why, God?" Elena felt her cheeks wet with tears. "Oh, Lord, what will happen to us? Did we not ask You not to provide the money for our escape unless You wanted us to leave? Did we not pray for You to close the doors if we should not do this? I feel betrayed! No! No! I cannot endure this! I know prison will be much worse than what we just went through! Oh, Lord, why did you not take us home with You when we were crossing the river? To have drowned would be better than this!"

The van stopped again. The scene that greeted their eyes when the doors opened made them all gasp in horror.

They were in an army camp! A Romanian army camp! Soldiers and officials swarmed the courtyard, all dressed in the familiar uniforms.

"Out! Out! Everyone out! This is not a tourist bus!" The words screamed at them were in their native language. Rough arms shoved the prisoners against each other as they scrambled out of the van.

This was a nightmare come true! Elena could not believe this was happening to her. She felt faint and sick to her stomach.

Again she found herself crying, "Please, Lord! Please, Lord! Oh, please, Lord!"

17
Prison

BUT WHEN THEY DELIVER YOU UP, TAKE NO THOUGHT HOW OR WHAT YE SHALL SPEAK: FOR IT SHALL BE GIVEN YOU IN THAT SAME HOUR WHAT YE SHALL SPEAK.

MATTHEW 10:19

"So! Here are the brave ones who know how to sneak out of the country. Stupid people! You thought you could get away with something like this. Hah! There are people all the time who think they can escape. Well, you will join them, rotting in prison!" The short, heavy-set officer waddled importantly up to the group of eight huddled together inside the locked compound. The van that had transported them was gone, headed back into Yugoslavia.

"Which one of you is Silvia Tarniceriu?" His voice sounded more like a dog snarling over his prey than like a normal human voice.

"I am," Silvia replied calmly, facing the officer.

"Get in here! Officer Radu, guard the rest. No moving, all of you!" He yelled his commands in all directions. Silvia followed him into an office.

Elena trembled all over. She still felt faint. She tried taking long, slow breaths as she stood in the cold February air.

What were they going to do with her? With all of them? They obviously knew Silvia. They must know her too. Did they know all about the rest of the group too? Who had told them? What would they do with them now? Take them to prison, like the officer had said?

She groaned within her spirit. Prison. The very place she had dreaded all her life. The place where her nightmares were born. How could she endure it? For how long?

"Dear Lord, I don't know what is going on. I don't know where You are in this experience, but please, God, can You send someone to show me that

You still care for me? I'm sorry that I even tried to escape if I shouldn't have done it. I don't know. I'm so confused. We thought we were doing what You wanted us to do. I just don't know." Elena knew her prayer made no sense, not even to herself. She just prayed. She had to!

Silvia came back outside. Elena searched her face for any signs of shock or pain. Had they beaten her?

As soon as her friend had rejoined the group, the leader was called inside. Silvia sidled up to Elena.

"That man in there," Silvia hissed in a low whisper, looking straight ahead. "He knew me! I went to school with him!"

Elena comprehended the words with difficulty. She kept herself from staring at Silvia. How was this possible?

"Elena, God is with us! He did not beat me! It is amazing! I told him about you. Praise God, Elena, we are not alone!"

Somehow, merely knowing they were not without friends, even here, made it easier for Elena to endure this suffering. Well, maybe the officer was not exactly a friend, but at least he knew Silvia! How remarkable!

Elena remembered her prayer. "Thank-you, God, for showing us that You have not forgotten us! All the way down here on the other side of the country from Iasi, You have sent this schoolmate of Silvia's! Thank-you, Lord!"

"So, you are Silvia's friend," the man behind the desk said in wonderment when Elena's turn came. "I couldn't believe my eyes when I read the name on Silvia's record. I said to myself, 'I know that name!' Now here you are, trying to escape with that girl." He shook his head. "I have been ordered to have you two beaten." Elena paled, but he continued. "I will try to spare you, but don't expect miracles. Listen. If you are alone with one of my officers here, cry and scream as if he were beating you even if he doesn't harm you. That way everyone else will get the impression he is beating you, and no one will know we didn't follow orders."

Throughout this rapid dialogue, Elena listened keenly. Her throat had become dry when he started speaking about beatings. She licked her parched lips.

"You are dismissed. I don't need to know any more about you than I already know. I just hope, somehow, that you will be all right. You won't be kept here long, so I have no way of knowing." He stood. "Well, that is all I can do. Go."

"Face the wall! Do not move! Do not speak!"

All eight were lined up in a cold room, facing a concrete wall. It was night. Everyone was exhausted after another journey in a closed van that lasted for several hours. But an entirely new set of officers and interrogators were waiting for them.

"You! Come!" Elena did not turn her head, but she heard the command and a rustle from the end of the line. One of the men must have left.

There was a shuffling of footsteps, and again the word, "Come!"

Elena understood. Each of them was being taken for interrogation. Silvia was taken before Elena felt the officer's hand on her own arm. "Come!" She was escorted into yet another drab room.

"What is your name?" the interrogator asked. His voice was almost friendly.

"Elena Boghian."

"Where were you born?"

"Patrauti, Suceava.

"When is your birthday?"

"April 23, 1953."

"Where do you live?"

Elena hesitated. Where did she live? She had no home. The collective farm seemed too far away and unreal to think of as home. Her friends in Iasi may as well have lived on the moon, so far away did she feel from them. For some reason, her mother's house in Patrauti seemed closest to home at the time.

"Where do you work?" The man's voice jerked her back to reality.

"Bratulesti."

He wrinkled up his nose. That village was too small for him to know about. He studied some papers and then said, "You may go."

She had not been beaten! Once more the Lord had been with her! A tiny surge of hope bloomed in Elena's heart. "Thank-you, Lord!"

Moving slowly in the darkness of the cell, Elena groped through her bag until her fingers touched the pouch where she had hidden her money. Fearful lest they meet up with some unforseen emergency, Elena had smuggled 500 lei across the river the night they had escaped. She had carefully guarded her bag and had managed so far not to let it out of her sight. Now, she was sure their things would be searched and any money confiscated.

Carefully, she withdrew the roll of money. It rustled slightly. She stopped moving and listened. She could hear the gentle breathing of Silvia and the other two ladies. Yes, they must be sleeping. There was nothing she would hide from Silvia, but the other two . . . the older woman, the leader's wife, seemed to be a devout Christian, but Elena was not too sure she trusted the daughter. It was better not to take any risks.

Opening the metal tube of shampoo she had brought along, she emptied the contents under the wooden bench. As the faint fragrance reached her nose, she regretted her decision only slightly. She did not know how long it might be before she would have shampoo again, but just now the money was more important.

Rolling the money into a tight cylinder, she wrapped it in a piece of plastic. Then she carefully inserted the wrapped money into the shampoo tube. Her fingers found the cap in the darkness, and she screwed it tightly onto the top.

Should she put the tube back into her bag? No, she would put it in her boot. It might be safer there, for probably her bag would be the first thing they would search and take from her. She could not imagine they would allow her to keep her bag in prison.

Prison! With a start, Elena realized what she was getting ready for. Until now, she had been trying to keep from thinking about the inevitable. Surely she was headed for prison—the place she had feared since her childhood! With a sinking heart, she faced the reality: even though they had not been sentenced yet, they would be sent to prison. Or worse! Of that she did not dare to think about just now.

Once more, Elena turned to God in prayer. She had no words in her desperate need, just deep groanings of her heart that cried out to Christ for help.

"Who met you at the train?" the spokesman asked sternly. Two other officers flanked the one at the desk. They were asking about the train station in Resita, where they had met their first contacts enroute to Yugoslavia.

"I—I was with Silvia," Elena answered.

"Don't you have a mind of your own? You always say, 'I was with Silvia.' Can you not speak for yourself?"

Elena did not reply. Weariness had taken control of her body, her emotions, and even her spirit. Nevertheless she was determined to say nothing that would incriminate anyone else, so to every question she had steadfastly answered the same thing: "I was with Silvia."

"Take her back," the spokesman told the guard curtly. "She is of no use. We'll get something out of one of the others."

All day long they had been taken in and out of the office for interrogations. Each time, they were alone. Different officers tried their ploys to gain information. Sometimes questions were fired at them in rapid succession. Other times they tried sly, subtle methods of prying out information.

There was no rest from the surveillance. When they were not being questioned, they had to stand at attention, facing a wall. They were not allowed to move. They were not allowed to talk to each other. Faint from hunger, weak from lack of sleep, and fatigued—beyond reason at times—Elena felt alone in her stupor. Nothing seemed real.

But a cry from the courtyard jerked her back to her surroundings. It was the horrible sound of someone being beaten!

"This is what happens to people who try to escape!" shouted one of their captors. "Maybe this will help you remember who helped you with your escape!" Then followed the awful moans and groans from the man who had led their escape across the river.

No! No! Elena could not bear it! But the nightmare continued. In horror, she heard the clubs striking against the man's body. His cries of pain were terrible to hear.

Then they heard the younger voices of the man from Bucuresti, the son-in-law, and even the teen-aged boy! The noise of the shouting, cursing soldiers, and the screams and protests from the beaten men almost drove Elena mad.

Would the women be next? How could she endure it? She thought she was going out of her mind just from hearing the ordeal the men were going through. What would she do if she and Silvia and the other women were beaten? Her toes curled inside her boots as she imagined the vicious clubs assaulting her body.

When the noise outside died down, her body grew rigid with fear. Without turning her head, her ears strained toward the door. Would they come for the women next? Chills of fear raced up and down her spine.

For the rest of that day, Elena was on edge, constantly expecting to be taken outside and beaten. Her head throbbed from the tension. Prickles of pain crept into her legs from standing so long. The loud voices, the shouts, the repeated interrogations—all were a part of her worst imaginable nightmare.

The following days jumbled into one long, unending horror. They were herded from room to room and rudely asked the same questions over and over. Nights were probably the worst. Elena could not sleep—whenever she did doze off, she would find herself jerking awake from some horrible dream.

About the third day, she found herself sitting at a table, a guard looming over her.

"Write!" he barked. "You must declare all your activities. Write down everything you did and sign your name." The guard walked away from the table and stood by the door.

Elena was too weary to think. She did not know what to write. When she tried to focus on the paper, the white sheet glared in front of her eyes. It was too bright in the little room. She could not concentrate.

"Write!" The guard was back at her side, screaming at her. "Write your report! You are going to be tried in court, and you must have a written report! Take that pen and write!"

The screaming noise seemed to come from a great distance, drifting down a long tunnel to her ear. Yes, it was directed toward her—that much she could determine in her near-stupor.

The guard paced back to the door again. Elena's head began to nod toward the table. A profound weariness shrouded her consciousness.

"Get up! Get out of here!" From the great distance again, Elena heard the shouts. Were they for her? She thought she was supposed to write.

Her chair was jerked back. She almost slid off the hard seat and onto the floor. Throwing out her hands, she caught hold of the edge of the table.

"Get out! If you can't do anything, go back to the cell." Stumbling along behind the guard, she left the room.

Trial. Courtroom. Had the guard said something about a trial? Would they be tried? The numbness overtaking her made it hard to think.

"Please, Lord! Oh, God, have mercy!" Silvia moaned in a low breath. Which day it was by now, Elena was not sure, but they had been escorted down the street to the court house. There, in the corridor, Silvia had recognized the man who met them at the train station when they had arrived in Resita. Elena glanced in the direction of Silvia's gaze. There was *Ginu!* Elena moaned.

Not Ginu! Husband of Mama *Leone*, the woman who had been a contact for their escape plans! Elena's heart went out to him. He had been so kind and solicitous when they arrived. He had prayed with Elena and Silvia and given them many kind and encouraging words. Now he was on trial too—because he had helped them!

Ginu looked down the hall and saw them. His eyes filled with tears of pity. He slowly closed his eyes and then tried to smile at them.

Oh, the suffering other people were going through because of them! Elena, in her weakened condition, felt a new knife twist in her heart. Not only were she and Silvia being punished, but anyone who had helped them was being punished too!

The courtroom scene was a confusion of activities and speeches that made very little sense to Elena. Why were so many people crowded inside? How many people were on trial?

For the first time, Elena heard the names of the leader and his family. Even the man from Bucuresti had a name. All the information about where they had lived, the work they had done, and other seemingly insignificant details, made Elena's head spin.

But she did hear her sentence. "Elena Boghian. Two years for illegally crossing the border."

Two years. Two years of prison. How many years had Bunica been in prison? How many stories of horror and atrocities had been told and retold in her childhood? The very thing that Elena most feared was happening to her. Just the few days she had already spent in custody were enough to give her a foretaste of what could lay in store for her.

"Silvia Tarniceriu. Two years for illegally crossing the border."

Could it be possible that the two of them might be able to stay together? So far in their ordeal, they had only been separated for a few brief times. *Oh*, Elena thought, *I could not bear it if we were separated.*

On the way out of the courtroom, Elena put her hand against the door jamb to steady herself. She was weak from the lack of food. Someone in the crowd must have noticed her weakness.

"Hey! Have these people had anything to eat?"

Soon afterward, cookies were passed around. Elena ate gratefully. A small act of kindness even in this dark place.

Then it happened. The last vestige of comfort was taken away from her.

The group of sentenced women was led down a concrete hallway. The guards opened a barred door, shoved Silvia and the older woman into the cell, locked the door, opened another door and shoved Elena inside. She was alone, away from Silvia!

The small room held four iron beds. Already seven women were inside. Two women in each bed! She would have to share a bed with a stranger! Elena's chest heaved with emotion.

The stale, putrid air inside the cell made her retch. Hostile eyes glared at her.

"You will have to share the bed with her." One of the inmates indicated a bed where a large woman lay prone, staring at the newcomer. "*Mari*, give her room."

The big woman made no move. She just continued staring at Elena.

Elena felt her tears spill over. She did not even try to hide them. Something broke inside her and torrents of salty water washed over her cheeks. Her shoulders heaved. She was worse off than the miserable dogs that roamed the streets. Even those curs had places where they could sleep. She had nothing.

Weakly, she slumped onto the floor and cried deep, heaving sobs. At first the other women were silent, but as she continued weeping, even their hard hearts were moved.

"Don't cry so, you will make yourself sick!"

"Now, now. True, this is bad, but it could be worse!"

Elena turned a deaf ear to their entreaties. Sobs wracked her body, her tears flowing beyond control.

Never in her entire life had Elena felt so wretched. The last smidgen of comfort was taken away from her when she had been separated from Silvia. Always, Silvia had been able to bring some comfort and cheer to her. Just to know she was not alone had meant more to her than anything else. How could she endure life alone?

Late that night, when the large woman had finally moved enough for Elena to stretch her weary body on the foul mattress, she found comfort in communion with God.

"My child," she heard Him say, "you are not alone. I am with you. I will never leave you nor forsake you. Though you may feel as though everything has been taken from you, Elena, I am still here. Trust me. I am your strength and confidence. I am your Saviour. I am Jesus Christ, who died for you, rose from the dead and gave you eternal life. I am waiting for you in heaven. I love you, my child." These sweet, gentle thoughts were a healing balm to the heart-sick girl.

In the darkness—wretched, and bereft of her best friend—Elena found the arms of Jesus sweet and wonderful. "Thank-you, oh my Lord, my Saviour, my Friend. Even though my earthly friend has been separated from me, You are still here. Thank-you for Your presence!"

"Everybody out! Immediately!"

The call startled the inmates sharing the cell. Elena leaped from her narrow space on the bed and joined the other seven crowding toward the door.

One by one, they were taken into an office for yet another interrogation. Elena wondered how many times she would be subjected to the same questions. Why didn't they share their information instead of constantly questioning them?

"What is your name?"

"What is your address?'

"What did you work?"

"Who helped you in your attempted escape?"

Elena gave her stock answer. "I was with Silvia." It had worked before. Whenever she was asked to give information about someone who had helped them, or anyone else, she continued with the same response.

During this interrogation, a guard stood by the door, ready to take her back to the cell. His eyes were fastened on this girl who was not the usual type to be in prison. He studied her carefully.

"Place your bag on the table." The officer looked through the bag. Then he turned to the guard. "Do a body search."

Elena gasped and her hand flew up to her mouth. No! How could she bear to have a man search her? Then she thought of the money she had hidden in her boot! What would they do to her if they found it?

"Sir," the guard spoke respectfully, yet firmly, "it is illegal for me to search a female inmate. It is against the policies of our division."

A tense moment followed. The officer glanced sharply at the guard, then looked at Elena's tall, spare figure. He looked back at the guard. There was no insolence on the young man's face, only a calm, serene look.

"Take her back," the officer ordered tersely.

"Thank-you, God! Oh, thank-you!" Joy welled up in her heart as she was taken back to the cell. "I know now that You are still watching over me!

Please keep me from the clutches of evil men! Plant a hedge around me, even here in this place!"

The cell was the same, she was still separated from Silvia, and she was still sentenced to two years in prison. But even in these squalid conditions, Elena found encouragement from the recent deliverance. God had kept her from the terrible indignity and immodesty of enduring a body search by a man. Oh! How good the Lord was to her! That she could praise Him and have such joy at a time like this was a miracle! Yes, the Lord was showing His goodness to her!

18

Mere Existence

Yea, though I walk through the valley of the shadow of death,
I will fear no evil: for thou art with me;
thy rod and thy staff they comfort me. Thou preparest a table
before me in the presence of mine enemies.

Psalm 23:4-5a

"Silvia! Oh, thank-you, Jesus! Silvia, how can it be possible?" Elena was crying with joy. She felt her friend's strong arms around her heaving shoulders.

"Oh, Elena! It is so good to see you again."

"How is it possible?" exulted Elena. "I thought I could not stand to be separated from you. But now, after God showed me that He is all I really need, I am with you again! This is so amazing!"

Silvia gave her another gentle squeeze. "I was praying for you, Elena. Then I asked the guard to let you come over here to be with me. At first, she did not pay any attention to me. But I was like the widow in the Bible. I didn't give up. I explained how we have been friends for years now and depend on each other. God softened her heart, because the first thing I knew, I saw you coming through the door! Now I understand why the Lord Jesus sent out His disciples two by two!"

The two prisoners settled themselves on a cot. This cell was no different from the one Elena had just left. It also held almost twice as many women as it was designed for. But this time, Elena did not mind. She was with her best friend on earth.

"Out! Everyone out!" A woman's voice rang through the corridor, cutting short their reunion.

Another inspection! Elena's mind flew to the money in her boot. There was sure to be another search. And with a woman guard coming, there was no escaping a body search. With a swift movement of her arm, she plucked the shampoo tube from her boot and looked about the cell. Almost without thinking, she shoved the tube under the skimpy pillow on the cot. Hardly a hiding place, but at least it was not on her person.

Trembling, Elena stood in line beside Silvia with the other prisoners. Sure enough, this time there was no escaping the humiliating body search. The female guard made sure there was no place on the prisoners' bodies where something could be hidden. Elena felt her face grow crimson as the guard's hands patted her all over. She kept her eyes straight ahead.

"Go in and search the cell," the woman ordered the young man who had accompanied her. Elena heard the words with dread.

The money! Now he would find the money!

She could not turn to see what was happening. She had to continue facing the wall. The woman had started to search Silvia. Elena felt cold all over. She did not know what was happening in the cell. Would he exclaim in surprise when he found a shampoo tube? Would he immediately suspect that it held more than shampoo? Would they be able to trace the money to her? Would that mean a longer prison sentence?

Perhaps she would have to be separated from Silvia again. Oh, how she was praying that they could stay together for the entire two years! Prison would not be so bad if they could at least be together.

She would be 29 years old when her two years were up. Two whole years of her life, wasted in prison. "Lord, You remember how I wanted to do something for You as soon as I became a believer. I was so happy to be able to help clean the church, to help with food preparations for the choir trips, and to record for the choir. Now what will I do here in prison? Do you have anything for me to do? I want to work for You!"

"Are you finished searching the cell?" The woman's voice was loud and brisk.

"Yes, ma'am," the guard answered crisply.

"Well, what did you find?"

Elena held her breath. Her heart began beating rapidly.

"Nothing, ma'am."

"Nothing at all?"

"No ma'am. No contraband. Nothing personal." His voice was clear and confident.

"Everyone back in," the guard ordered. She had finished her job.

The inmates hurried back inside. The door was shut and the key turned in the lock.

Back at her cot, Elena immediately reached under the pillow. Her searching fingers touched the shampoo tube. Her heart raced.

"Oh, thank-you, Lord!" she whispered gratefully.

"Elena! What is the matter?" Silvia asked, looking at her face.

First looking around the room to make sure no one was paying attention to them, she replied in a low voice, "I hid my shampoo tube under the pillow. They didn't find it!"

Silvia gave a little chuckle. "Elena, I know it's terribly hard on you to be in this dirty prison. I, too, know the joy I would have to wash my hair with real shampoo again, but you look so white and scared! All that about a shampoo tube?"

"No, Silvia! Let me tell you what I did." She moved closely to Silvia's ear and told her how she had hidden the money inside the tube.

"Then you just put it under the pillow?" Silvia was incredulous.

"I couldn't think fast. I didn't want it on me. I prayed that God would keep it safe, and He did!"

"Elena, what if it happens again? Do you think it's safe to try to conceal that shampoo tube on yourself all the time?"

"I don't know. What do you think?"

Silvia was silent. Then she said, "Let's ask God for guidance."

The two girls prayed. They opened their hearts for direction from the Lord.

"I think I could open a little place in the hem of my wool coat," Silvia said after awhile.

While Silvia opened up a small space in the hem of her coat, Elena managed to get the 500 lei out of the shampoo tube. Then, in the dimness of the cell, they folded the money and inserted it into the hem.

"See if you can find where it is," Silvia whispered to Elena when the task was finished.

Elena carefully felt all around the hem. The thick fabric did not reveal anything!

"The Spirit of the Lord led you to think of that," Elena said gratefully. "I feel much better about it now."

"What shall I do, Silvia? I can't stand the filthy talk anymore!" Elena turned her anguished face toward her friend. "Oh, I never imagined that prison would be this horrible! No one ever told me about this!"

"Let the cleansing Word come and keep your mind on the right things," Silvia encouraged. "We must continually pray and ask the Lord to keep us pure, both in body and in mind."

A burst of raucous laughter came from down the hall where the male prisoners were incarcerated. Their loud calls came clearly into the women's cells.

Several of the women from their cell laughed and stepped to the bars. They began calling in response. Lewd conversations followed.

"Come, let's sing," Silvia suggested. The two girls turned their backs on the noise, and Silvia began to sing the songs they both loved.

Visions of their times in church and with the young people's group came like a healing balm to their hearts. They sang softly, but with deep feeling.

"Listen to them sing," one of the women in the cell exclaimed. "Hey, what are you singing about?"

Silvia turned to the questioner with a smile and began singing louder.

Jesus, lover of my soul,
Let me to Thy bosom fly,
While the nearer waters roll,
While the tempest still is high.
Hide me, O my Saviour, hide,
Till the storm of life is past;
Safe into the haven guide,
O receive my soul at last.

Several of the women laughed uneasily. Others scoffed. The loud calls from down the corridor died out.

As the two girls huddled on their cot, they continued to sing and encourage each other. God made a hallowed spot there in the prison for His daughters to draw strength and courage through His Spirit.

"Silvia, remember how Jesus prayed in John 17 that we would not be taken out of this world, but be kept from the world? I know He can keep us, even in this dreadful place."

Silvia nodded, smiling. "Elena, that is so true. We must keep our faith and trust in Him! He will never leave us, nor forsake us."

During the long days of idleness, loneliness and boredom crept into Elena's life. Her natural energy had no outlet, increasing her frustration and aggravating the pent-up feeling. Then came more interrogations. Numbness invaded her life and threatened to destroy any joy from the Lord.

Then they were transported to another prison—a women's prison, where rigid schedules and a strict regimen were relentlessly enforced. A prison that stole more of their vanishing identity and individuality.

"Everyone undress." There were no explanations, just shouted orders. Rumpled prison uniforms were thrust at them.

Elena looked in dismay at the baggy clothes. They did not fit her slight, tall frame at all! Too-short sleeves exposed most of her lower arms, and the shapeless skirt was too short.

"Take it and put it on! What do you think this is, a dress shop?" The woman guard had no patience with any complaints. "Keep moving! Go on, get dressed quickly!"

The constant noise and movement, the shouting, screaming guards, and the heavily guarded compound were Elena's worst nightmares come true. The place she had feared and dreaded as a child was now reality.

"Eyes forward! Forward, I say!" The guards shrieked at them if they so much as glanced one way or the other. The prisoners were ordered to work in groups wherever they were needed, under constant, strict surveillance by armed guards. And dogs! At times Elena heard the fierce barking of the German Shepherd dogs that guarded the perimeter of the prison. Whenever she saw the canines pacing beside the guards, she kept as far away as possible.

"Line up!" The command rang from the front of the group of inmates. Elena immediately tensed. They must be getting ready for transport.

The guard paced importantly in front of the line of women, taking a careful count. Then they were herded into the back of a closed truck, where an armed guard accompanied them.

Jouncing through the city streets, Elena wondered where they would be taken that day. The dullness that wanted to creep over her spirit threatened to make her just another prisoner, another number. She was at least comforted to be beside Silvia.

"Out!" The command came, brutal and unfeeling. Elena longed for a kind word, a friendly person, or at least a smile from someone. All the hatred and loud shouting, cursing and foul language created a sordid environment that was difficult to cope with.

Uninterestedly, Elena looked to see where they were. She could not see any identifying feature in front of the gray building where they had been deposited. It looked like another factory, she decided.

A group of factory workers, dressed in blue aprons, approached their band. Elena studied their faces. Those women were free! They could go where they wanted and be about their business without a guard. Already, that seemed a marvel to Elena. Already, she felt herself completely removed from free society.

Then she saw her! *Florica!* What had been just another face in the group of factory workers now took on an identity! A jolt of excitement shot through her.

Florica recognized her! She was sure! Just a slight nod of the dark-haired girl in their direction was enough to reassure Elena that Florica knew who they were.

Tears swam in Elena's eyes. To see someone familiar outside of prison was a ray of sunshine in her gray life!

"Move in!" The command sliced through Elena's thoughts.

"Did you see Florica?" Elena whispered to Silvia as they shuffled through a door into the canning factory.

"Yes!" Silvia nodded her head. Her eyes, too, were swimming in unshed tears.

The menial task they were set to do suddenly seemed as nothing. To see that one friendly, familiar face was one of the most wonderful things that had happened to them since they were in prison.

Carefully scrubbing rust from one of the tins of canned tomatoes, Elena remembered where they had first met Florica.

The children's choir had given a program at a church in *Braila*, where Florica was a member in the choir. She had become friends with the girls from Iasi.

A giggle from one of the inmates caught Elena's attention. She turned to see what was happening.

One of the women cleaning tins had somehow managed to open a can. She was busily eating tomatoes from the can and passing it around to the other prisoners.

Elena glanced hastily at the guard. She was at the far end of the room, chatting with one of the factory overseers.

More cans were opened. Someone thrust a can in front of her face.

Elena took a few bites and again glanced fearfully at the guard. She shuddered and then shook her head. The other inmate shrugged and ate the tomatoes herself.

They saw Florica again that day. This time they were on their way to another area to scrub more tins. They had to pass through the factory where the employees were busily filling tins with food.

As soon as they came into the factory, Elena eagerly scanned the faces again. Then she saw Florica!

It was evident that Florica was watching for them. As soon as the line of prisoners began filing through, she stepped forward where she could see clearly.

A surge of emotion ran through Elena. To see a friend! To see someone who loved them! She tried to smile in Florica's direction to let her know how much they appreciated seeing her, but she did not dare to look openly. She only risked one more quick glance backwards as they went into the next room.

The image of Florica gazing after them stayed branded upon Elena's mind. A cheerful face, smiling at them and nodding her head slightly—it was as though an angel had come to cheer Elena. To let her know they were not forgotten by their Christian friends.

The burlap bag was filled with potato pieces. Elena tugged at the heavy bag with her cold hands. It barely moved.

She gave a sigh and looked at the other workers, all slinging their bags off the truck and heading toward the plowed field.

Again, she pulled on the bag. She felt her strength fail her. But one look at the armed man standing guard over the group of prisoners put a fear into her that gave her a surge of adrenaline. She jerked the bag toward her, but still she could not lift it!

She had to get it off! Daily there were beatings for the inmates who slacked their duties. She had never been beaten, but the fear was always there.

Her hand slipped on the rough sacking and she felt the fibers tear into her fingers. The stubborn bag refused to move. Tears of fear and frustration made it difficult to see.

She heard the heavy boots of the guard coming toward her. Elena winced in fear. With downcast eyes, she watched his boots come closer. The rubber club hung from his belt.

"What's wrong, girl?" The guard's voice came in a surprisingly sympathetic tone.

Elena glanced briefly at him. "I can't—I can't lift the bag. It's too heavy for me!" The words came out in a rush.

"Here, let me." The guard moved to the truck. With an easy swing he lifted the bag and shouldered it, then headed for the field.

Elena followed him in amazement. How could it be that he was showing mercy to her, a prisoner!

"Thank-you!" she said breathlessly when he had put the bag beside a trench. She grabbed potatoes from the bag and pushed them into the ground.

Silvia had been watching. As soon as she saw Elena begin to plant potatoes, she managed to slip across the rows and plant some in Elena's row to help her friend catch up.

Elena's breath came in gasps. She hurried, but the bag was still too heavy to lift, so she dragged it across the ground. She was conscious of the guard watching her. This made her more nervous than ever. Would he report her?

Then the furrows ended. There were not enough rows prepared for the potatoes.

"Take the shovels and dig holes," the supervisor instructed. He threw down a pile of short, straight shovels from the truck.

Adding to their difficulty, the ground had been broken when it was too wet. Huge, hard clods of dirt made even walking difficult, much less digging holes for the potatoes.

Elena stepped on the shovel, trying to force the blade into the stubborn soil. Her light weight was hardly enough to push the tool into the clods.

"Here, let me help you." Silvia was at her side. With strong, swift movements, she prepared the holes for Elena. Then she went back to her own row and dug a series of holes for herself.

Elena planted her potatoes, then tried again to dig holes. It was no use. She was too weak, too distraught from the trauma of imprisonment.

"No, no!" she protested feebly as Silvia once more came to help. "You must not do my work. You don't get enough good food either to give you strength!"

The group of women toiled all morning in the brisk spring air, chopping at the hardened ground, dropping in the potato pieces.

Drop potatoes into the hole. Cover them up. Go to the next hole. Drop potatoes into the hole. Cover them up. Go to the next hole. No hole. Elena tried to straighten her back to hunt for the shovel.

"Let me," Silvia took Elena's shovel. Her movements, too, were slower now in the afternoon. She pushed vigorously down on the shovel.

"Silvia, don't," Elena said tonelessly. "Let me go. I don't think they will kill me, but I just can't keep up."

Silvia did not answer. She marched ahead and dug some more holes for Elena. Before she went back to her own row, she briefly rested her hand on Elena's shoulder. "Remember Jesus' promise: 'Lo, I am with you always, even unto the end of the world.' " Then she went back to her work.

Elena's mind became numb. Her movements slowed down and she dropped further and further behind, in spite of Silvia's help. She no longer protested when Silvia helped her, although she noticed that the two of them were far behind the others.

Not once had the guard yelled at them. He had kept his distance, but his eyes rested more than once on the two girls who labored together.

"Number 224 and number 226, report to the guard at the gate."

Elena glanced at the number on her uniform: 226. Silvia was number 224.

"Clean this office." The command came briskly as they followed the guard.

Elena looked at their escort. It was the same man who had been kind to her the day before in the potato field.

"I will lock you in here and you must clean everything. Check all the boxes, especially the box under the desk, and put any trash into the stove and burn it." His voice was stern, but as they looked into his eyes, they saw kindness and pity there.

"Sweep the floor, clean the walls, and put everything in order." Then he went out and locked the door behind him.

Silvia and Elena looked at each other in amazement. What a relief after the difficult work they had done the day before! The office was small and hardly needed cleaning.

"Why did he say especially to check the box under the desk?" Silvia wondered out loud. She bent down to pull out a brown cardboard box from underneath.

"Pecans!" Elena gasped. She felt her mouth water.

Silvia looked around for something to crack open the nuts. A metal paper weight on the desk top worked just fine. She cracked open a nut and offered the nut meats to Elena.

"Do you think we should?" Elena hesitated.

"Absolutely," Silvia said, popping a piece into her own mouth. "Why do you think he specifically mentioned the box under the desk?"

"Silvia! God is good to us! He has sent someone who has taken pity on us!"

As Elena crunched the savory pecans, she marveled at how good they tasted. It was wonderful to have something to eat besides watery soup and stale bread.

"But we have to clean!" Elena jumped up from her kneeling position and looked around for cleaning supplies.

"You stay right here beside the stove and crack nuts for us," Silvia instructed. "I will dust and straighten the furniture, although there is hardly anything to do. I do think that kind man planned this expressly for our benefit!"

It took less than thirty minutes for Silvia to clean the office. Then, for more than two hours, the girls rested and munched on the nutritious pecans.

"How good this feels," Elena murmured. "Away from the crowd of prisoners, being able to rest, and even having nuts to eat. This gives me more strength than I ever imagined."

"You know, the guard really did think this through," Silvia mused. "We can easily get rid of any evidence that we were eating nuts by throwing all the shells into the fire. And the fire, fueled by pecan shells, keeps us warm, and even cozy! May God reward him for his kindness."

The girls named the kind guard "Gabriel," for to them he was a messenger from the Lord to help them. Once when they were sent outside to the fields to weed the State Farm vegetable plots, he intentionally assigned them to work among the new green onions. "Thin any of the onions that need it," he told them, his eyes again conveying more than his words. The green onions were delicious! The girls secreted several in their clothes and ate them with the hard bread they were given for their lunch break.

Another day, when the sky was dark with clouds and a chill wind penetrated through their prison uniforms, "Gabriel" built a warm fire with trash. From somewhere he produced potatoes and put them to roast among the ashes. At lunch break, he allowed the inmates to retrieve the hot potatoes from the ashes.

Elena savored her roasted potato. She even cleaned the charred skin of her potato and ate the crispy shell. The warmth of the potato and the warmth of the kind deed spread through her like sunshine.

In her prayer time, Elena regularly thanked God for this bit of cheer in their lives. "You are good to us! I know You have somehow sent 'Gabriel' to remind us that You have not forgotten us. Lord, I am still in complete dismay that I am in prison! I have nothing to do here but to exist. No reason to live. I would much rather die and come to You in heaven. But I do thank You that You have not forgotten us! I still praise You for being my Saviour! Teach me, Lord, what You want me to learn."

19
Light in the Darkness

REJOICE NOT AGAINST ME, O MINE ENEMY: WHEN I FALL, I SHALL ARISE; WHEN I SIT IN DARKNESS, THE LORD SHALL BE A LIGHT UNTO ME.

MICAH 7:8

Elena dreaded Sundays in prison. At first it had seemed like a day to look forward to, but she had soon learned differently. Because they were not taken to the fields to work, they had to endure the entire day in their cell, and yet they were not allowed to rest on their bunk beds. The fifty cell mates usually paced the floor restlessly, and the filthy language always seemed worse on Sundays.

On one particular Sunday, a television had been brought in for the inmates to watch a nationalistic program. Elena and Silvia paid the program little attention, for the propaganda was mostly rhetoric and boring besides.

They were sitting on the hard benches in the middle of the room when, suddenly, music sounded from the television speakers, interrupting the tedious broadcast. One of the women had been fiddling with the knob and found another channel. The music and the scenes on the screen were obviously from another country. They all, including Elena and Silvia, watched in fascination as an announcer moderated an event in an unfamiliar language.

"I think they are having a singing contest," Silvia said after a moment.

Sure enough, various women took the stage by turns and sang a song. Spellbound, the prisoners watched the program.

"Americans," Elena said softly. She studied each contestant's dress and mannerisms. They looked happy and relaxed, smiling into the camera as they sang.

Then a young woman appeared on the screen and began to sing. The melody sounded familiar to Elena. Yes, she knew that tune!

"She's singing 'Amazing Grace!' " Silvia said in a hushed voice. "Oh! How beautiful!"

As the lovely strains of music filled their prison cell, it was as though heaven itself had opened a door and allowed the women a glimpse of its glories. The healing balm of the song ministered to their sad, lonely hearts. Though the words were in English, the song was so familiar to them that they could sing along with the Romanian words.

". . . I once was lost, but now I'm found, Was blind, but now I see!" Tears rolled down Elena's cheeks. Not tears of sadness this time—tears of joy!

"When we've been there ten thousand years, Bright shining as the sun; We've no less days to sing God's praise, Than when we first begun!" The uplifting message penetrated the deepest part of Elena's heart.

"Yes, that's right!" Elena rejoiced. "Time here is nothing compared to eternity! Our two-year sentence will be as nothing in heaven! Thank-you, Jesus, for reminding us so beautifully!"

"What is going on in there?" The harsh voice of the guard brought them all back to reality. With a flick of the dial, they were back to the Romanian station and the tiresome propaganda.

But Silvia and Elena did not mind. That brief window into life outside prison, indeed, outside Romania, had brought them the comforting song of hope and faith. They thanked God for sending them that message.

The continual barrage of smutty, filthy talk was a constant grief to the girls. The aged wife of the guide who led their escape shared their cell. She, too, was deeply grieved by the language the other inmates used. More than once, all three of them covered their ears with blankets at night as indecent conversations and innuendos swirled around them.

"You all just think you are holier than we are," the other women would taunt them. "Your minds think the same things we do, you just think you're too holy to admit it." It seemed to infuriate them that the three would not join in their vile speech.

One Sunday, the guide's wife and Silvia were sitting on the hard wooden benches, singing. Elena drank in the words of the hymns and listened with eager ears. Suddenly she noticed everything else in the room was completely quiet. She cautiously looked around. Alarmed, she saw a group of women standing in a huddle, whispering to each other and shooting venomous looks their way. She could feel the hatred emanating from them.

Fights among the inmates were not uncommon. At certain times, when no guards were expected, a dominant group would suddenly take control over the rest. If there was any resistance, a fierce scuffle was sure to break out. These fights were fast and furious and almost completely silent. By the time the guards realized something was amiss and came to check, the fights were over. Often the losers were minus some hair, and scratches and twisted limbs were not uncommon.

"Silvia!" Elena hissed. "I think we are going to be beat up!" she whispered in fear.

After a quick glance, Silvia said to her two companions. "Let's pray!"

Elena bowed her head and began praying out loud. She heard Silvia and the guide's wife praying desperately too.

In her cries to heaven, Elena poured out her petition for protection. At any moment, she expected to feel the blows of the antagonists. She continued to pray.

A rough shove caught her in the back. She cried out but continued to pray. Angry voices washed over her like a flood of muddy water. She bowed her head for the expected blows.

Then she heard Silvia began to sing. Pure and clear, her voice lifted above the turmoil around them. "Rock of Ages, cleft for me, Let me hide myself in Thee . . ."

There was a lull in the cacophony of noise behind them. Silvia continued to sing. "Jesus, Jesus, how I trust Him! How I've proved Him o'er and o'er! Jesus, Jesus, precious Jesus! O for grace to trust Him more!"

No more pushing. No more swearing. Only a profound stillness behind them. A stillness and a peace that were surely effects of the words of the song.

Silvia sang some more. The guide's wife joined in.

What had begun as a potentially ugly scene for the believers turned into a triumphant moment of victory. God had protected them once more, this time through the power of song!

"You! To the right!" The guard in this new prison was a man, and Elena knew immediately that he was not one to grant any favors. In fact, he looked like someone who would make life as miserable as possible for any of the newly-arrived inmates.

"Please, Lord, allow Silvia and me to stay together!" This had been

Elena's constant prayer throughout the entire two-day journey to this prison. They had been moved once again.

The journey to this prison had been an experience beyond words. The train car in which they had been locked was severely crowded and suffocatingly hot. The women had received almost no food or water, and Elena had wondered more than once if they would die from the terrible conditions. But finally they had arrived at this prison. Now, with about fifty other women, they were being herded into a corridor and assigned to two cells.

"You! To the left!" There was no apparent logic in how the guard decided who should go where. Elena wildly thought of asking to stay with Silvia, but another look at the guard made her retract that idea immediately.

Pointing straight at Silvia, he brusquely ordered, "To the right." Without hesitation, he pointed to Elena, "To the left!"

Elena stumbled into the cell. She felt ill with disappointment. Her chest heaved in anguish. Why hadn't God answered her prayers? What more would she have to endure? Would she never see Silvia again for the remainder of her prison term? Why? Why? Why?

"Hey! Over here!" A young woman with sad brown eyes called to her. At first, Elena was not sure if the greeting was meant for her. She looked intently at the lady. No, she did not know her.

Hesitantly, Elena went over to where the young woman was sitting on a cot. With a beckoning motion, she indicated the cot next to her. "Here, you take this one."

Elena, her heart still heavy with the sorrow of being separated from her friend, sank onto the thin mattress. The room around them was a flurry of movement as the inmates shuffled about, claiming their territories or staking out new ones.

"Don't be so sad, young lady," the dark-eyed woman said to her. "I think you will be all right. When I saw you in line, I prayed that you would come to my room. I need someone I can talk to and you looked like that someone. You don't look like someone I would have expected to see in prison. Why are you here?"

"I—I escaped from Romania and was sent back by the Yugoslavian government," Elena said simply. Was this person sincerely sympathetic? Did she really want to be friends?

"Oh." The exclamation fell from her lips without much emotion. "Why did you want to escape?"

Briefly, Elena explained that she had been shadowed by the secret police because of her work in smuggling Bibles and with the children's choir. Hardly ever was it safe to share such information with anyone, but for some reason she felt safe with this woman. Too much suffering was etched on her new friend's face for her to be an informer.

"Call me *Veronica*," she answered Elena's query as to her name.

"I believe in God too," Veronica said after Elena finished her story. "At least I used to. Now I don't know what will become of me."

Elena's sympathy went out to the sad-faced woman. "Tell me about it," she urged.

With a deep sigh, Veronica groaned. "I feel so condemned! I feel so wicked! I wish I knew what to do with my guilt. I wish I could die, but I'm afraid to die." She buried her head in her hands. "I—I don't think Jesus can ever forgive me for what I have done!"

"Oh, what is it? If you want to tell me, perhaps I can pray with you about it. I—" Elena hesitated, "I have had some difficulties of my own and maybe it will do you good to talk about it."

Veronica straightened her shoulders, took a deep breath, and began her story. "I am a nurse. A trained nurse. I worked in a hospital.

"One day, an engineer in a high position approached me privately. She wanted me to do something for her.

"She said she needed an abortion, but she could not go to a doctor. She told me I had to do it. I protested and told her that I did not want to. I didn't have the training.

"She didn't listen to me. She insisted that I could do it. She threatened to ruin my career if I wouldn't help her." Veronica swallowed painfully and closed her eyes.

"Elena, that lady died! I tried to do what she wanted me to, but I didn't really know how, and she died! She died in my arms with her blood all over me! Oh, I will never forget it—it was awful, awful . . . " Her hard, dry voice cracked with emotion. She stopped speaking.

Elena's eyes filled with tears. Her own heart ached with the pain that Veronica carried.

"I can't be forgiven! My sin is too great!" Veronica's voice was filled with anguish. She leaned forward and bowed her head.

Elena leaned toward the distraught woman. "Veronica, God *can* forgive you. We read in the Bible that if we confess our sins, He is faithful and just to forgive our sins. Remember, that is why Jesus came to earth. To forgive our sins and make us as white as snow."

Veronica raised her head. "But isn't that talking about sinners repenting? I was already a Christian and I should have known better. I am now suffering for the sins that I knowingly committed. How can God forgive such a sin?"

Elena thought a moment. "Do you remember the thief who was crucified beside Jesus? He asked Jesus to remember him, and Jesus told him these blessed words: 'Today you shall be with me in paradise.' Jesus freely forgives *all* those who sin, not just those who have never been believers. I know this, Veronica, because I have sinned too. And I know God has forgiven me."

"How do you know? How can anyone be sure that God forgives our sins?"

"First of all because the Bible says so, and the Bible is true. Also, because of the freedom from guilt that comes along with confession of our sins. We must claim God's forgiveness by faith and believe that God never goes back on His promises."

The other prisoners had settled in for the night. Elena and Veronica sat huddled together, talking in low tones.

Elena bowed her head. "Dear Lord, I pray for Veronica. Help her to claim the forgiveness You offer to her in the name of Jesus. You see her sorrow. You see her desperation. Reward her with Your presence in her heart. I pray this in the name of Jesus Christ, our Lord."

"Oh, thank-you, Elena!" sighed Veronica. "I know it was God who planned for you to come to this cell instead of going with your friend. How I thank Him for you!"

In the darkness of the night, Elena felt a warm glow burn in her heart. She was glad God had wanted to use her to be a messenger of hope for Veronica. She missed Silvia sorely, but the peace in her heart came directly from God.

"Let my friend come in with me," Elena heard Silvia plead. "She is not strong and we need to be together. We wouldn't make things difficult for anyone." Silvia spoke politely, yet beseechingly to the woman guard.

Elena heard no reply. Her heart yearned across the bars for her friend. True, she had Veronica, and yes, they spent time together in prayer. Elena rejoiced to see her new friend's faith growing. But in spite of this blessing, sadness and depression had steadily crept into her heart and mind. She had not realized until now just how much she had depended on Silvia to encourage her and keep her spirits up.

Perhaps the lady guard would have mercy on them. Elena could not see down the corridor, but she could hear the jangling of keys fading away. Elena sighed in disappointment.

But in a moment, the guard had returned.

"Out! Number 36." Elena was Number 36.

Hope rising within her, Elena followed the guard. Oh! She was going to be reunited with Silvia!

The guard unlocked the door to a cell and motioned Elena to enter. A wave of foul-smelling air met her. She hesitated.

"Get in! You wanted to move, now here you are!" The woman clanged the door shut behind her and turned the key in the lock.

A fetid odor assailed Elena's senses. In the murky light, she could see a group of bedraggled women huddled together in a corner. Their dark brown faces looked at the newcomer with hostility. They spoke to each other in a foreign tongue.

Vagabonds! Gypsies! Elena looked wildly back toward the door. Where could she go?

Immediately on her right she saw a vacant cot. She stumbled toward it, her eyes welling with tears.

"Don't cry, young girl." An old woman spoke to her from the next cot. "You must not break down. You must make your own life wherever you go." She studied Elena more closely. "I can see you have had a good life. Now, somehow, you are thrust in here and you think it is very bad. Yet, you must trust that God can see you even in here." The woman made the sign of the cross as she spoke God's name.

Elena listened to the kind words. Even in this putrid, filthy place, she had found someone sympathetic.

"I don't know why you are here, but God does." Again the woman signed the cross. "You must not despair, for that is giving up. You must keep on living, one day at a time. What if you were serving time for something you didn't do, like I am? Oh, perhaps you are innocent too, I don't know. But six years is a long time to spend in prison for a crime one did not commit."

Elena listened to the flow of words. Somehow, there was comfort in just listening, not being asked questions.

"You see, I came to jail to save my sister. She was working in a hospital and performed an illegal abortion and the patient died. Well, my sister is married and has a family, so when it was time for her to be put on trial, I went instead. I guess they didn't really check into her identity too much, for even though my sister is taller and more slender, they tried me instead of her and sentenced me to six years in jail. I've been here for two now and I get lonely sometimes."

Elena was aghast! How was such a story possible? Was this woman making it up?

"How—how could you do such a thing for your sister?" She stared incredulously at the woman.

"I told you. She has a family and I'm just a single woman. No one misses me." She went on. "I have learned to take one day at a time. I know the food is horrible and there is hardly enough water to take a bath, but somehow I get along. Just as you will, deary."

A stench of bad meat burning choked Elena's breath. Somehow, the Gypsies had managed to light a fire in the corner used as a toilet and were trying to fry some rancid bacon over the smoky flames. The nauseating smell almost made Elena gag. She covered her nose with her hand.

How could she stay here? Why, oh, why had she not been satisfied to stay where she was? There she did not have cell mates like these dirty women. She shuddered.

"Why are you so sad, young woman?" It was the old lady again.

"I wanted to be put into the room where my friend is," Elena said in resignation. "But when she asked that I be moved, they put me in here instead!"

"Ah!" the woman nodded understandingly. "Sometimes it is better not to ask for favors, for then the guards will do just the opposite! They don't want us to be comfortable!"

Elena knew the truth of the old woman's words. More than once she had seen it happen. Any indications the prisoners gave of their preferences were often noted by the guards only to see to it that just the opposite happened. She felt crushed.

"But like I said, you must not despair. Make your own life by what's inside you."

Elena nodded. "That's true. I know that my faith in God will take me through the most difficult times, but sometimes I forget. I'm glad God has reminded me."

"Oh, you believe in God!" Once more, the woman crossed herself.

"Yes, I not only believe in God, but I believe in Jesus Christ as my Saviour." Elena shared her testimony with the old woman.

Even though the conditions did not improve, once more Elena found someone she could share with. The old lady's Orthodox beliefs kept her from accepting Elena's testimony completely, but as the days wore on, they had many opportunities to speak about their experiences. In her daily prayers, Elena asked God to use her to bring the woman to a complete understanding of faith in Jesus Christ.

Elena shuddered and covered her ears with her hands. It was evening, and the curfew bell would soon ring. Her cell mates were squabbling fiercely in one corner of the room. Angry voices penetrated her consciousness.

"Oh, Lord, how long? How long must I endure this? I know You've promised to stay with me and to be everything I need, but I am still in despair in my situation."

A noise at the door of the cell arrested everyone's attention. A female guard entered.

"Number 36, get your things and come with me."

Elena jumped up from her cot, her heart racing. What was happening? She quickly took her bag of personal items and followed the guard through the door. She waited while the guard locked the door.

Down the hall they trod, Elena following with dread.

The guard stopped in front of another cell door, unlocked it, and said, "Go in."

Elena stepped inside. Instantly, she was engulfed in a hug!

"Silvia!" Elena gasped. Her eyes wet with tears, she embraced her dearest friend on earth.

"Oh, Elena, God has answered our prayers! Come, you will have to share a cot with me!" She led Elena over to her bed.

"How did this ever happen?" Elena found it difficult to comprehend. "I had just been telling God that I didn't know if I could take it any longer, locked up in that cell with those wicked, quarreling women. Silvia, it was simply terrible!" She shuddered.

"I'm sure it was," Silvia sympathized, then launched into her tale. "After you were moved to that cell, I studied the guards for several weeks, looking for a kind one. When I thought I found one who seemed to feel sorry for our predicaments and softer toward the inmates, I asked her if she could make it possible for my friend, which is you of course, to be in the same room as I am. She did not say anything, and for several days I waited. And prayed! Tonight she asked me if I would be willing to share my cot. I said I would share it with you. Then she left!

"I was praying furiously while she was gone. Then suddenly you were here! I mean, you are here!" Silvia laughed and hugged Elena again.

"To be with you again is the best thing that could happen to me while I am in prison," Elena said fervently. "God knows how much I need your strength and encouragement."

Elena grasped the hoe by the handle and chopped away at the weeds. Her coarse prison shirt, too warm for the summer weather, chafed her skin. Perspiration trickled down her forehead and into her eyes. Straightening, she wiped her face and rubbed her aching back.

The row of women, hoeing the ankle-high corn, moved across the field. Silvia was in the row beside her.

In a way, it was good to be outside in the fresh air and sunshine. She could draw deep lungs full of air, untainted with fetid smells and foul, clammy air. But after several hours of working in the sun, Elena felt her strength ebb away. The poor food they were served in prison had at first been so repulsive to her that she had hardly eaten anything. Her body weight had dropped immediately. Now she forced herself to eat what was offered in order to keep up her strength. But the poor diet and the constant mental anguish she endured robbed her of her usual stamina.

Elena chopped at a stubborn weed with her hoe. She was lagging behind. She would have to work faster.

The voice of the armed guard who kept pace with the prisoners arrested her attention. She looked over to see who he was talking to. An official had just arrived.

There was a forceful discussion between the newly arrived official and the guard.

"Boghian and Tarniceriu!" the guard shouted. "Come here!"

Clutching their hoes, the two girls stepped across the rows of corn.

"Drop the hoes!"

With a surprised look at each other, they dropped their hoes and stood in front of the men.

"Yes, these are the two!" The official looked at his papers. "They are the ones who tried to escape from Romania."

"We did escape," Silvia corrected him. "We were turned over to the Romanian police by the Yugoslavian government."

"Shut up!" the official roared. Then he turned to the guard. "Take all the prisoners back to jail. Keep these two escapees well under guard. They are too dangerous to be allowed to work outside! They must stay inside the prison!"

Even though it was early afternoon, the prisoners were herded back into the transport truck. Elena did not have much time to think about the recent developments, for the truck was too full.

Straddling the backless benches in the bed of the covered truck, the women had to fit themselves as tightly as possible against the person in front of them. Still, they could not get all the prisoners inside far enough to close the metal gates in the back.

"Get in there!" The shrill commands and curses seared across Elena's mind. She tried to scoot closer toward the front.

Then she heard the snarling of the German Shepherd dogs the guards kept with them. Screams and cries of fear echoed inside the closed truck as the inmates desperately shoved forward.

The gates were swung shut and locked. Elena was squashed between the lady in front of her and Silvia, just behind her. They were to sit that way all the time they were in transport. Anyone who would turn her head to look out the back would surely be yelled at by the armed men who guarded the rear.

Packed tightly inside the roaring truck, faint and almost sick from the poor diet, Elena felt her mind go into a stupor. She did not even have the will to mentally protest.

This was life in prison. "Help me, Lord, to somehow endure the rest of my prison term. I can only put my trust in You!" The four months since she had been imprisoned and shunted from place to place were like a blur to her. The time ahead looked like a tunnel without a light. All darkness. With all her mental effort, she cried out to God, "I need You! I just need You!"

20
Strength Through Suffering

Blessed be the Lord,
who hath not given us as a prey to their teeth.
Our soul is escaped as a bird out of the snare of the fowlers:
the snare is broken, and we are escaped.
Our help is in the name of the Lord, who made heaven and earth.

Psalm 124:6-8

Sewing machines on either side of Elena hummed busily. The women inmates in this room were sewing heavy garments for factory workers. The stiff material was bulky, and difficult for Elena to handle.

"Come on, sew faster!" the overseer behind Elena prodded.

Elena bent over her machine and tugged at the fabric. She pressed the foot pedal and tried to guide the fabric under the flying needle for a straight seam. But as she reached back to get a fresh grip, the stiff fabric skewed sideways and the needle raced across the material at crazy angles.

"Stop!" The cry from the overseer caused the other seamstresses to look at what was the matter. "You can't sew that way! You have no sewing skills whatsoever!" Elena felt her cheeks burn. She tried to keep the tears from forming in the corners of her eyes.

The exasperated overseer yanked at the offending garment. "Now pick out that seam and do it over!"

Elena gathered up courage and looked at the overseer. "Can I please do something else?"

There was a sharp intake of breath from the woman and the surrounding inmates. The general manager of the sewing operation came over to see what was happening.

"She is useless here," the overseer said. "This is her third day and she has made absolutely no progress in her sewing."

The manager looked at Elena's discouraged face. "Come with me," she said briskly. "Sew buttons onto these jackets." A pile of finished work jackets were lying on the work table.

Elena threaded a needle and found the marked spot. Her fingers shook as she pushed the needle through the heavy fabric.

Back and forth, over and under she sewed. Button after button.

"Ouch!" she cried out involuntarily as the sharp point of the needle pricked her finger. She put her injured forefinger into her mouth. When she looked at it again, a small bead of blood dotted her skin.

Doggedly, she kept on sewing. She favored her pricked finger and that slowed her down. By mid-morning she had finished the first jacket. Already, a second finger bore the marks of the needle. Her other fingers were sore.

Several times she looked over to where Silvia was busily working at the sewing machines. It had not taken Silvia long to pick up the skill.

Elena sighed and picked up another button. Holding it against the jacket front, she stitched the first stitch. Ouch! Again, she had pricked her finger.

A small group of women were in one corner, marking the fabric before it was cut. Then it was placed onto a table where a mechanical cutter, guided by a worker, cut the layers of material.

"Lord, if only I could have a job like that! I could mark the fabric. That would be something I could do. Could You make it possible for me to do something I could do well?"

The overseer came over to inspect Elena's work. She looked at the lone jacket on the table. She watched Elena struggle to pull the needle through the fabric.

"You don't have the hands of a seamstress," she said finally. "Your fingers are too long and thin. Look how you have pricked them with the needle!"

Elena did not need to look. She had tried not to look. Or feel. She bent lower over her work.

"Come here." The overseer led her over to the group marking patterns. "Number 78, show this woman how to mark patterns. Maybe that's something she could do."

Elena felt hope grow within her. Her heart beat faster, this time with pleasure. She felt confident she could do this!

It was not long before Elena became proficient in her new job, taking her place among the other pattern markers. Her nimble fingers easily matched the edges of the fabric and, with sure, swift strokes, she followed the pattern placed on the fabric.

The days that followed were almost pleasant. Elena's co-workers in the pattern corner were mostly intellectual women who had worked in offices or financial institutions. Elena found out that most of them had been convicted of embezzlement—some unjustly.

They had special favors from the guards. A number of them received food parcels regularly from family or friends "outside." They shared these treats liberally with Elena.

"Oh, look! Sausages!" an excited lady exclaimed one day, after she drew her parcel out from under her work apron.

"Heat them up on the stove!" another suggested.

Elena was bewildered. What stove? She glanced around the large room, the familiar scene catching her attention again. The sewing machines were whirring busily. Hand seamstresses finished the garments, while the two overseers stood at the far end of the room. A sort of contented hum came from all the activity and noise of the machines. Were it not for their prison uniforms, Elena mused, all of them might merely have been workers in a factory. *Working for no wages*, Elena thought wryly. But there was no stove in sight.

She reached for another pattern when she smelled something so delicious it made her stomach muscles twitch.

The lady who had received the sausages saw Elena look around. She winked at Elena and wiggled her eyebrows. She glanced down at the side of her table. Elena followed her glance.

She almost had to laugh. An aluminum cup was sitting on the floor with a hot iron setting on top of it. Sausages, simmering in water, gave out the most delectable smell.

Elena glanced back at the lady. She casually lifted her hand to her nose and glanced toward the overseers who were still at the far end of the room.

With a grimace, the lady nodded. She took a scrap of fabric and picked up the hot aluminum cup. Switching off the iron, she placed it back on the stand.

Not long afterwards, Elena felt something warm thrust into her hand. She knew what it was right away. With a surreptitious glance, she made sure neither of the overseers were close by. She popped a bite of sausage into her mouth.

Oh, the taste of that warm sausage! Not since she was in prison did she taste anything so good! The food parcels she and Silvia had been able to receive from their families at long intervals had always been opened by someone, and nothing as good as meat had ever been allowed to slip through to them.

Continuing with her work, Elena gently nibbled at the sausage. The savory juices tasted so good! She tried to refrain from eating too fast, wanting the delicacy to last as long as possible. When another piece was thrust into her hand, she did not put it into her mouth. She wrapped it in a piece of fabric and put it into her pocket. This one was for Silvia!

If working conditions during the day improved, life in the cells during the evening and night certainly did not.

"Boghian! Tarniceriu!" The call was heard with dread. "Come into the hall."

Elena followed Silvia out into the corridor. They were met by a guard who seemed to hate everyone on the face of the earth. Especially everyone in prison.

"No, no!" Elena found herself praying. They were headed for the isolation cell! Dreadful stories circulated about the terrible conditions of the isolation cell where prisoners were sometimes locked for days on end.

Her mind whirled busily. Had they found out that she had eaten sausages at work? Would they be punished for sharing the tidbit she had smuggled to Silvia?

The door to the isolation cell stood open. A foul odor blasted their senses. "Get in there and clean the room!"

With dread, they entered, holding their breath. The guard shut the door, locked it, and left.

"Oh, Silvia! I can't stand the smell!" Elena wailed in a whisper.

"Where are the cleaning supplies?" Silvia asked, looking around them with a shudder.

They stood helplessly inside the door, not wanting to look, yet unable to keep their eyes from roaming the cell.

Truly, this was the most nauseating place they had ever been in. There were no bathroom facilities for any unfortunate person locked in here. The reeking human excrement in one corner spoke quite eloquently of the prisoner's plight. Forced to be in here, day after day, would surely drive most inmates into complete submission.

"Why are you standing there? Do you want to be locked in there for days?" The guard was back, looking through the barred door.

"We have no cleaning supplies," Silvia said patiently.

"Cleaning supplies! Hah! This is a prison! You will get no cleaning supplies! Clean everything up and put it into that bucket! If you are not done by suppertime, you will stay in here until it is done." Then she strode off.

Fear spurred them to action. Gagging and retching, they used some filthy rags they found and set to their gruesome task. Knowing the guard would return soon, they quickly did the best they could and filled the bucket with refuse. Time and again, Elena thought she would have to throw up, but determinedly kept working.

A disgruntled "Humph" was all the guard said when she came back. She unlocked the door and led them back to their cell.

The cold water spigot in their bathroom provided a trickle of water for them to wash, but they needed soap and hot water! Lots of it!

They had neither. Just cold water. Weeping in revulsion, Elena tried to clean her hands. She washed and rubbed them over and over again. She did not even want to dry her hands on anything. She could not bear to touch her clothes with her hands.

She felt like a leper. "Unclean, unclean!" The words rolled over and over in her mind. Neither she nor Silvia could eat any of the food that was served that evening. They could not bear the thought of touching anything with their hands. Even that night as they lay side by side in their bed, Elena could not rest. Her hands felt defiled, like they were not even part of her body.

Days melted into weeks, weeks into months. Summer was wearing on, and still, life in prison for Elena was a dark tunnel with no ending. Work in the sewing factory was the only normalcy, for there she felt useful and productive. Only the presence of guards and locked doors kept reminding her that she was still in prison.

Evenings were the worst. Pressed into cleaning duty, she was warned that if she didn't clean the floors well, she would have to kneel down and lick them clean. That scared her into a frenzy of scrubbing that left her knees sore, her muscles aching, and her heart weary.

The night watches were another dreadful experience. Every prisoner had to take her turn being on watch for certain hours of the night. Introduced as a means of safety for the cell mates, it turned into living nightmares, especially if the hours of watching were between midnight and the rising bell in the morning. Leaning against the side of the bunk beds, Elena found herself falling asleep on her feet more than once. She always managed to be awake, however, whenever the guard outside in the corridor looked in the cell to see if someone was on duty.

She tried to use these hours for prayer and meditation. Reciting Bible verses over and over encouraged and strengthened her. Recalling songs and parts of poems, praying, crying out to the Lord for courage and strength, Elena battled through the wearying hours while sleep fought a vicious battle for her consciousness.

"Every August, as you well know, our benevolent leader, *Ceausescu*, grants amnesty to prisoners deserving that status. Tomorrow morning someone will come to your cell and announce the names of those who will be released. For those fortunate ones, remember to be thankful to our kind ruler for his consideration of you."

An excited murmur broke out in the dining hall. Elena stared at Silvia as her friend stared back. Would they be among the ones to be freed?

She hardly dared to put her thoughts into words. As soon as she was back in her cell, Elena asked, "Silvia, what if you are released and I am not? Or what if I am released and you are not?"

Silvia did not answer. She just stared back at Elena.

After that, they hardly spoke. Each was lost in her own thoughts. The entire room was in an abnormal hush.

As Elena lay in the darkness that night, her mind traveled back to their attempted escape and consequent imprisonment. That was six months ago. Six long months that reached back into another life. Elena saw herself working at her job, attending the university, competing at sports, living at the boarding school, and growing up in her childhood home.

What was happening to her mother? Where were her siblings? If she should be released, whatever would she do? Where would she live? Would it be possible to go back to work anywhere? Would their old friends be glad to see them? Questions pounded her brain.

For the last half year, she hardly had to make any decisions. Few choices were available to her. She had been told what to do, with every detail of her daily existence ordered and forced upon her. How could she cope with making decisions again?

A sense of wonder crept over her. Never in her wildest imaginations would she have thought she could ever feel this way.

Prison had become a way of life for her. Her work, her duties, and her companions had become the norm! In spite of all the horrors, she had actually gotten used to it!

She remembered the money in the hem of Silvia's coat. Would it be enough to buy train tickets to take them back to—where would they go? Elena felt dizzy.

What if they would not be released? Or what if, like she had said, one of them would be released and the other would stay behind?

Oh, it was too much like judgment day! Everyone was hoping to be released—some would leave and others would not.

"Lord, I have to give this to You. Trying to figure out what will happen is robbing me of my peace. I cannot bear it. I cannot even pray for my release. I just ask, Lord, that You come and assure me of Your presence!"

Throughout the long, sleepless night, Elena tried to commit her future, her life, into the hands of God. Random thoughts drifted through her weary mind like untethered kites.

The sound of the door unlocking the next morning snapped all the inmates to immediate attention. An important-looking man, flanked by two armed guards, came into the cell.

"I will read the names of the prisoners who will be released," he began. "You must not riot or in any way create a disturbance." His ponderous voice slowly prolonged the moment.

Elena stood frozen beside Silvia. She licked her lips nervously as she watched the speaker.

"I will read your names alphabetically. If your names are called, step outside into the corridor."

He began to read the names. The entire room of sixty women was as silent as a tomb.

One name was read. A woman burst into tears and started forward. Soon another joined her outside the cell.

"Boghian, Elena."

Elena's hand flew to her throat. She was called! Her heart leaped with joy!

"Go!" Silvia whispered to her.

Wildly, Elena looked at Silvia with appealing eyes. Then, remembering what she was supposed to do, she walked toward the door. She was outside her cell!

She wanted to wait to see if Silvia's name would be called, but as soon as a group of ten were gathered in the corridor, they were marched toward the far end of the building.

"Take your possessions and leave the uniforms in this room!"

Elena eagerly reached for her clothes. Her own clothes! She had not seen them since she had been forced to wear the despicable uniforms. Her fingers lingered over the soft fabric of her blouse.

The pictures of her family! Her Bible! Her jacket! Almost delirious with emotions, Elena lifted her few belongings.

"Go! You must leave now."

Elena glanced wildly around for Silvia. She was not in sight. Oh! Had she been kept behind? What should she do?

Elena followed several others toward the gate that guarded their part of the prison. It stood wide open! They walked quickly through that one, made a left turn, and headed for the front gate that opened up to the outside. To freedom!

They quickened their pace. Only ten more meters to the gate!

"Stop!" A man's voice came from behind them. "No, Boghian! You may not leave! Stop!"

Elena turned in horror. Surely the command was not for her!

"Boghian! You must stop!" He yelled to the guard at the gate. "Do not set her free!"

She stopped. A numbness began in her heart and crept all throughout her body. Something terrible was happening!

"There was a mistake," she dimly heard a man explain heartlessly. "Your name should not have been called. You must complete your sentence for having tried to escape our country. Report back to your cell!"

Weeping silently, Elena turned. Back to the room she had so recently vacated.

Take off your own clothes. Put on the hated uniform. Never mind that the uniform that was thrown is not the same one you took off just fifteen minutes before. Never mind the smell of another woman's sweat clinging to the dirty outfit. Put it on.

The sight of her pictures and her small Bible brought on an emotion that caused Elena to make a bold move. When the guard was not looking, she slipped the pictures under her too large uniform. She did not dare take the Bible because the guard began looking suspiciously at her.

A guard took her back to her cell and locked the door behind her. Elena found herself in a strangely empty place. All the other inmates had either been released or sent out to work. Elena sank onto her bed. Her legs were trembling and she had no idea what to do.

Was Silvia free? Did she realize by now that Elena had not been released after all? Or had her name never been called? Was she somewhere in the sewing factory?

The sound of the cell door opening came clearly to her in the quiet cell. Silvia came in.

"Oh, Elena!" she cried. "I thought you were free! Your name was called! Why are you back?"

It took awhile to piece together what had happened. Silvia's name had also been called, but she, too, had been called back before she had reached the last gate!

At first they wept, as the realization dawned on them that they would probably serve the rest of their prison sentence. Then they tried to figure out why this had happened.

"Do you suppose," Elena asked, "that they did this just to further torment and persecute us? I would much rather not have had my name called at all, than to have gone through this emotional turmoil: wondering whether my name will be called, having it called, getting my things, and walking out only to be sent back to this cell again."

Silvia agreed. "Elena, I don't know if this was all planned or not, but I do know that there are no surprises with God. That's why we can trust that He never makes any mistakes. He must have allowed this to happen to strengthen our faith somehow."

Elena nodded. "I know. But it is strange. As much as the reality has set in, I'm surprised I don't have a greater sense of loss. I wonder if I ever really believed that we'd get out of here. And Silvia, I'm willing to be where the Lord wants me, even if it's in prison!"

The next day they were sent back to the sewing factory. Elena once more occupied herself marking patterns. The day seemed no different than any other day.

That night, however, Elena could not sleep. When Silvia began her night watch after midnight, Elena joined her. She had suddenly remembered her pictures. After everyone else was asleep, she showed them to her friend.

The two looked at the pictures. They flipped through them again and again.

"You look funny here," Silvia chuckled, holding up a picture that showed Elena strutting around a sports stadium with a group of gymnasts.

Elena looked over Silvia's shoulder. She saw herself, a straight, slim young girl of twelve, holding a flag.

She giggled. "I know it's me, but it feels as though that's a person not even related to me! Only someone I knew at one time. Isn't that strange?"

"If that's not you, nor feels like you, how about this?" Silvia gave Elena a slight pinch.

Elena giggled and said, "I know it sounds strange but that's the way I feel!"

Whether it was a reaction to their dashed hopes or the opening of the window into her past that made Elena feel giddy, she did not know. But soon she and Silvia were laughing and giggling like school girls, stifling their laughter with their hands lest they wake the sleeping women.

"Boghian! Tarniceriu!" The guard spoke through the cell door the next evening. "There has been a mistake. You will be released tomorrow."

Silvia and Elena looked at each other. Silvia rolled her eyes and grimaced.

"Not this time," she said grimly to Elena. "I will not let them torment me again with promised freedom. If they think they can trick us over and over again, they are wrong." She plopped down beside Elena.

"Oh, Silvia! What if it's true!" Elena couldn't help but feel a small fountain of hope bubble up inside her.

"I'm praying that God will simply give us peace wherever we are. I haven't given up hope in God, but my hope in man is not very strong right now."

They were both worn out and exhausted from having lost so much sleep the night before. The two girls fell into slumber. Quietness descended upon the cell.

"Boghian! Tarniceriu!" The same guard was at the door.

Elena rubbed the sleep from her eyes.

"Come with me!" The two girls looked at each other in fear. Then they went to the door and waited until it was unlocked. They filed out into the corridor and into the same room they had been in a few days ago.

"Here are your clothes. You are released."

Again. They began to change their clothes, slowly this time.

"I don't have any of my clothes here," Silvia said. "My family took my things with them when they came to visit."

"Wear some of mine," Elena offered an extra outfit from her bag.

Silvia tried on the skirt and blouse. They were too small, but she gave a shrug and wore them anyway.

They left the prison uniforms on a pile on the floor. Elena shuddered as she looked at the clothes. How soon would she be putting the same clothes back on?

The first gate was open. Side by side, they walked through it and turned left again. The front gate, high and forbidding, loomed ahead of them. But it was standing open far enough for a person to slip through. A guard was in the little guard house, watching their approach.

"If this is another game, I sure hope they enjoy it," Silvia said grimly.

Elena did not answer. She could not keep hope from surging through her. They were so close! Just a few more steps!

Her ears strained for an order from behind them. She did not dare look back. Was that a noise? Her nerves felt as tightly strung as a stretched wire.

They were passing through the gate! Silvia was actually outside, and now she was too! Taking a deep breath, Elena tried to stay calm.

They heard the gate close behind them. They continued their walk. Would the guards wait longer this time? Would they suddenly come from behind and force them back?

Away from the prison they walked. One step at a time. They did not speak. They did not look back. They just walked forward, one step at a time.

The fields outside the prison looked enormous. The horizon stretched on and on. The air seemed suddenly cleaner, the sunshine warmer. They were free!

"Elena! Silvia!" Two people ran toward them, calling their names!

It was *Daniel Branzei* and his wife, Dana. The pastor from Bucuresti!

The girls began running too. They all began crying and laughing at the same time.

"Oh, girls, you are finally released! We have been waiting for you for three days!" Welcoming arms reached for them. They embraced and wept with joy. They were with friends! They were free!

Dashing the tears from his eyes, Daniel explained. "We read in the newspapers that the prisoners were being granted amnesty. Since so many people from the West had been praying and writing letters to our government, we knew the pressure was on to have you released. So, when we checked at the office in Bucuresti, we found your names posted on the list of released prisoners. We came here to greet you, but you were not among those released. So we went back to Bucuresti and demanded to know where you were. They didn't answer us right away and I told them we wouldn't leave their office until we were given an answer. After awhile they came back and told us there had been a mistake and that you would be released. So we hurried back, and now here you are!"

Elena could not believe it. They were free! Then she realized how they must look. She smoothed her hair and tried to straighten her wrinkled skirt.

"Come," the couple urged them. "Come back with us to our house. You can rest there before you go back to Iasi."

"Daniel," Silvia began, "I don't know if we are going back to Iasi. We don't know if we will be welcome back there again. We are—jailbirds, you know." She laughed a little.

Daniel stared at them. "What are you talking about? Not welcome! Oh, girls, you have no idea how many people are just waiting to hear from you! The believers have been praying for your release for months. People from many countries have been following your plight ever since your capture. Genovieva and many of her American friends have been writing letters to their congressmen and to our government."

Elena felt bewildered. For so long, they had felt forgotten by their families and friends. Now, suddenly, they found out what all had been happening since their arrest. People across the world had been praying and intervening for them. They had been far from forgotten!

"Aren't you hungry?" Dana asked in concern. "Are you feeling ill?"

Elena and Silvia shook their heads. They looked at the laden table and compared it with the prison food.

"No, thank-you, Dana. It—it's just too much. We haven't had anything like this for six months." Elena gestured toward the food and the house, trying to explain. "It's still so hard to believe that there could be a place like this."

"Yes, yes," Daniel sympathized. "It is a big change, too fast."

"Come, girls, I will show you where you can sleep. I'm sure you are weak from all the excitement." Dana was the perfect hostess, doing everything she could to make them comfortable.

The Branzei house was nothing more than a modest home, but it felt like a palace. Elena felt like a queen! She had taken a bath before supper and found herself almost forgetting how. All that water for one person! Soap! Shampoo! A large towel just for her!

Then all the months of living in dirty, unsanitary conditions flooded her memory, and she began scrubbing feverishly. She washed her hair twice, scrubbed her fingernails vigorously, and almost rubbed her skin through trying to get herself completely clean. Only the fact that Silvia was waiting to bathe finally made her emerge from the bathroom.

Now, after supper, ready for bed in the room prepared for them, the two girls were overwhelmed.

Elena burst into tears. Silvia, her own eyes wet, hugged her. "Don't cry, Elena. We are out! We are free! God has delivered us! Come, let's thank God for bringing us out, for freeing us . . ." Silvia's words trailed away. Overcome with emotion, she also began to weep.

The two friends knelt beside the soft bed and poured out their hearts to their Saviour, the Lord Jesus Christ. Their Deliverer!

21

Free or Not?

For to me to live is Christ, and to die is gain.

Philippians 1:21

"Elena! Silvia!" The group of people at the train station were as exuberant as any crowd could be under the shadow of communism. They waved flowers and called out to the girls as the train came to a stop in Iasi.

Elena was passed from one welcoming embrace to another. Laughing and crying, she accepted arm loads of flowers.

"Ah, Elena!" A foreign couple stepped forward.

"Mair! And Les!" Elena eagerly embraced her friends. "How is it possible that you are here? All the way from England!"

"Oh, Elena!" Mair exulted. "God has made it possible for us to see you! We were so worried that we would have to leave before you arrived! It is God's providence that we are here."

Les Peters gave Elena a hug. "We need to tell you how it happened. We will talk later."

As many as could went to the house where Genovieva's family lived. The Sfatcu home was always a ready haven for anyone who needed shelter or comfort.

Elena sat next to Silvia in the Sfatcu house. Their friends crowded around them. Les and Mair Peters, feeling very much a part of the welcoming group, were beaming at the happy reunion.

"Now tell us," Silvia turned to the English couple. "How did it happen that you are here at this time?"

"Well," Les began, "we were in prayer for our persecuted brothers and sisters, especially here in Romania, and the Spirit of God told us to come and visit.

"We motored across Europe and entered Romania. When we arrived here in Iasi, we asked for you two girls right away. You can imagine our disappointment when we found out you were not here, but in prison."

Elena felt her eyes fill with tears. She followed Les' words intently. Teodor, Genovieva's brother, was interpreting for the group.

Mair stroked Elena's hand and took up the account. "We had not heard," she said softly. "We wanted to see you so badly! Then we heard that you were to be released.

"We were so excited! But when you didn't come we didn't know what to do. Our visas would not allow us to extend our stay beyond today. And today you came!"

Someone began praying. Others joined in. Elena could not pray out loud, for her heart was too full for words. But in her spirit, she prayed. She rejoiced in her salvation. She thanked God for His abiding faithfulness and His loving care during the entire ordeal in prison. She even thanked God for allowing her to go through the pain of separation from her friends in order that she might learn to grow more completely dependent on her Saviour.

"Elena and Silvia, here is a package of clothes for you." Mair pushed a parcel into Elena's arms as she prepared to leave. "We were led to bring them along, but we didn't know who to give them to. Now we know!"

"Oh!" Elena gasped. "Thank-you!" They all waved good-bye as the Peters drove off in their car.

"Look, Silvia! A skirt and blouse for you! It looks like they should fit just right." Elena handed the clothes to Silvia.

"And an outfit for you!" Silvia laughed as she handed a suit to Elena. "How did they know our sizes?"

The clothes did fit. Perfectly.

"How good God is," Elena marveled. "Not only did He orchestrate our release from prison in time for us to meet the Peters, but through them He also provided clothes for us that fit perfectly!"

"I know we are no longer in prison," Silvia said one evening a few weeks later, "but I still sense a cloud of oppression hanging over me. I know we're still being shadowed by the secret police. More than once I've seen a man following us."

Elena was silent. "Oh, Lord," she prayed in her heart. "How long will it be before we are in trouble with the police again? How can we be delivered from this persecution?"

They had been able to rent a room from one of Silvia's relatives for a small sum. Neither of them were able to find jobs. At first, the directors of the places where they applied assured them they could come to work. But usually by the next day, the girls were told that no, they were sorry, there were no openings after all. Both girls realized that whenever the directors checked with their superiors, they were told not to hire them.

"We will not beg," Silvia said emphatically. "God will provide for us. But sometimes I wonder what we would eat if it were not for Tata and his daily bread."

"Silvia," Elena said hesitantly, "do you think anything will come of our requests for visas to go to the United States?" After they were released from prison, before leaving Bucuresti, Daniel had taken them to the American Embassy where they had applied for visas.

Silvia did not answer immediately. "I don't know," she said at last. "We are like people without a country. We can't work here and we can't leave. I feel as though we are suspended between two worlds." She looked around their small room. "At least we have a place to stay."

A gentle knock at the door startled them. Elena's hand flew to her throat.

"Who is there?" Silvia asked softly from inside the door.

"Teodor."

A sigh of relief escaped Elena's mouth.

"Come for a walk with me," Teodor said softly. "Both of you."

Elena looked at Teodor with wide eyes. Then she looked at Silvia.

It could only mean one thing. Another shipment of Bibles had arrived. Teodor needed help to unload them.

Silvia immediately prepared to leave. An inner battle raged in Elena. How could they do such a thing? They were already being watched! They had just come out of jail! They were already under suspicion for having met foreigners! Wasn't it foolish to endanger their lives further?

Whosoever puts his hand to the plow and looks back is not fit for the kingdom of God. The words came clearly to Elena.

Her response was immediate. She would go along and help. She would do whatever God gave her to do.

Silvia smiled at her. Elena knew she had seen her turmoil. She smiled back.

Yes, Elena decided, even if it meant arrest, she was willing to be a part of the work of the Lord. Gladly, even eagerly, she followed the other two out the door, ready to be involved in something worthwhile again. The danger was great, but her trust in God was greater. She was willing to risk her life for Him—had not her Saviour given His life for her?

The work was hard. The Bible packages needed to be moved quickly. It was long after midnight before they finished and Teodor walked them home.

"Good night, and God bless you for helping," he said as he turned to go.

"Good night, Teodor," they said. Closing the door, they opened the package addressed to them that they had found in the shipment.

"Songbooks!" Silvia said in awe. "Genovieva's songbooks!" She lifted Volumes I, II, and III out of the package.

They both paged through the children's books. Colored pictures illustrated the songs. Silvia softly hummed several tunes.

"Here is something else," Elena said, looking inside the package. "An envelope!"

She opened the envelope. "Oh, look, Silvia! Someone sent money for us!" Elena quickly counted the bills. "What a gift, just when we were desperate! This is a month's wages!"

"What?" Silvia gasped. "Oh, Elena! We can eat!"

Folding the money to her breast, Elena knelt down beside the cot. Silvia joined her and the two girls pledged their trust and confidence to God once again. Step by step, they were being fashioned and shaped to put all their faith in the One who promised them His unfailing love and care.

Elena shivered and hunched over, trying to shield herself from the chilly autumn wind that blew down from the hills. She held on to the side of the horse-drawn wagon with one hand to steady herself.

The horse plodded steadily on. Elena was not sure where she was, but she did not ask the pastor, *Gheorghe Mitrofan*, or his wife, *Catela*, any questions. She was not in charge; she was merely going along to gather information.

It had all happened so smoothly. In her daily prayers, Elena continually asked God for a purpose in her life. There seemed to be no reason to live in Romania anymore. No jobs were open to her—she and Silvia had both tried numerous times.

They had decided to apply for passports to leave Romania. True, it was risky to remind the government of their existence, but it was also risky to stay in a country that refused to give them work. Anyone without a job was considered a parasite in the country and could be arrested. Yet, they could not get jobs because of their prison records.

The officer in Suceava had been scornful when Elena applied for her passport. She had definitely felt his antagonism, and hopelessness threatened to overtake her. But she had gathered courage and applied anyway.

Meanwhile, Genovieva had written her and asked her to gather addresses and information about poor, Christian, village families who needed assistance. She would need to smuggle these addresses back to America through the Bible couriers who came into their country.

That was why Elena was on the wagon with the Mitrofans. They had agreed to help her contact poor families from a village they worked in.

Elena smoothed her dark skirt, sprigged with little flowers. She had tried to dress like the villagers, wanting to blend in with the local people.

The houses lining the road as they entered the village were all enclosed behind wooden fences. Wisps of smoke struggled from the chimneys. A flock of geese, hissing and honking, crossed the street ahead of the wagon.

"Whoa!" the driver yelled to his horse. The wagon came to a halt. Gheorghe nodded at Elena, and she got off with him and his wife. Darkness was already falling around the village, gathering all the shadows to itself.

Elena followed the couple as they walked down the sidewalk. She skirted a water puddle on the packed dirt walkway.

"This is the first place," Gheorghe said as he pushed open a wooden gate. It screeched protestingly.

The little house was scarcely more than a hut. The roof came down around the walls, shading the windows and creating deep shadows under the eaves.

The pastor knocked on the front door. There was no answer.

"Perhaps no one is at home," Catela said softly. She stepped to the window and tried to peer inside.

Elena heard a soft shuffling sound. Then the doorknob turned and the door opened a crack.

"Pace!" The pastor said in a cheerful voice. "It is Gheorghe and Catela Mitrofan and a friend. May we come in?"

"Ahh! The pastor!" The door opened wide. "Come in, come in!" welcomed the elderly woman. They filed inside.

In the dim light Elena took in the tiny, one-room dwelling. A mud stove took up a large part of the room. On the warming shelf lay an old man. His eyes were bright as he looked at the visitors.

"Look who's here," the woman said as she went over to her husband. "It is Brother Mitrofan and his wife. And," she turned curious, friendly eyes toward Elena, "who are you?"

Elena introduced herself. She sat beside Catela on the bed.

Pumpkin seeds were roasting on top of the stove. She looked around the room. It was clean and tidy, but it was obvious that these people were very, very poor.

"We came to pray with you and to bring you greetings from the brethren," Gheorghe said lovingly.

Something moved under the cot where Elena was sitting. She glanced at Catela, then gave a sudden gasp as a small, pink form shot out from under the cot, right between her legs!

Disturbed by the visitors, the little pig circled the room, complaining with a series of low grunts. Then he disappeared under the table.

The woman chuckled. "Our son gave him to us. That was the runt of the litter and we want to keep him over winter before we sell him. But we keep him warm in here. It's too cold to keep him outside at night anymore."

"Is your son working now?" Gheorghe asked.

"Yes. He is working in the fields with the corn. But there is very little pay and no food. We keep their children here during the day because Maria works too."

"How many children do they have?" Catela inquired.

"Six. Ioan is eight and the baby is not even half a year old. They are a lot of work for us, but we do what we can."

Elena's eyes misted in tears. Memories of her own childhood came to her vividly.

"What did you have for your supper?" wondered Gheorghe.

The old woman sighed. She turned her head toward her husband. "Well, we had some beans that I cooked. They are hard for him to digest, but that is all I had."

"No mamaliga?" Catela asked. Even poor people had mamaliga.

"No, we are out of corn meal." The words were not said in a complaining way, but merely stated as the truth.

"We will pray and ask the Lord to provide for you," Gheorghe said. He led them in a prayer as they knelt on the dirt floor. The old man sighed and closed his eyes.

"Silvia! Such poverty! We visited more than twenty homes and there are many, many poor families there. We have only begun!" Elena told her friend.

Her pen flew over the papers. *Names. Addresses. Number of children in the family. The needs. Clothing. Bedding. Food. But mostly, nutritious food.*

"Have you already sent out some lists?" Silvia asked softly. She glanced toward the window of their rented room.

Elena nodded. "With the last visitors," she answered in a low voice.

Week after week, she went into the villages with different pastors. The pastors provided the addresses and she gleaned information from their visits. Then she carefully recorded the details and hid them until someone from the West arrived and she could safely send it with them, across the border and on to Ohio.

Each time she tried to warn the visitors of the risk they were taking. "It's extremely dangerous for you to be caught with these addresses. If you are not willing to take the risk, don't do it. But if you are, the poor families will be ever so grateful to you, for they will receive food parcels from sponsors in America."

No one refused. Elena never knew how many lists actually got back to Christian Aid for Romania, but she knew that many did. The poor families began receiving food parcels.

"Oh, thank-you! God has blessed us so richly!" With tears, people thanked her if she visited their homes after a package had arrived. Mothers knelt on the floor in front of her, kissing her hands.

Elena often knelt with them, and together they thanked the Lord for the kindness of the Christians in America who willingly shared with them.

Elena's own financial problems were solved through this work. Even though funds did not come regularly, there was always enough to buy food. Visitors slipped money to her along with notes from Genovieva.

Dangerous work? Definitely. But Elena continued, trying to be as cautious as she knew how, yet willing to travel many weary miles by bus and wagon and even on foot to gather addresses and information to help her people.

She continued to go to the government office in Suceava and inquire about her passport. She felt the net closing around them. Silvia was going to the office in Iasi; she, too, was waiting for a passport.

They knew it was dangerous to continually visit the passport offices.

Each visit they made again reminded the government of their presence, and invited further surveillance and hostility. Yet they felt they must. It would only be a matter of time, they sensed, before they would once more be in the hands of the law and imprisoned.

"Sir, I have come to inquire about my passport," Elena felt a calm boldness that was not at all like her former self. Something about having gone through the rigors of prison gave her a feeling of resignation about the whole matter. What would happen would happen.

"You are crazy! Get rid of your wild idea about leaving the country!" the officer yelled at her.

"I can't get a job here. I may as well leave," Elena said clearly. "Please tell me what the status is of my application."

"You want to talk to us? Well, you may soon be talking to us from behind bars!"

Elena did not flinch at the threat. "Can you please tell me where my application is?" she repeated.

"Get out!" The words were flung at her. "Stop coming here!"

"Now what is it that you want us to do for you?" The officer's rude tone grated unpleasantly on her ears.

This time she had been called to the office. Elena had gone with a dim hope that maybe her passport was being processed.

"I want to receive my passport for immigration," Elena said.

The officer fumbled under the desk. Then he asked pleasantly, "Do you want to immigrate to the same place where your visitors from last week live?"

Elena felt prickles running up into her scalp. They knew about those visitors? She had given them lists of names! Names of needy families.

"Is that where you want to immigrate to? From where did your visitors come?" The officer reached under his desk again.

"What does that have to do with my passport?" Elena asked boldly. "I refuse to answer your questions, for you are recording this conversation."

The officer tried to look surprised. Taking his hand out from under the desk, he said smoothly, "Why would I do such a thing?"

Elena did not reply.

"You are the one who tried to escape. Where did you get the money to pay those criminals who helped you escape?"

Elena looked at him steadily without saying a word. She was sure the tape recorder was still recording the conversation. Or rather, his questioning.

"Here, take this paper and state why you want to emigrate. Write that you tried to leave illegally and that you were caught. Write the names of the people who helped you and who were with you."

Elena took the paper. She crumpled it and dropped it back on the desk. "I have already been punished for the crime of trying to escape. I do not believe it is legal for you to try to get a statement from me on this matter. I am here today to check on my passport status."

No longer did the officer try to speak pleasantly. "Get out of here!" he roared. "You will never get a passport! You live in Romania and you will die in Romania." He paused, then said ominously, "Maybe sooner than you think!" He shoved her out of his office.

They could no longer stay in their rented room. It was too dangerous, not only for them, but also for their landlady.

"Every week someone comes and asks about you," she told Silvia. "I'm sorry, but this is making it too dangerous for me and my family."

The girls did not want anything to happen to anyone else because of them so they stayed with various friends or lived in the room in the church where Genovieva had lived. They kept on the move to make it difficult for them to be shadowed.

Again and again, they applied for passports. In response, they were given seemingly impossible tasks, such as getting signatures from different officials.

But they kept trying. Whenever she could, Genovieva wrote that she and her friends were doing all they could to put pressure on the Romanian government to release them. She also wrote, "David Troyer and his wife Erma told me to tell you that they are building bedrooms onto their house. Three bedrooms. One for Silvia, one for Elena, and one for Genovieva. There will be three desks in the office. One for Silvia, one for Elena, and one for Genovieva."

This moved them deeply. By faith, this family was preparing for their arrival, believing God somehow would work a miracle so they could immigrate to America.

"Well," Elena said one day as they once again were thrown out of the passport offices. "God parted the waters of the Red Sea for the Israelites, and I know He can still do miracles for us."

22
Left Behind for a While

With men this is impossible; but with God all things are possible.

Matthew 19:26b

Silvia, followed by David and Erma Troyer, walked into the office. Tensely, Elena clutched her purse to her chest.

So much had happened so suddenly. The visitors from America had come to Romania to see if they could in any way speed up the process for Elena and Silvia's passports. The Troyers, along with Paul and Barbara Ann Miller, had traveled with the girls to the Bucuresti passport office.

Now, Elena was left to wait with Paul and Barbara. "Please, to sit," she motioned to her guests.

"No, no. You sit down," Barbara Ann protested.

"You must to sit down," Elena said, as firmly as her broken English allowed. She motioned the couple to the two chairs outside the office. "I sit here," Elena perched herself on the window sill, moving a potted plant to one side.

They heard loud voices from the office.

Elena bowed her head. "Oh, merciful Father! Please help us!" That was all she could think to pray. Words failed her.

It was now over a year since she and Silvia had been released from prison. Life was getting more difficult all the time. They were openly followed as they tried to go about their duties. They were constantly interrogated about their foreign visitors and harassed whenever they went to check on the status of their passport requests.

Paul and Barbara Ann, seeing the tension that Elena was under, bowed their heads also. They, too, longed to see the girls released. Genovieva had told them of the difficulties the girls were experiencing. They sensed the cloud that hovered over the girls as they lived constantly under the threat of arrest and imprisonment.

Elena's thoughts churned. Would the government grant them passports? Would they be gracious and kind while the visitors were here, then make it difficult for them after the guests left? What would happen if they were continually denied? Would they carry out their threats and arrest and imprison them again?

Suddenly the door opened. One look at her friend's face, and Elena knew that Silvia had good news. A smile covered her face as she excitedly told them, "They promised me a passport! Oh, Elena, you must go in and ask about your passport too! We must leave together!"

Spurred on by Silvia's good news, Elena entered the office. When David and Erma tried to follow her, they were ordered out.

Elena's heart sank. They had been allowed to accompany Silvia!

"What is your name?"

She swallowed. "Elena Boghian."

"What do you want?"

"I want to check on the status of my passport. I am Silvia's friend." The words wanted to tumble out. "We are applying for immigration passports. Silvia and I want to leave together."

There was a long, cold silence. Then, in measured tones, the officer spoke. "You are trying to leave the country. You, who have received so much help from the State. You have been educated by the State. You have been clothed and fed by the state in your childhood. Now you want to leave! Do you realize how much you owe the State?"

Elena blinked her eyes rapidly. She opened her mouth to get more air. "I—I want to leave with Silvia. Please."

"Leave? You will not leave!" The officer raised his voice. "You have cost the State twenty thousand dollars! There is no way you can leave without paying your debt to the State!"

Feeling as though someone had punched her in the stomach, Elena reached out for support against the wall. A low moan escaped her.

"Now go! Go tell your American friends that you cannot leave until your debt is paid!"

Elena stumbled from the office. She tried to compose herself, but could not.

"Oh, Elena! No!" Silvia moved up alongside her.

Tears blinding her steps, she allowed them to lead her out of the building.

She began sobbing.

"Elena! What did they say? Why did they deny you the passport?"

"They said—" she gasped for breath. "They said—I have to pay for my education first." Elena turned her tear-streaked face away and broke out in fresh sobs.

"Oh, Elena! How is that possible?" Silvia turned to their guests and relayed what Elena had said.

There was a sympathetic murmur of voices from the little group. But there was nothing any of them could do.

The four visitors from America had to leave for their return flight. Before they left, they tried to encourage the distraught Elena. After they had prayed together, the Americans left for the airport.

The two girls returned to Iasi on the train.

Silvia did not try to comfort her stricken friend with words, but kept a tight hold on her arm. When Elena could not control her emotions, she gently placed her hand on Elena's head and drew the weeping girl to her.

"Elena! Look at this." Costica held out a newspaper. "See? This article says that anyone who wants to leave the country has to pay for their education first. In US dollars, mind you!"

Elena looked. In dollars! How utterly impossible! It was illegal for Romanians to even own foreign money. Now the government was demanding dollars for payment! How ridiculous!

She pushed the paper away. There was no way she could even think of paying for her release. She still had debts to pay for their prior escape. In addition, she had no job. The only money she had was what she received from Ohio for gathering addresses of the poor families.

To watch Silvia preparing for her departure was torture. Silvia had offered to stay, but Elena had been firm on that point. "No, Silvia, you must go. There is no use for you to stay here when you have the opportunity to leave. You must go. If you stay, there will just be another person for the secret police to shadow."

It was two months before Silvia's paperwork was completed. Finally, all the proper documents had arrived and Silvia made plans to leave. Her ticket was dated for her to leave in two weeks.

Silvia's many friends and relatives came to the Sfatcu home to say farewell. There were farewell songs and impromptu prayer meetings. The well-wishers crowded the small house.

Elena tried to keep her emotions in check. She and Silvia had spent the night at the Sfatcus and Elena had cried most of the night. Her lips felt numb.

"Mama Sfatcu! Telephone for you!" someone called, holding out the receiver toward Genovieva's mother.

"It's Genovieva!" Maria Sfatcu called out. An excited hush fell over the room.

For some reason, Elena felt the tears welling up again. She buried her head and began to sob.

"Yes, Silvia is coming!" Mama Sfatcu said loudly into the telephone. "Soon she is leaving for Bucuresti! Yes, we love you too, Genovieva! Yes, I will tell your friends you send greetings. Elena? Oh, Genovieva! Talk to her! She is crying so much we are afraid she will be sick! Talk to her, Genovieva!" She turned from the phone. "Elena! Come! It is Genovieva!"

Elena gulped back a sob and took the receiver. She stepped around the corner. "Hello!" she said as loudly as she could into the phone.

"Elena! How are you?"

Elena's face crumpled. "Oh, Genovieva, my hope for living is gone. I don't know what will happen with my life! I don't know how to start again. I don't know what to do!" The tears flowed faster.

"Elena! Don't cry! Listen to me. Maybe this is not a closed door. The door may still open. If it is God's will, you will come to America!"

"Genovieva, do you understand? I would have to pay twenty thousand US dollars for my education first. Twenty thousand! I can never pay that. I still have other debts I do not know how I can ever pay. It would take the rest of my life to pay this big amount."

"Elena, we have a Father in heaven who is rich. This is nothing for Him. He specializes in impossibilities. Be encouraged and take everything to Him in prayer."

For some reason, a small spark of hope flickered within Elena's heart. She thanked Genovieva for her encouragement.

The future stretched out into the unknown. Elena occupied herself in gathering addresses and faithfully copying them for *Christian Aid for Romania*. Whenever she spent time with Silvia, which was often, she tried to join in her friend's excitement in leaving for America. But it was always with a heavy heart that she was reminded of the painful parting that was imminent.

"I don't know why God is leading us apart this way," Elena said sorrowfully one day. "Perhaps it is to teach me to depend totally on Him. Maybe I have been gathering too much strength from you, Silvia. I thought I had learned that lesson when we were separated that time in prison. I guess I need another lesson."

"Oh, Elena!" Silvia protested. "Don't you realize how much your faith in Christ has challenged me? You were always steadfast in your trust in God. Just to have you as my friend means so much to me. I will miss you so!" Thoughtfully, she said, "I think this is the most difficult time I have experienced. I am torn between the desire to leave and the desire to stay here with my family and friends." She paused again. "But one thing I know, I want to be in the center of God's will. Wherever He leads me."

The day of Silvia's departure finally came. Along with a group of friends, Elena accompanied Silvia to Bucuresti. While they were in a friend's house in the city, the telephone rang. "Elena, it is for you!" The hostess handed her the phone.

In surprise, Elena took the receiver. "Hello!"

"Elena, this is Genovieva! Oh, Elena, I have good news for you! We have been praying and contacting people here in America about your situation. Elena, listen! God has moved in the hearts of our friends and they have raised twenty thousand dollars for your release! The money is being wired to a bank in Romania where it will be available to the government when you are released!"

Elena couldn't speak. The shock of the stupendous news engulfed her entire being. Twenty thousand dollars! How was such a thing possible?

"Elena, are you there?" Genovieva's voice brought her back to reality.

"Yes," Elena said weakly. "Oh, how can I ever pay it all back?"

"No, you don't understand. This money is a gift. You will not need to pay it back. This is for your release."

"Genovieva!" Elena gasped. "Oh, Genovieva! Silvia is leaving today! And now you have given me this news! How can I take it all in?"

Genovieva chuckled. "Well, I guess you'll just have to."

Placing the telephone back in its cradle, Elena stood for a moment without speaking. She looked around the room at all her friends. She felt dizzy. What was happening to her? Was it really possible that she had just spoken to Genovieva? Had she heard correctly that money was being sent to Romania for her release?

"Elena!" Silvia burst through the door. "There you are! Who was on the phone?"

"It—it was Genovieva! She told me the Americans donated the money I need to pay for my education!"

Silvia gasped. "Oh, Elena! That is wonderful! This makes parting so much easier!" She hugged her friend.

The following hours flew by in a blur. Silvia bade them all farewell, then boarded the plane. Her last words to Elena were, "I will be waiting for you. Come soon!"

Elena's new-found hope made the good-byes a little easier. "*Come soon!*" That was something worth hanging on to.

"*Sora* Maria, how can I take the money?" Elena asked in anguish. She had come to ask advice from this Godly sister whom she greatly admired and respected. "When I think of all the poor people I have visited in the villages, I know this money could be used to give them much-needed food. But if I take this money for my release and give it to the government, they will just use it for themselves. I am torn apart by my dilemma."

"Have you asked God what He wants you to do?" Maria asked gently.

"Yes! I have prayed and fasted and still am not settled. I tell God that I want only what He wants, and all the time I feel guilty to have all this money spent on me. At first I could only think of leaving Romania and going to America! But gradually, this other thing—this guilt—began to plague my life."

"Since you are willing to do whatever God wants you to," Maria said thoughtfully, "you are in the right frame of mind to find out the will of God.

"One thing we should keep in mind. We think of money as much or little. With God, it is not so. A thousand lei to Him means no more than one leu. Remember the poor widow who cast in only a little coin? Jesus said that she gave more than all the rest. It was the attitude she had."

"Oh, I see!" mused Elena. "I hadn't thought of it that way." She paused. "What I do think of all the time is the kind and generous people who gave the money. I know that God sees their generosity. Surely He will reward them for being willing to help me. They don't even know me!"

"That's what the community of believers does— cares for each other."

Maria continued wisely, "Elena, they cared enough to give you the money. I think you ought to accept the gift and make preparations to leave. Surely this is all the hand of God, and He must want you in America for a reason."

Elena nodded. "I guess I feel guilty that our government will get all those good people's money. I will have to sign a paper stating that I consent to give the money in the bank to the State. It grieves me to have to do this."

"You will have the strength to do the right thing," Maria placed her hand on Elena's shoulder. "Come, let's pray about this matter. I have every confidence that God will lead you in the right direction."

Elena left Sora Maria's apartment, more settled about her course than ever before. "God, I thank You for Your wonderful love to me. Thank-you for speaking through Sora Maria! Thank-you for guiding me in this matter."

23
A Goal Reached

And he said unto them, Verily I say unto you,
There is no man that hath left house, or parents, or brethren,
or wife, or children, for the kingdom of God's sake,
who shall not receive manifold more in this present time,
and in the world to come life everlasting.

Luke 18:29-30b

"*Domnisoara* Boghian," the officer at the passport office said politely, "we are working on your passport for immigration. We will notify you as soon as the paper work is done."

Elena marveled at the transformation! Before, whenever she had asked about the status of her passport, she had been treated rudely and sarcastically. She remembered the times when she had been threatened by this very man.

"Your friends in America must be very rich," the officer continued, looking at her intently. Elena could see curiosity on his face. She was sure he had never encountered anything like this before.

"My friends in America are believers. They really care what happens to us here in Romania," Elena told him sincerely. "That is what happens when God rules people's hearts."

"Twenty thousand dollars!" he said admiringly. "That is a lot of money for one person." Then he added, "But there is one more thing that must be taken care of. You must sign this paper renouncing your Romanian citizenship. By signing, you are testifying that you voluntarily give up your rights and privileges as a citizen. You will no longer enjoy the benefits of our country, you will not be allowed to obtain a job, and you will need special permission to visit here."

Elena swallowed. This was more difficult than she had imagined. To give up citizenship of her own country! To declare that she no longer belonged in the place where she was born! Was she denying her heritage? Her family had been in Romania for as long as anyone could remember. Could she renounce all this?

She picked up the pen. Yes, she would sign. Jesus said in the Bible that His kingdom is not of this world. It is a heavenly kingdom. Yes, it was difficult to think of leaving the land of her birth and of her fathers, but she felt confident that the Spirit was leading her to make this move. With a sure hand she signed her name: Elena Boghian.

"You must pay us a fee for this paper," the officer told her.

Pay to give up her citizenship! How strange! Then she realized that this was probably just another way to get more money from her before she left. She paid the fee and left the office.

As she walked out onto the sidewalk, she felt different. She was no longer a citizen of Romania! That fact made her surroundings seem unreal. The street was the same, the linden trees lining the sidewalk were the same, and the people walking along the road were the same. Yet they all looked different. These things no longer belonged to her. She was now a stranger without an earthly country.

The hot September sun bore down on the streets of Suceava as Elena climbed the familiar steps to the office. The passport agency had called and told her to come in. In spite of the assurance that she would get her passport once the money was paid, she still felt apprehensive. Would they really let her leave? They could "change their minds" as they had done so often before. Even the threat of another jail term hung over her like a dark cloud. She no longer had her Romanian ID card. She could be arrested simply because she did not have a form of identification.

"Boghian, Elena!" The same officer was there. This time his voice was cold and distant. "Here is your passport."

Elena reached out and took it. She looked intently at the official document, then back at the officer. How was this possible? She had not signed for the money to be transferred from the bank to the passport agency! Now she was handed her passport with no mention of the money she owed the state! Had they somehow confiscated the money?

She could not leave without knowing. "What—what about the money?" she stammered.

"Take the passport and go! We don't need the Americans' money! Get out!" The anger in the officer's voice made Elena recoil. She turned and quickly left.

Even as she was running down the steps outside, the amazing thought continued to fill her mind. The money was safe! For some reason, she did not have to pay!

"I have the passport!" She was laughing and crying at the same moment.

Her sister Lidia and her husband, *Gicu*, were the first ones to hear the good news.

"They didn't even make me sign for the money! They just gave me my passport and told me to leave. He said they didn't need the Americans' money!" Elena tried to tell them everything that had happened. She could barely control her emotions. The relief of finally getting her passport and the shock of not having to pay for it overwhelmed her.

As soon as she could, she called her friends in Iasi and told them the wonderful news. She made a call to America and relayed the marvelous message that she had her passport and the money was still in the account at the bank.

Oh, how Elena rejoiced! The heavy weight that had made her hesitate to accept the money for her ransom was gone. Now the money could be returned to the donors or used to help needy people.* Oh, praise the Lord! Her heart sang!

There was a nip in the autumn air as Elena darted up the two steps into her childhood home. "Mama!" she called excitedly. "The youth from Iasi just got off the bus! I'm going to meet them!"

Elena dashed back outside, running out through the yard and into the street. She turned the corner and saw the street filling with people.

"Elena!" called her neighbor *Miziuca* as she saw the hurrying girl on the sidewalk. "Are you getting married?"

"No, Tanti Miziuca!" Elena bubbled. "My friends are coming to see me!"

Miziuca stared in astonishment as more than thirty youth swarmed toward them.

Elena greeted them joyfully. These were her friends! Her brothers and sisters!

"We want to take a hike!" they cried.

"Let's go up the hill!"

"Remember, Elena, where you took us the other time!" Their voices filled

**By this time, the law that required all emigrants to pay for their education had been cancelled.*

the street with life and laughter.

Elena's siblings and the young people from the village joined the visitors. The crowd crossed the river and began climbing the steep slope up the hill.

"This is the same hill I climbed so often in my childhood," Elena told her friend, *Magdalena*. "So many memories and scenes come back to me. Memories of going with Bunica to see the sick and the old ones. Memories of picking mushrooms and gathering firewood. Oh! The woods and hills of my youth! Will I ever see you again?"

They stopped for a rest. The village of Patrauti spread out below them. Elena could see her mother's house. She identified the familiar streets and homes of the neighbors. A lump rose in her throat.

Someone began to sing. The words and the melody soothed the emotions in Elena's breast.

For over an hour they sang and quoted Scripture verses. The harmonies rang out over the hills around them. They felt free! What if someone would see or hear them and report their activities? For the moment, they did not care. God was in their midst and nothing could disturb them.

Then they went back down to Elena's home and filled the little house with laughter and joyous singing. As many as were able crowded into the tiny kitchen and helped Elena's mother with the cooking.

Elena looked at her mother with love. "You enjoy all the activities, don't you, mama dear?"

Viorica looked at her daughter. "Yes, I enjoy all the young people. But my heart is saddened that I will not see you again!"

"Oh, Mama! Don't say that! I can't bear the idea yet!"

Elena's sister Lucia came into the kitchen. "Elena, some of us want to walk to the monastery. Shall we go now?"

Out into the streets they went, singing as they walked. When they reached the monastery, they filed inside.

"Please, sing for us!" a nun urged them. "I heard you singing in the streets, and you must sing here!"

The acoustics were wonderful. As the choir sang song after song, more and more nuns appeared in the doorways and stood in rapt attention.

"Oh, do not stop!" the nun in charge protested after the singing stopped. "We are getting a recorder to record the singing!"

With glad hearts, the choir continued. Truly, it was a surprise to be welcomed at this place. They used the opportunity to sing of their faith and trust in God.

Then they went back home to fill the little house with more singing and to spend the night. What did it matter that the house was filled to overflowing? Surely this is how it must have been when the early church was started.

The moving train picked up speed. Elena hung out the window, waving and waving. Face after face was lifted and "Good-bye! God bless you," echoed from person to person.

All Elena could do was wave. Tears streamed down her cheeks as the station in Suceava was left behind. She was on her way to Iasi to bid farewell to her friends there. Her airplane tickets had arrived and she was to leave December 10. Once the tickets had arrived, things happened in rapid succession. She had attended her last service at her mother's church and told the people good-bye. Thankfully, she was spared the farewells with her family just yet because most of them insisted they would come to Bucuresti to see her off.

Elena had turned her work with the needy families over to her brother Nicu. Her carefully-kept records, her contacts, her system of acknowledging receipt of the food parcels—all were entrusted to him.

The several days in Iasi were filled with intense emotions as Elena went to her church for the last time. The pastor, *Iosif Morcan*, asked her to speak to the people after the service.

"I want you to know how much you mean to me," Elena said in a quavering voice. "You have taught me what it means to have a family. A family of believers. You welcomed me when I was a timid, scared university student in need of knowing Jesus Christ in a personal way. Your friendliness and welcome reached out to me like loving arms. I will never forget that.

"To the children in the choir, I will always remember the wonderful times we had together, singing and traveling, sharing the love of God with many people. May you continue to grow in your understanding and love of the Lord." She turned back to the congregation.

"When Silvia and I were released from prison, you did not spurn us but continued to love us and support us. Thank-you!" Her voice cracked with emotion. She saw Sister Maria wipe her eyes.

"No matter where I am, I want to serve the Lord. He has saved me and I want to give everything to Him wherever I go. Now that I am leaving my people and my country, I feel the need of Him more than ever. Please remember me and pray for me." She sat down, spent.

"Elena!" It was dear Sora Maria addressing her young friend. "I want to give you a scripture verse to take with you as a farewell from me. In Genesis 22:14 we find the term 'Jehovah jireh.' That means 'in the mount of the Lord it shall be seen.' Remember when you were so troubled about the huge amount of money donated for your release? Remember how I told you that if the Christians from America gave this amount in the name of the Lord, then the Lord would use the money in His work even if it had to pass through the hands of the Communists? Elena dear, even as God has already moved in this matter, so remember that as you trust in God, all things shall be seen as He designs. 'Jehovah jireh!' "

Elena smiled through her tears at Sora Maria and nodded her head. She would never forget this dear sister who had been such an encouragement to her.

" 'The Lord watch between "us" and thee, when we are absent one from another,' " Pastor Morcan read from Genesis 31:49. "Elena, you have been living in uncertainty, but the Lord has kept His hand over you and protected you. He has been watching over you." He smiled at Elena. "Surely He will continue to watch over you in America too."

Visions of the kindnesses of Iosif and *Sanda* Morcan drifted through Elena's thoughts. When she and Silvia had been hiding from the police, many people had been afraid to give the two homeless girls a place to live. But the Morcans had been willing to let them stay in a back room of their home, regardless of the danger to themselves.

"'Let thy garments be always white; and let thy head lack no ointment.'" It was Sanda reading Ecclesiastes 9:8. "Elena, the Lord will clothe you with white as you keep your heart pure before Him."

Another woman rose from the pews. It was Mama Sfatcu. How Elena's heart yearned toward this second mother, who had sheltered her so often in the little house beside the Botanical Gardens. " 'The Lord hear thee in the day of trouble; the name of the God of Jacob defend thee . . .' " As Mama Sfatcu continued to read Psalm 20, Elena thought of how often God had used the Sfatcu home as a place of sanctuary. Yes, God had used this family to safely harbor her more than once in her days of trouble.

"Here is my encouragement for you, Elena," said *Danut Manastireanu*, the young people's Sunday school teacher. " 'I thank my God, making mention of thee always in my prayers, hearing of thy love and faith, which thou hast toward the Lord Jesus, and toward all saints; that the communication of thy faith may become effectual by the acknowledging of every good thing which is in you in Christ Jesus.' Philemon 4-6." He looked at

Elena. "Your faith has been an encouragement to many in our fellowship. We want to continue to hear of your love and faith in faraway America."

A young man rose to address Elena. It was Teodor, Genovieva's brother. He read from Ecclesiastes 7:14. " 'In the day of prosperity be joyful, but in the day of adversity consider . . .' I have seen Elena joyful, and in her adversity I have seen her consider the hand of the Lord." He turned to face her. "Elena, continue to consider the Lord and trust Him regardless of what happens in your future."

Smiling and weeping by turns, Elena absorbed every word. She wanted to memorize every precious detail as her brothers and sisters spoke their parting words to her. These people were a part of her life! How could she bear to leave them? It would be like leaving a part of herself behind.

She stayed with the Sfatcu family while waiting to leave for Bucuresti. Every evening until her departure, many friends came to bid farewell. If the secret police were still watching, they certainly saw the crowd of people come to spend time with Elena. But they did not interfere. The hand of God must surely have been with His people during this time.

The Branzai house in Bucuresti was crowded with people. All the chairs were full. Many of Elena's friends sat on the floor. Outside, night had already fallen, but sleep was far from anyone's mind. Time was relentlessly moving toward the next day and the moment Elena would begin her journey to America.

" 'He that dwelleth in the secret place of the most High shall abide under the shadow of the Almighty,' " Elena's mother read from Psalm 91. Her voice trembled as she continued reading the well-known Psalm.

Elena bowed her head and listened intently. How often had she heard her beloved mother read those verses? ". . . abide under the shadow of the Almighty!" Truly, if anyone had learned to do that, it was Viorica. Throughout her widowhood, she had learned to trust fully in her Lord. Now, she was passing these verses on to her departing daughter.

"We, too, have verses to read to you, dear sister," Gicu said soberly when Viorica had finished. "My verse is from Psalm 37. 'Delight thyself also in the Lord; and He shall give thee the desires of thine heart. Commit thy way unto the Lord; trust also in Him; and He shall bring it to pass.' Elena, continue to commit all your ways to the Lord and let Him bring into your life those things He wants to give you."

Lidia's soft voice followed her husband's. " 'Be thou my strong habitation, whereunto I may continually resort: thou hast given commandment to save me; for thou art my rock and my fortress . . . For thou art my hope, O Lord God: thou art my trust from my youth.' This is my prayer for you." She smiled an encouraging smile that caused Elena's heart to constrict. What a precious sister Lidia had been to her!

Then her niece Gina, Gicu and Lidia's daughter, read Isaiah 54:10. " 'For the mountains shall depart, and the hills be removed; but my kindness shall not depart from thee, neither shall the covenant of my peace be removed, saith the Lord that hath mercy on thee.' " The young girl smiled at her aunt. Elena smiled back.

One part of Elena felt this could not be real. How could it be that these were her last hours with her family and friends? Was she really leaving them all the next day? But another part of her was alert and attentive. She did not want to miss any of the encouraging verses that were given her. Busily, she wrote down the Bible references as the voices continued.

"I know that this verse will be more meaningful after you leave, but I want you to remember I Thessalonians 2:17. 'But we, brethren, being taken from you for a short time in presence . . .' " Mari's voice trembled. She swallowed and continued, " '. . . in presence, not in heart, endeavored the more abundantly to see your face with great desire.' " Elena reached over and grasped her youngest sister's hand. How sweet and precious Mari was to her!

Elena's brothers, Nicu and George, read their verses. " 'Cast not away therefore your confidence, which hath great recompence of reward.' "

" 'And the peace of God which passeth all understanding shall keep your hearts and minds through Christ Jesus. But my God shall supply all your need according to His riches in glory by Christ Jesus. Now unto God and our Father be glory for ever and ever. Amen.' "

Teodor Sfatcu quoted Psalm 121. " 'I will lift up mine eyes unto the hills . . .' "

His married sister Aurora read from Numbers. " 'The Lord bless thee, and keep thee . . .' Remember these verses, dear friend, as we part. And when you are in difficult times remember Isaiah 57:15. 'For thus saith the high and lofty One that inhabiteth eternity, whose name is Holy; I will dwell in the high and holy place, with him also that is of a contrite and humble spirit, to revive the spirit of the humble, and to revive the heart of the contrite ones.' "

Aurora's husband *Virgil* read from Psalm 139. " 'Whither shall I go from

Thy spirit? or whither shall I flee from Thy presence? . . . Even there shall Thy hand lead me, and Thy right hand shall hold me.' "

There was a stir from the three girls who sat at Elena's feet. With wistful eyes they looked at Elena. "Here are the verses we chose to read for you," *Mariana* said softly.

"Mine is from Ecclesiastes 3: 11," Carmen said in her clear voice. " 'He hath made everything beautiful in His time: also He hath set the world in their heart, so that no man can find out the work that God maketh from the beginning to the end.' I chose that verse because we cannot know what all God has in mind for His children. We do not know His ways, but we know Him." A pink flush spread over her fair cheeks.

Liliana read from Ephesians 6. " '. . . Above all, taking the shield of faith, wherewith ye shall be able to quench all the fiery darts of the wicked.' "

Then Mariana closed with Exodus 14. " '. . . The Lord shall fight for you, and ye shall hold your peace . . . . lift thou up thy rod . . . . go on dry ground through the midst of the sea.' Just as the children of Israel marched through the Red Sea on dry ground, the Lord will continue to make a plain path for the feet of our dear Elena."

"Thank-you, girls," Elena whispered huskily. These three girls had traveled from Iasi to Bucuresti to say good-bye. What sweet memories Elena had of the girls' choir and of hearing the pure voices of these girls as they lifted praises to God.

Elena closed her eyes, struggling to control her emotions. Feelings she had never before experienced were stirring deep down inside her, threatening to overwhelm her. "Oh, Jesus," she breathed, "be with me! I need You!"

"*May the Lord watch over you . . .*" Someone had begun a song. Softly the voices surrounded Elena. The words etched themselves deeply into Elena's heart. Yes! This journey was of the Lord. He would watch over her. He would give her strength to go through the wrenching good-byes of tomorrow. He would go with her into an unknown land. An unknown land, yes, but not an unknown God! Elena knew God. He was the known, the constant, the One element that would never change, no matter how uncertain her future was.

December 10, 1983. "Elena! Good-bye! God bless you with a safe journey!" Voices called from the small crowd of friends and family that traveled to the airport to see Elena off.

Eyes red from crying, Elena gave a farewell to each of them. Finally, she turned to her mother.

"Mama! Oh, Mama! How can I leave you?" She folded her mother in her arms. Viorica, a head shorter than her daughter, clung to her. Both were weeping. It was difficult for Elena to remove herself from her mother's embrace.

"Lady, it is time to go!" The stern voice of the ticket agent pulled them apart at last. Elena pushed her tickets and passport under the bars in front of the agent. She turned back to her mother.

"Here, Mama! Here is something for you!" She placed an envelope into her mother's hand. Then, retrieving her documents, she turned and walked toward the waiting airplane.

Viorica watched her daughter disappear. Then with trembling fingers, she opened the envelope. A picture! A picture of Elena!

She gazed at the likeness of her daughter who had just disappeared, perhaps forever. She turned the photograph over. There was something written on the back! Eagerly, she read:

December 1983

For my beloved Mother

Ruth 2:12 "The Lord recompense thy work, and a full reward be given thee of the Lord God of Israel, under whose wings thou art come to trust."

Genesis 31:49 "And Mizpah; for he said, The Lord watch between me and thee, when we are absent one from another."

When you are in trouble or on trial, tell the Lord:

** "My Father, I don't understand You, but I trust in You!" —and you will see that He will help you.*

** The harder the suffering, the greater will be His compassion toward you. Carry your cross and don't reject His help by complaining about the cross.*

** Someone is watching over you and will not leave you alone. Someone understands your fears and trials. - (God with His eternal love toward us!)*

** Trust in the power of prayer: prayer can change circumstances, trials, people, and things. The power of prayer has no margin!*

** "Delight thyself also in the Lord; and He shall give thee the desires of thine heart." Psalm. 37:4*

With deep love and missing you always,
the fourth flower from the bouquet of nine,
Elena

Epilogue

When Elena came to America in 1983, she did not know the English language. But she soon started to learn it and began working under Christian Aid Ministries (then Christian Aid for Romania). She wrote letters of thanks to those who gave money for her release from Romania, wrote receipts for other donations to CAM, and went on speaking tours with Silvia Tarniceriu. In 1984, she started to help send medicine parcels to Romanian doctors.

After Elena became a US citizen in November 1989, she tried to visit her family in Romania. But she was turned back without explanation after Romanian border officials searched the car for almost four hours. Little did she know that, two months later, the Communists would lose power in Romania, and she would be able to return with three trucks of humanitarian aid. This time, the same people who turned her away in November 1989 not only let her enter, but also gave her vouchers for gas, hotels, and restaurants. Only God can bring such changes!

Elena's mother, Viorica, came to live in the states in 1986. Two of Elena's sisters, Lidia (married to Gicu Cotlet) and Lucia, live here too.

May 30, 1992, marked a special day for Elena and Cornel Marza. It was their wedding day. They met in California, where Cornel had lived since 1984.

For some years, the couple spent part of each year in Romania and part in Ohio. They also traveled to Haiti and other countries to evaluate CAM's medicine distribution program.

Since 2001, Cornel and Elena spend most of their time in Romania. They are responsible to coordinate CAM's medicine program there, which helps thousands of people.

As a CAM staff member, Elena is faithful, energetic, and hardworking. Her goal is to understand where God wants her to be and obey His will. She wants to see the needs around her and be ready to do what God wants to bring a bit of His love to those who suffer.

About the Author

Harvey Yoder and his wife Karen live in the beautiful mountains of western North Carolina. They have five children, all of whom are married, as well as eight grandchildren. A teacher for many years, Harvey is now a licensed real estate agent in addition to being a prolific writer. He has traveled extensively while gathering materials for his many books, most of which have been published by Christian Aid Ministries. Harvey finds it especially fulfilling to write the inspiring accounts of faithful believers whose stories would otherwise remain unknown. His greatest desire in writing is that his readers will not merely be entertained by the stories, but rather be motivated to seek God with all their hearts.

Harvey enjoys hearing from readers and can be contacted by e-mail at harveYoder@juno.com or written in care of Christian Aid Ministries, P.O. Box 360, Berlin, Ohio, 44610.

Map of Romania

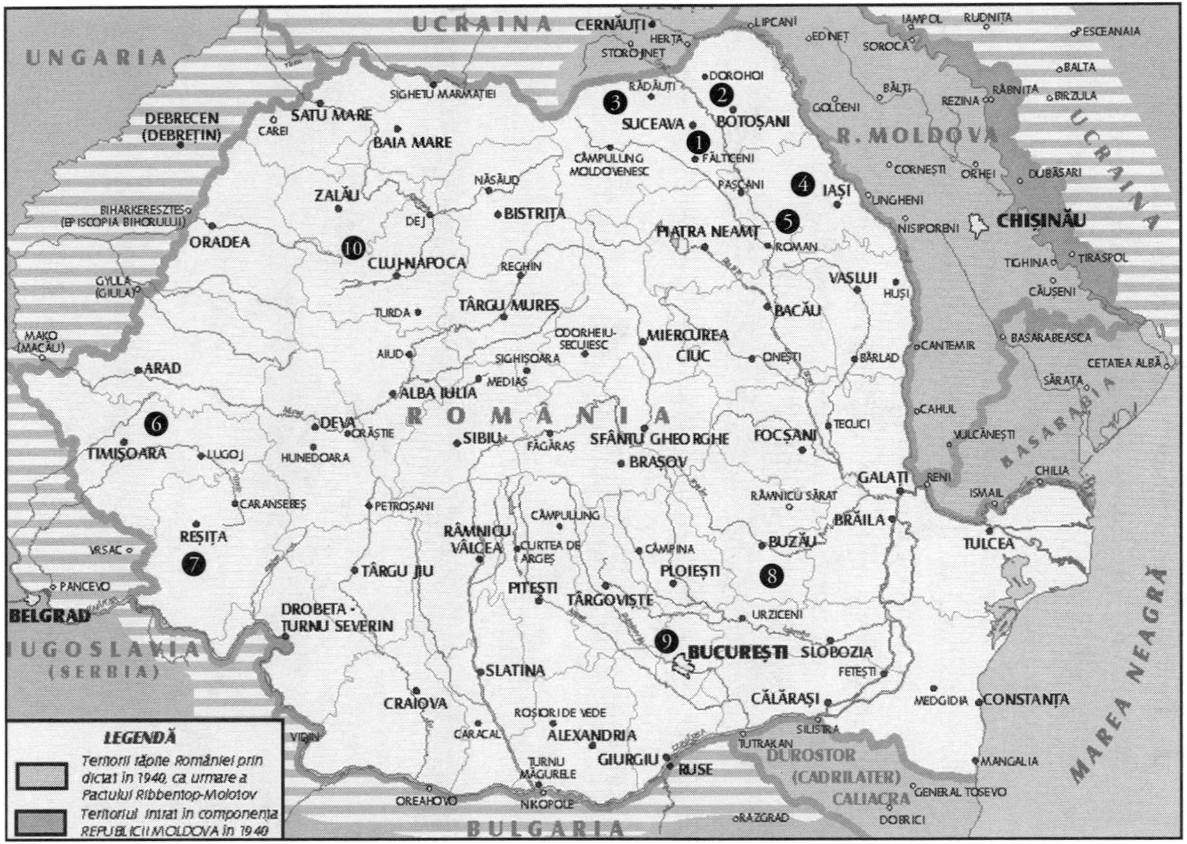

1. Patrauti (where Elena was born, and location of Christian Aid Ministries' warehouse)
2. Siret (boarding school)
3. Radauti (high school)
4. Iasi (college)
5. Bratulesti (where Elena worked on a collective farm)
6. Timisoara (first attempt to escape, and location of one prison where Elena was held)
7. Oravita (near where Elena made a second attempt to escape, and location of her first court trial)
8. Targsoru Nou (location of the third prison where Elena was held)
9. Bucuresti (the "gate" to the USA)
10. Cluj

Glossary

Romanian pronunciations in alphabetical order.

Alexandrina	(Ah lehx ahn DREE nuh)
Ana	(AH nah)
Andrei	(AHN dray)
Aurora	(Ah oo ROH rah)
Boghian	(Boh GYAHN)
borşch	(borşch) – soup
Brăila	(Bruh EE lah)
Brânzei	(Brn ZAY)
Brătulești	(Bruh too LESHT)
București	(Boo kuh RESHT) — capital of Romania
Bunica	(Boo NEE kah) — Grandmother
Burdujeni	(Boor doo ZEHN) — a suburb of Suceava
Carmen	(CAHR mehn)
Castanilor	(Kah STAHN ee lohr) — Chestnut
Catela	(Koh TEHL uh)
Catrina	(Kah TREEN ah)
Ceausescu	(Chow SHES koo)
Costache	(Koh STAH keh)
Costel	(Koh STEHL)
Costică	(Kohs TEE kuh)
Cruceru	(Kroo CHEH roo)
Dana	(DAH nah)
Daniel	(Dahn ee YEHL)
Danuț	(Dah NOOTZ)
Doamna	(DWAHM nuh) — Mrs.
Domnișoara	(Dohm nee SHWAH ruh) — Miss

Dorel	(Doh REHL)
Elena	(Eh LEHN ah)
Enache	(Eh NAY kay)
Eugenia	(Yoh GEHN ee ah)
Florica	(Floh REE kah)
foarte bună	(FWAH teh BOO nah) — very good
Gabriel	(Gah bree EHL)
Genovieva	(Jehn oh VYEH vah)
George	(JOHR jay) — short for Gheorghe
Gheorghe	(GYOHR geh)
Gheorghiţă	(Gyor GEETZ ah) — nickname for Gheorghe
Gicu	(JEE koo) — a nickname for Gheorghe
Ginu	(JEE noo)
hectar	(Hehc TAHR) — about 2.5 acres
Iaşi	(Yahsh)
Ilie	(EE lee eh)
Ioan	(Y' WAHN)
Iosif	(YOH seef)
lei	(LAY) — Romanian currency
Leone	(Leh OH nay)
leu	(LEH oo) — Romanian currency, singular
Lidia	(LEE dee yah)
Ligheria	(Lee GEH ree ah)
Liliana	(Lee lee AHN nah)
Livia	(LEE vee ah)
Lucia	(LOO chyah)
Magdalena	(Mahg doo LEHN uh)
mămăliga	(muh muh LEE gah) — cooked cornmeal, a Romanian staple
Mănăstireanu	(Mah nahs tee REE AHN noo)
Margareta	(Mahr gah REHT ah)

Mari	(MAH ree) — short for Maricica
Mariana	(Mah ree AHN nah)
Maricica	(Mah ree CHEE kah)
Mircești	(Meer CHEHSHT)
Mitrofan	(Mee troh FAHN)
Miziuca	(Mee ZYOO kuh)
Morcan	(Mohr KAHN)
Moșu	(MOH shoo) — term of endearment or respect for an elderly man or grandfather, used in small eastern Romanian villages like Patrauti
Nicolae	(Nee koh LAH eh)
Niculina	(Nee koo LEE nah)
nu înțeleg	(noo IN tzee lehg) — "I don't understand."
Nuți	(NOO tzi)
Oltean	(Awl TEE AHN)
pace	(PAH cheh) — peace, used as a greeting among the Romanian evangelical believers
Pătrăuți	(Pah trah OOTZ)
Pavel	(PAH vehl)
Petru	(Pet ROO)
Radu	(RAH doo)
Reșița	(REH sheets ah)
Reveca	(Reh VEH kah)
Rodica	(Roh DEE kah)
Sanda	(SAHN dah)
Sărăriei	(Suh ruh REE yay)
Securitate	(sehk oo ree TAH tay) — Secret Police
Sergiu	(SEHR joo)
Sfatcu	(SFAHT koo)
Simeon	(Sim ee AWN)
Siret	(See REHT) – a city in northern Romania, very near the Ukrainian border

Solonar	(Soh loh NAHR)
Sonia	(SOH nee ah)
Sora	(SOH rah) — sister
Suceava	(Soo CHYAH vah) — a city about 8 miles from Patrauti
Tanti	(TAHN tee) — a term of endearment and respect for a woman or aunt
Tărniceriu	(Tuhr nee CHEHR yoo)
Tata	(TAH tah) — Daddy
Teodor	(Teh oh DOHR)
Timişoara	(Tee mee SHWAH rah)
Turliuc	(Toor LYOOK)
Valerica	(Vah leh REE kah)
Vasile	(Vah SEE leh)
Veronica	(Veh roh NEE kah)
Vica	(VEE kah)
Vighenia	(Vee GEH nee ah)
Viorel	(Vee oh REHL)
Viorica	(Vee oh REE kah)
Virgil	(Veer JILL)

Christian Aid Ministries

Christian Aid Ministries was founded in 1981 as a nonprofit, tax-exempt 501(c)(3) organization. Its primary purpose is to provide a trustworthy and efficient channel for Amish, Mennonite, and other conservative Anabaptist groups and individuals to minister to physical and spiritual needs around the world. This is in response to the command ". . . do good unto all men, especially unto them who are of the household of faith" (Gal. 6:10).

Each year, CAM supporters provide approximately 15 million pounds of food, clothing, medicines, seeds, Bibles, Bible story books, and other Christian literature for needy people. Most of the aid goes to orphans and Christian families. Supporters' funds also help clean up and rebuild for natural disaster victims, put up Gospel billboards in the U.S., support several church-planting efforts, operate two medical clinics, and provide resources for needy families to make their own living. CAM's main purposes for providing aid are to help and encourage God's people and bring the Gospel to a lost and dying world.

CAM has staff, warehouse, and distribution networks in Romania, Moldova, Ukraine, Haiti, Nicaragua, Liberia, and Israel. Aside from management, supervisory personnel, and bookkeeping operations, volunteers do most of the work at CAM locations. Each year, volunteers at our warehouses, field bases, DRS projects, and other locations donate over 200,000 hours of work.

CAM's ultimate purpose is to glorify God and help enlarge His kingdom. ". . . whatsoever ye do, do all to the glory of God" (I Cor. 10:31).

Additional Books
Published by Christian Aid Ministries

God Knows My Size! / *by Harvey Yoder*
How God answered Silvia Tarniceriu's specific prayer
251 pages $10.99

They Would Not Be Silent / *by Harvey Yoder*
Testimonies of persecuted Christians in Eastern Europe
231 pages $10.99

They Would Not Be Moved / *by Harvey Yoder*
More testimonies of Christians who stood strong under communism
208 pages $10.99

Where Little Ones Cry / *by Harvey Yoder*
The sad trails of abandoned children in Liberia during civil war
168 pages plus 16-page picture section $10.99

Wang Ping's Sacrifice / *by Harvey Yoder*
Vividly portrays the house church in China
191 pages $10.99

A Small Price to Pay / *by Harvey Yoder*
Mikhail Khorev's story of suffering under communism
247 pages $10.99

Tsunami!—*from a few that survived* / *by Harvey Yoder*
Survivors tell their stories, some with sorrow and heartbreak, others with joy and hope.
168 pages $11.99

Tears of the Rain / *by Ruth Ann Stelfox*
Poignantly honest account of a missionary family in war-torn Liberia
479 pages $13.99

A Greater Call / *by Harvey Yoder*
What will it cost Wei to spread the Gospel in China?
195 pages $11.99

Angels in the Night / *by Pablo Yoder*
Pablo Yoder family's experiences in Waslala, Nicaragua
356 pages $12.99

The Happening / *by Harvey Yoder*
Nickel Mines school shooting—healing and forgiveness
173 pages $11.99

In Search of Home / *by Harvey Yoder*
The true story of a Muslim family's miraculous conversion
240 pages $11.99

HeartBridge / *by Johnny Miller*
Joys and sorrows at the Nathaniel Christian Orphanage
272 pages $12.99

The Long Road Home / *by Pablo Yoder*
Will prayers and the Spirit's promptings bring young Pablo "home"?
456 pages $12.99

Miss Nancy / *by Harvey Yoder*
The fascinating story of God's work through the life of an Amish missionary in Belize
273 pages $11.99

Into Their Hands / *by Harvey Yoder*

Bible smugglers find ingenious ways to transport Bibles into Romania and the former Soviet Union.

194 pages $11.99

A Heart to Belong / *by Johnny Miller*

A Heart to Belong (sequel to HeartBridge) continues the story of God's sustaining grace as the Millers love and guide the children of the Nathaniel Christian Orphanage in Romania.

302 pages $12.99

The Way to God and Peace

We live in a world contaminated by sin. Sin is anything that goes against God's holy standards. When we do not follow the guidelines that God our Creator gave us, we are guilty of sin. Sin separates us from God, the source of life.

Since the time when the first man and woman, Adam and Eve, sinned in the Garden of Eden, sin has been universal. The Bible says that we all have "sinned and come short of the glory of God" (Romans 3:23). It also says that the natural consequence for that sin is eternal death, or punishment in an eternal hell: "Then when lust hath conceived, it bringeth forth sin: and sin, when it is finished, bringeth forth death" (James 1:15).

But we do not have to suffer eternal death in hell. God provided forgiveness for our sins through the death of His only Son, Jesus Christ. Because Jesus was perfect and without sin, He could die in our place. "For God so loved the world that he gave his only begotten Son, that whosoever believeth in him should not perish, but have everlasting life" (John 3:16).

A sacrifice is something given to benefit someone else. It costs the giver greatly. Jesus was God's sacrifice. Jesus' death takes away the penalty of sin for everyone who accepts this sacrifice and truly repents of their sins. To repent of sins means to be truly sorry for and turn away from the things we have done that have violated God's standards. (Acts 2:38; 3:19).

Jesus died, but He did not remain dead. After three days, God's Spirit miraculously raised Him to life again. God's Spirit does something similar in us. When we receive Jesus as our sacrifice and repent of our sins, our hearts are changed. We become spiritually alive! We develop new desires and attitudes (2 Corinthians 5:17). We begin to make choices that please God (1 John 3:9). If we do fail and commit sins, we can ask God for forgiveness. "If we confess our sins, he is faithful and just to forgive us our sins, and to cleanse us from all unrighteousness" (1 John 1:9).

Once our hearts have been changed, we want to continue growing spiritually. We will be happy to let Jesus be the Master of our lives and will want to become more like Him. To do this, we must meditate on God's Word and commune with God in prayer. We will testify to others of this change by being baptized and sharing the good news of God's victory over sin and death. Fellowship with a faithful group of believers will strengthen our walk with God (1 John 1:7).